THE GOLDEN APPLE
OF SAMARKAND

---

*For my daughter Joanna whose
self-awareness, empathy,
humour and moral compass
are an inspiration.*

*For my grand-daughters
Anousha and Lidia to help them
always look for the bigger picture.*

THE GOLDEN APPLE OF SAMARKAND

A True Story of Splendour, Tragedy, Humour and Hope

Lala Wilbraham

UNICORN

This edition first published in the UK by Unicorn
an imprint of the Unicorn Publishing Group LLP, 2021
5 Newburgh Street
London W1F 7RG

www.unicornpublishing.org

10 9 8 7 6 5 4 3 2 1

ISBN 978-1-913491-80-2

Cover design by Piotr Suchodolski
Interior design by Vivian@Bookscribe

Printed in Turkey by FineTone Ltd

TABLE OF CONTENTS

FOREWORD

THIS IS A true story, a memoir cum family history, a tale of splendour and extravagance, philanthropy and public service, patronage, great visions, tragedy and loss. It is also a tale of great courage, love, humour and hope.

It has at its centre the estate of Lentvaris in Lithuania, my paternal grandmother's childhood home, which in 1850, came into her family, the Tyszkiewicz (pronounced *Tish kay vitch*)

The Tyszkiewicz were Catholic Poles, in Lithuania for centuries and in 1569 they were given the title of Count and the right to vote in the Lithuanian Parliament, both hereditary. Notwithstanding the fact that they held high offices in the Church, in Politics and at Court for generations, I see some of the themes in this account as universal. Ultimately it is a story of clinging to one's moral compass in spite of the ever-shifting loyalties imposed by history and geography, of willing oneself to be a Phoenix and not losing one's core. These themes are as relevant today as they were centuries ago. Wherever you are in the social spectrum or along the continuum of time, no matter which continent you come from and what caused you to be displaced and ripped from your roots, it is about still knowing who you are, learning to belong again and clinging to hope.

I won't include a full bibliography because my book is not a scholarly work. I have of course relied on many learned tomes and I will list those that have been particularly useful to me, not least Dr L. Narkowicz's *Tyszkiewiczowie Rodem z Landwarowa* (The Tyszkiewicz from Lentvaris), 2013. Dr Narkowicz's sources are ample and detailed: national archives, articles from the press, published memoirs, and historical analyses across several centuries and countries.

I myself have of course accessed extensive family archives, letters, memoirs, photographs, diaries and verbal accounts. The latter were largely responses from my mother, my aunt and my two grandmothers to my constant pestering from an early age: *Tell me how it was when you were little. Tell me how it was during the war. Tell me how it was before you left Europe.* And they did.

Last but not least are my own memories of a colourful and eccentric childhood spent in South America as the child of Polish émigrés.

Of course, memory alone isn't a sufficiently reliable source so being able to confirm facts by consulting scholarly tomes was essential. Below is a list of some of them.

Tyszkiewiczowie rodem z Landwarowa (*The Tyszkiewicz from Lentvaris*) *by Dr L Narkowicz, 2013, ISBN 978-83-7543-304-3*

Nicholas and Alexandra by Robert K Massie, 1968 Victor Gollancz

The Romanovs by Simon Sebag Montefiore, 2017, Weidenfeld and Nicholson

God's Playground, A History of Poland Vol II by Prof Norman Davies, 1981, Clarendon Press

The Polish Way by Adam Zamoyski 1987 John Murray

Poland by Adam Zamoyski 2009 William Collins

Close of a Dynasty by Vice Admiral Sir Francis Pridham KBE, CB 1956, Allan Wingate

Stefan Tyszkiewicz by B Kaczorowski (ed) 2008 Wielkie Biografie (Great Biographies) Odkrywcy, Wynalazcy, Uczeni (Discoverers, Inventors, Scientists) ISBN 9788301151089

A History of Brazil by E Bradford Burns 1993, Columbia University Press

A History of Brazil by Joseph Smith, 2002, Pearson Education Ltd

The Almanach de Gotha

Although a list of personal acknowledgements is at the end on pg x, I want to mention here the following institutions that were invaluable to me:

The Sikorski Museum in London
The Association of Polish Nobility in Warsaw
The Sovereign Military Order of Malta

The Fondazione Marco Besso in Rome
The Édouard André Club in Lithuania
The National Centre for Research and Heritage Records in Poznań.
The National Archives in Warsaw
The Patents Office in London
The Kretynga Museum in Lithuania

A FEW NOTES ON NAMES:

I have decided to use the Lithuanian version of place names for those towns and estates on what is now Lithuanian soil, as that is what they're known as today. Hence 'Lentvaris' for my grandmother's childhood home, rather than the Polish 'Landwarów'. See chart of Polish vs Lithuanian names in Appendix One.

A FEW INDICATIONS OF PRONUNCIATION:

WŁADYSŁAW= Vua diss uaf (*w=v, ł=w*) MARYŃCIA= Ma rin tscha
TYSZKIEWICZ= Tish kay vich (*Sz = sh as in shoe, cz = ch as in church*)
JÓZEF= Yoozef (*J=Y, ó= oo*)
WANDA= Vanda
MYCIELSKI/MYCIELSKA= Mitch**e**lski/Mitch**e**lska (stress on the letter *e*)
POTOCKI/POTOCKA = Pototski/Pototska

Note that in Polish, surnames have a gender, plurals and endings that denote whether women carry the surname from birth, by marriage or as spinsters. You will be relieved to know that I will only use the masculine and feminine variants. I'll give you a couple of examples below just to exasperate you:

Lubomirski (masculine single); Lubomirska (feminine single); Lubomirscy (masculine plural and/or mixed plural as in The Lubomirskis); Lubomirskie (feminine plural). For most surnames ending in consonants (like my grandmother's surname Tyszkiewicz) there are also variations for Tyszkiewicz women depending on whether they have the surname by birth or by marriage. I will stick to Tyszkiewicz throughout.

PROLOGUE

JUNE 2017, THE COTSWOLDS

I play with the diamond ring on my finger and, as usual, it's not only its intense sparkle that mesmerises me, but the distant world it conjures up for me, the man who chose it, the woman who wore it; and *Lentvaris,* their estate near Vilnius, in Lithuania. The mere sound of the name of my grandmother's childhood home fills a space somewhere in my chest with intense nostalgia, a somewhat curious emotion since I've never been to Lithuania and my family isn't Lithuanian but Polish.

Throughout my childhood in Brazil, in the 1950s and 60s, this word – *Lentvaris* – evoked vivid images of the heyday of my father's maternal line and still does today. The splendour and extravagance were breath-taking, and yet, although central to my grandmother's world and to her parents' love, Lentvaris was and is so much more. Throughout the decades of conflict and political turmoil it was the point of reference for my grandmother's family, the symbol of her parents' union, but also their personal stage on which were played out the much wider patriotic struggles of Poles and Lithuanians everywhere, and their dogged personal battles to defend national traditions, regional identity and a sense of self.

In June 2017, in Cirencester, my mongrel Linda barks at the sharp clap of the letterbox. We both make a dash for the mail and I just beat her to it: there's a letter from Brazil, another from Poland, a jokey postcard from a friend in Yorkshire, an invitation to dinner. So far, so predictable. But then a grey envelope slips from my fingers onto the kitchen table and immediately intrigues me. The stamp says *Lietuva* (Lithuania). It's an invitation from the Édouard André Club and from Vilnius University to a conference in one of my grandmother's family's estates. I do know who Édouard André was because my grandmother told me in the 1960s, when I was a teenager: in 1898, the year of her birth, Édouard André was the most prolific and versatile designer of parks and gardens in the world, and my grandmother's father, Władysław Tyszkiewicz, commissioned him to design his garden and park in Lentvaris.

I recall the many conversations with my grandmother over the years, sharing the hammock with her in our little garden in Brazil, with my parrot, Messalina, pecking at Bougainvillea buds above our heads. There were many days like this, with bright sunlight, cool shadows and soothing sounds: the buzz of a bee, the squeak of the hammock hook against the rope, distant kitchen noises, my dog yawning. I recall well running my finger along the paths of a crude aerial view of the park in Lentvaris, drawn by my grandmother on a scrap of paper to show me the favourite paths she and her siblings ran along. Whenever I briefly inhabited the magical garden of their childhood, these little moments entranced and hurt in equal measure. The devastation that two world wars wreaked on Poland and Lithuania and the irrevocable destruction of my grandmother's world, could never quite be pushed aside. Even in my early teens I had that hybrid feeling about myself, that question mark hanging over the notion of being an émigré. That garden, those parks, that word – *Lentvaris* – were with me then, and live in me now.

I'm not just a product of my DNA. I'm a mixture of my Polish Catholic ancestral history, of my relationship with my immediate family, my Brazilian upbringing, my fifty years in the UK. Brazilian music wafts through my Cotswold house, a box of Polish fudge lies next to the tin of Earl Grey; my own memories of the tropics jostle with vignettes of visits to Poland before and after the fall of Communism, and with images of rows of ancestors in the vaults of a basilica. But it goes far deeper: I've visited what was lost by the other side of my father's family, the Mycielskis, who lived in the West of Poland near the German border, but I've never been East, to Lithuania. Life in the Tyszkiewicz estates is alive in me, no question about it, but it lives through my grandmother's accounts, national and family archives, memoirs, books, parish records, old newspapers, letters, photographs.

Now, long after my grandmother's death, when I myself am an old woman, an invitation arrives which will allow me to take a few more steps towards this part of my family and these roots; and all because one day, in 2017, I suddenly felt compelled to turn to the internet and google Édouard André.

Something wonderful happened at that moment: Florence André (Édouard André's great-granddaughter) materialised on the screen, talking about André's own garden in La Croix-en-Touraine. I promptly emailed her, and she shared my delight: *her* great-grandfather had designed *my* great-grandfather's garden well over a hundred years ago and now we'd found each other. She told me about the correspondence between Édouard André and my forebears in the Tyszkiewicz family and rejoiced in the fact that they had made time to understand each other's visions and to collaborate in harmony to fulfil them.

The invitation that arrived in my house in Cirencester is the result of this newfound friendship between us, the two great-granddaughters. Although the topic of the conference is *René André, A field of creativity of landscape architects,* and is about Édouard André's son, it comes with a promise from Florence André to see first-hand, with her by my side, the restoration work carried out on the four parks and gardens of my grandmother's family's estates. All of a sudden, Lentvaris that always felt as distant and remote geographically as it did in time when I was growing up in South America, seems just around the corner from Cirencester. With an unsettling flutter in my chest, I google flights and hotels, and phone the dog sitter. I shall finally visit the magical world of my grandmother's childhood, Lentvaris, that paradise loved and lost. I owe it to her, and I owe it to myself.

CHAPTER ONE
THE BEAR, THE UNDERWATER WOOD AND THE DWARF

IF IT HADN'T been for a large live bear attached to a porch by a long chain, it is quite possible that the estate of Lentvaris would never have come into my grandmother's family. Notwithstanding the fact that these were the 1850s, as bizarre ideas go, this one takes the biscuit. It concerns the acquisition of property and we can safely assume that no estate agent was involved!

Taking possession of a large inheritance when you're but fifteen years old, could give you weird ideas, go to your head, and lead you to waste it all. My grandmother's grandfather, Józef Tyszkiewicz (1835–1891), lost both parents at a very young age and he certainly came up with a somewhat unusual plan. Oddly enough there seem to have been no trustees to rein him in, only advisors and lawyers with few powers over his decisions.

His inheritance was considerable and he surprised everybody with his abilities, unexpected in one so young. Over the years he made a great success of managing his affairs and expanding his domain. Yet it all started with a preposterous plan of action. Pretty well immediately after receiving his inheritance he set his heart on the estate of Lentvaris and developed the *idée fixe* that he'd simply *have* to buy it. The small problem was that it wasn't for sale. It belonged to an old lady, a Mrs Izdebska, who lived in what was then a (mainly wooden) castle with a moat, in a wonderful undulating setting near Vilnius. He pestered the old woman assiduously until she finally agreed to sell him *half* of the property. They had separate entrances within yards of each other and I can't quite envisage how the interior was divided. This did not bother the young Józef as his brother owned the nearby estate of Trakų Vokè where he could stay in comfort and with which he vowed one day to share a border.

Part-ownership was only the first step as Józef Tyszkiewicz had every intention, right from the start, of eventually buying the other half. Lentvaris would be his, even if the only way were to wait for Mrs Izdebska's death. Fear not! He didn't proceed to plot her murder. And he wouldn't have to wait for the old lady's demise. He came up with a much more expedient solution: all he needed was a bear.

The bear was attached by a long chain to a heavy iron ring by the door and the chain's length was of paramount importance. It had to be worked out exactly, to within a few centimeters, to be long enough for the old lady to just squeeze past the beast when entering her own doorway in the entrance hall. Being a diligent young man, Józef Tyszkiewicz apparently found out that this was within his legal rights because at no time did the bear lay a paw on her part of the hallway. I'd have loved to be a fly on the wall when he was discussing this delicate matter with his lawyer.

I have to admit this wasn't the nicest thing to do (to bear or geriatric), although some might possibly say that there was one saving grace: the petrified old woman, who after a while couldn't wait to sell, was paid considerably more than she would by then have accepted. This delightful if appalling episode is described in *Nad Prypecją Dawno Temu* by Kieniewicz. Sadly, history doesn't relate what happened to the unfortunate bear...

Józef Tyszkiewicz was thrilled to take possession of Lentvaris which in the seventeenth century had been a settlement belonging to the Polish-Lithuanian House of Sapieha. Later, following the partitions of the Polish-Lithuanian Commonwealth, it had become part of the Russian Empire. In 1850 it belonged to the Izdebskis and as soon as Mrs Izdebska's packed her bags and left, Józef, as the new owner, set about improving the place.

For a start his romantic dream of grand vistas of streams and lakes, led him to turn the moat into a 6 km canal. The water came from the natural Trakai lake and, with the impatience of youth, he had the area flooded without allowing time to cut down all the trees that were in the way. For decades fishermen's nets kept getting entangled in the underwater branches. Maybe they still do.

Several lakes in the vicinity helped Józef Tyszkiewicz create the very decorative artificial lake one can see in a 1876 drawing of Lentvaris by Napoleon Orda, which shows also the extent of the buildings on the estate a quarter of a century after Józef took possession. The area of the lake was 600 hectares (1,482.63 acres)

All the creative effort he poured into developing and perfecting Lentvaris does resonate with me because notwithstanding the centuries during which the various branches of the Tyszkiewicz family held high offices in the Church, in Politics and at Court, Józef, as the first Tyszkiewicz to own Lentvaris, defined from the start, the importance of the magical place his granddaughter, my grandmother Róża, was eventually born into, in 1898.

Lentvaris by Napoleon Orda

Lentvaris retained a huge significance to the family down succeeding generations, even to those of them who were forced to live in exile with no chance of ever revisiting it for many years after World War Two.

My grandmother's father, Władysław Tyszkiewicz (1865–1936), Józef's son, spent the first five years of his life in Lentvaris where the list of those on his parents' payroll between 1864 and 1866 gives some idea as to their lifestyle. I know their names, which pleases me because they immediately become real people rather than just another role fulfilled in the Tyszkiewicz household – estate manager, personal secretary, accountant, writer, architect, architect's assistant, doctor, two resident herbalists, the countess's *dame de compagnie*, nanny, governess, butler, the count's valet, the countess's valet, chef, sous chef, large floating number of kitchen maids, the countess's maid, the herbalist's maid, nursery maid, kitchen maid, chambermaid, upstairs maid, downstairs maid, large floating number of young maids when needed, four coachmen, main stable boy plus several stable helpers, three blacksmiths, gamekeeper, gamekeeper's helper, six foresters, four security guards, head gardener, five under gardeners, three farm workers plus floating number of farm-hands as needed, bee keeper, three shepherds, leather worker, carriage builder plus assistant, three carpenters, two caretakers, chimney sweeps, tutors and masters for the children. Also on the payroll were several retired employees (carpenters and children's tutors), and six impoverished relations and friends.

There is one more person I'd like to add to the list of those living in Lentvaris in 1865, the year of my great-grandfather's birth. His name was Józef Szczenulewicz. He doesn't figure on the payroll because he received no salary. He was the resident dwarf.

It is horrifying to think that at worst Józef Szczenulewicz was a pet, at best a totally dependant protégé. He ate with everyone in the dining room, travelled with the Tyszkiewicz to visit relations on far flung estates, often accompanied the family on their holidays, had comfortable quarters and the best medical care. All his needs were met. What he didn't have was freedom.

It is a well-documented fact throughout history that dwarves were often favourites and/or jesters in the courts of kings and noble households, amusing the guests, frequently with music and political satire. In the eighteenth and nineteenth centuries the Tsars and noblemen of Russia and Lithuania kept them, often, but by no means always, treating them with kindness and affection. Dwarves were owned and sometimes traded or given as gifts. In what today is the most grotesque politically incorrect concept, I derive some comfort from the knowledge that by all accounts my family treated their dwarves well and that, although they didn't have the fundamental right of freedom, frequently the alternative was far worse: many others were destitute, kept out of sight in remote parts of the countryside, or sold by their poor families to the circus.

In Jarosław Pietrzak's *'Karły na polskich dworach królewskich i magnackich od szesnastego do osiemnastego wieku'* ('Dwarves in the households of Polish Kings and magnates between the sixteenth and eighteenth centuries') the author mentions amongst countless examples, a dwarf called Krzysztof who was so loved that he was painted by the great Polish painter Matejko in the 1870s. In the seventeenth century, Queen Henrietta Maria's dwarf (Sir Jeffrey Hudson) was painted by Van Dyck. In the sixteenth, seventeenth and eighteenth centuries, the Habsburgs had dwarves in Vienna, Madrid and Brussels. Jarosław Pietrzak also mentions a cast iron coffin in St Dorothy's Church in Slavuta in the Ukraine, with the remains of a much-cherished dwarf, Little Mr Jacob (Pan Jakubcio) who died in 1857. He was 'dwarf-in-residence' at the Potocki Palace and his plaque reads: 'A faithful confidante and friend'. In this context, it isn't difficult to imagine that dwarves very much figured in performances offered to guests at the time of my great-grandfather's birth. Lentvaris was a wonderful place for entertaining visitors who needed to be received in style.

Visitors came in droves to Lentvaris due largely to Józef Tyszkiewicz's generous contribution to the erection of a station there and his gift of land and buildings to the Railway. The main line from St Petersburg to Warsaw via Vilnius benefitted immensely from this and there were trains also travelling towards Kaunas where in 1860 Tsar Alexander II placed the final stone.

The full train journey from St Petersburg to Warsaw covered approximately 1,250 km (over 750 miles) but if you were travelling first class it wasn't a tedious one. The beds were extremely comfortable, the bathrooms very well appointed and the food excellent. For the aristocratic children, the visits to the restaurant car were one of the highlights, not least because their parents and governesses allowed them the freedom to stroll up and down the first class by themselves, chatting to people in various carriages on the way. One of the most memorable pleasures was undoubtedly in the last carriage which had a vast window from which the enchantment of the ever-changing landscape could be enjoyed and where one could feel the heady speed at which the express travelled: 35 km (21 miles) per hour!

Having Lentvaris as the ideal watering hole to break one's journey, was hugely appealing to every family member, friend and indeed acquaintance of the Tyszkiewicz. People would constantly invite themselves for a night or two en route to the balls in St Petersburg or the Opera season in Warsaw. And they were well entertained: the Tyszkiewicz threw lavish parties with concerts, dancing kossacks and performing dwarves, and the estate was perfect for swimming, riding, hunting, shooting and fishing. There was boar, lynx, badger, wild cat and the occasional bear. Game birds were abundant too as were the varieties of fish and crab in the lakes. Even Tsar Alexander II was partial to a spot of hunting *chez* the Tyszkiewicz.

Not surprisingly, the constant stream of guests became exhausting for my great-grandfather Władysław's parents and in 1870, when he was five, they finally decided to take a step back from the social frenzy that Lentvaris had become. First, they moved to their summer residence in Palanga, on the Baltic coast, with 18 km of glorious beaches and dunes. It was a blissfully peaceful retreat which they decided to develop for health and recreation; they built a *Kurhaus* (health spa) in 1877 when Władysław was twelve, with restaurant, games room, hot and salt baths, a theatre, and a casino. To attract people from Latvia they bought a boat to ferry them to and from Libava to Palanga.

The really exciting thing for my great-grandfather Władysław was his father's decision to build a pier in Palanga which took place in 1884 when he was nineteen. Profitable it undoubtedly was as it brought tourists and commercial boats. But the peaceful retreat changed forever. (Today, thoroughly restored, Palanga pier is one of the main attractions in what has become the most popular and busiest beach resort in Lithuania.)

At the time that the pier was being built, my great-grandfather, Władysław Tyszkiewicz, was about to depart for St Petersburg. Since the last unsuccessful military uprising against Russia in 1863, when Poland had become part of the Russian Empire, it was natural for Polish noblemen to do their studies in the Russian capital.

Władysław's and his siblings' initial education had been at home with resident tutors who taught them Arithmetic, Geography, Literature, Polish and Russian language along with History, English, French and German. Music figured too and their master was the conductor of the Lentvaris orchestra. They were also instructed in the art of letter writing as correspondence both official and informal was seen very much as an essential skill.

In the early 1880s, Władysław was no longer a child and his law studies awaited him. He wasn't embarrassed to say that he'd miss his mother who he was close to all his life. Not that he was a mummy's boy. On the contrary, he was the only one of his siblings to stand up to their father's military discipline, drilled into them virtually from birth, with the expectation of subordination and obedience. He was no wimp, but he was also a kind and generous child, agonising over the privations of the poor. His sister Helena described an occasion when, 'as a small boy he emptied the entire contents of his wallet into a beggar's cap. That's what he was like his whole life. He had a good heart.' Indeed, as an adult, not only was he to become very involved in philanthropic causes on a very large scale but he also sought to achieve social change at political level. There were countless mentions of his tireless social and political activities. Just one example of many, is this quote from the Vilnius newspaper *Kraj* (1902, nr 50): 'Count Władysław Tyszkiewicz is relentlessly driven by the family's all-consuming commitment to public service.'

But first, Law School. Little did he know that this was also the first step in his journey into the arms of a beautiful princess.

CHAPTER TWO

CUPID, HORSES, PHILANTHROPY AND A NEW TOWN

WŁADYSŁAW TYSZKIEWICZ FELL in love, hook, line and sinker, when he was twenty-three, in 1888. Cupid did a sterling job, seeing that the seventeen-year-old girl in question was miles away at the time, and had never met the besotted young man.

Władysław had graduated from the Law School in St Petersburg in 1886 and gone on to do his articles at the Ministry of Justice in Riga. His best friend there was Prince Konstanty Lubomirski from Kruszyna. One evening, in Konstanty's apartments, Władysław spotted the photograph of the prince's beautiful sister and from that day onwards he begged his friend to introduce them at the first possible opportunity, whilst in the meantime allowing him to have her photograph. In those days this was a most inappropriate request, *pas du tout comme il faut*, but after a while, Konstanty Lubomirski relented. There was a very strict condition though: that nobody else would be shown the picture. His sister's image was not to be ogled by all and sundry.

When telling me this well-worn family story in Brazil in the 1960s, my grandmother Róża, Władysław Tyszkiewicz's daughter, produced one of her rudimentary little drawings to illustrate her description of the extraordinary contraption her father had designed. Of course, he had commissioned it before she was born but he'd kept it and she'd seen it.

He took no chances. He needed to make sure that he, and only he, would be able to look lovingly at the image of his beloved, the girl with the tiny waist and perfect cheekbones, the princess he'd never met but knew he'd marry. The special picture frame he commissioned had a delicate laced silk curtain which could be drawn over the face that had launched his thousand heartbeats.

You may well now wish to pause, sigh and smile at such Slav devotion. Go ahead. I don't care! He was only twenty-three and he was in love. And as it turned out, he adored his Maryńcia. He adored her before he met her, even more after they were finally introduced, and throughout their forty-four year-long marriage until he exhaled his last breath. Before all that though he didn't half have to put up with an awful lot of dithering!

Princess Maria Krystyna Lubomirska (for that was Maryńcia's full name) was not one to make up her mind in a hurry and for four whole years she said 'maybe' to poor Władysław's frequent proposals of marriage. For Maryńcia, Lentvaris was the Back-of-Beyond, 284 km from the buzz of Warsaw and a daunting 645 km from her family home in Kruszyna. She was quite taken with the young man, saw his qualities, his kindness and his charm, but how would she ever survive living so far East?

I can empathise with her dithering. When Władysław started wooing her in 1889 she was only seventeen, adored by her parents and spoiled endlessly by four devoted brothers. The thought of being parted from them all, so very far from home, must have been extremely unsettling. That was the one thing causing her delaying tactics. Running a chateau or a palace didn't faze her. It was her 'normal' as she was from the House of Lubomirski. In the 17th century her great (times six) grandfather had been made Prince of the Holy Roman Empire by Ferdinand III and the Lubomirskis were related to almost all the dynasties ruling Europe: Capetirn, Bourbon, Liudolfing, Wittelsbach, Hohenzollern and Rurik. Several Lubomirskis at various historical moments had been contenders for the Polish throne and many lived in residences like Wiśnicz or Łańcut, not to mention Wilanów, known as 'The Polish Versailles'. (In 2011 there was an exhibition there entitled 'The Lubomirski Family in Wilanów-Politics and Private Life' which displayed their presence in Wilanów Palace in the eighteenth and nineteenth centuries).

Maybe if Władysław's family hadn't had such long-established roots in Lithuania he might have considered moving nearer to Warsaw and Maryńcia's home in Kruszyna, but the links of this Polish family to that part of the world, and the responsibilities that went with them, were deep and strong. These roots went back to 1569 when Zygmunt August (King of Poland and Grand Duke of Lithuania) signed a decree giving a certain Wasyl Tyszkiewicz the title of Count of Łohojsk (later Count Tyszkiewicz) and the right to sit in the Lithuanian Parliament, both hereditary. My grandmother Róża remembered being told as a child about this ancestor, Wasyl who, having thrashed about with club, sword and lance on various battlefields with boundless ardour for his monarch had been so generously recompensed for his services to the Nation. The Tyszkiewicz were very much Polish and their home language Polish not Lithuanian, but after centuries of living in Lithuania my grandmother's father felt that Lithuania was where they had to stay. The dithering Maryńcia knew that too. She would never have asked Władysław to move.

The link between Poland and Lithuania went even further back than the sixteenth century. The crown of the Kingdom of Poland and the Grand Duchy of Lithuania were in a *de facto* union since 1386 when the Polish Queen Jadwiga, also known as Hedwig, made a dynastic union by marrying Lithuania's Grand Duke Jogaiła, who then became King of Poland. Because she was the ruler in her own right, he was crowned king *jure uxoris* which means 'by right of his wife'.

Two hundred or so years later, the Polish Lithuanian Commonwealth proper was established, and it became one of the largest and most populous countries of sixteenth and seventeenth century Europe. In the early seventeenth century, the Commonwealth spanned some 450,000 square miles (1,200,000 km2) and had a multi-ethnic population of 11 million. The Polish Partitions (the first in 1772 and the second in 1793) dramatically reduced the country's size. (After the third Partition of Poland in 1795 the Commonwealth ceased to exist as an independent state.)

Although it was in the sixteenth century, during this bi-confederation of Poland and Lithuania, that the Tyszkiewicz rose to great prominence, it was by the nineteenth century that my great-grandfather's father (the infamous Józef of the chained bear) had become one of the richest men in Lithuania. He and his wife, Zofia Horwatt (1838–1919) who had been wealthy in her own right, showed great competence in finances, but material luck had also been on his side since he and his brothers had inherited an additional fortune from an uncle who had died without issue. Alas, my great-grandfather Władysław, was one of eight heirs (there had been twelve children but four had died in childhood). Yet inheriting Lentvaris, several farms and smallholdings further afield, and an extraordinary amount of land in Polesie, meant he'd be able to look after his high-profile wife.

The land Władysław's father had bought in Polesie and had left to him and to one other son, was 100,000 hectares (247,105,38 acres). The area, also called Polesia, is one of the largest forest areas on the continent, starting from the farthest edges of Central Europe, into Eastern Europe and Western Russia. Although it was a staggering amount of land, Władysław's father had not only bought it very cheaply but he'd done so in spite of a decree from 1865 that forbade Poles to acquire land in that area. This rule had been sidestepped because Józef Tyszkiewicz, having been in the cadet corps in

St Petersburg as a child, had later chosen a career in the Russian Army which afforded him preferential treatment. This was seen by some as a lack of Polish patriotism not least because at one point, Józef was adjutant to Muraviev, the Russian Governor General of North Western Poland, known as 'The Hangman'. I'm glad to say that after the failed 1863 Uprising, which had aimed to restore the Polish Lithuanian Commonwealth, Józef Tyszkiewicz seriously annoyed Muraviev by leaving not only his post as his adjutant, but by turning his back on the Tsar's army, as he could no longer square that career with his own personal loyalties and indeed identity. Whatever the means by which the land in Polesie had been acquired, my great-grandfather Władysław quickly sold his share, in order to invest the proceeds into perfecting Lentvaris. Maryńcia capitulated and finally said 'Yes' to Władysław's endless proposals of marriage and they were married in 1892 when she was twenty-one.

I wonder whether it was before or after their wedding that the 1892 issue nr 29 of the newspaper *Kraj* reported on a robbery in which several passengers in the second class on the train that travelled through Lentvaris, were chloroformed and relieved of their possessions! Whatever the case, my great-grandparents' wedding was a happy event, albeit a low key one because of the bridegroom's father's death a few months before in 1891.

The welcome for the young couple was warm and there were scores of people to greet the newlyweds with bread and salt, garlands of flowers, banners and a band. The 1 km long road from Lentvaris station to the great house was lined with well-wishers, not just family and friends but local staff and tenant farmers. Count Władysław Tyszkiewicz was bringing home his Countess (demoted from Princess by the Polish system. Had she married a Mr Bloggski, she'd have become Mrs Bloggska, pure and simple.) Whatever her title, everyone wanted to see the new chatelaine and her entourage (several families of well-known and trusted servants she was bringing from her home in Kruszyna). The guests were offered a lavish lunch and given lumps of sugar on departure symbolising wellbeing and prosperity.

When my grandmother's parents, Władysław and Maryńcia Tyszkiewicz, arrived in Lentvaris after their wedding, they hit the ground running. Władysław was well aware of Maryńcia's attachment to her doting family and well before he heard that long awaited 'yes', he had promised her a future with frequent get-togethers and holidays with relations and friends. To help her settle in, he'd give her everything she had at home and more, so not long after their wedding, in order to make Lentvaris worthy of her status, he started removing the wooden parts of the castle but soon decided on more radical action: to build a brand-new building, very much with his wife's input, exactly as she wanted it. They moved into a house on the estate for the duration and started planning.

The energy and productivity of the young couple are impressive. In that first year of marriage apart from conceiving their first baby, they turned to an important philanthropic cause: the fire brigade. The fire control arrangements in the area were dire. The nearest fire stations were much too far, in Vilnius and Trakai, and in 1892 Trakai had only one fireman so the Tyszkiewicz made sure that Lentvaris would offer an efficient fire

My great-grandmother, Princess Maria Krystyna Lubomirska ('Maryńcia') (1871–1958)

service with four departments: town, railway, factory and estate. In case of a bigger fire these would communicate by telephone and join forces. This private fire service was entirely financed by my great-grandparents and was the best for miles with large numbers of highly trained fire fighters and first-class fire extinguishing equipment made in the family's wire factory.

At the same time as dealing with the fire brigade, the couple threw themselves into developing the already top-grade stables as soon as possible. Maryńcia was an extremely accomplished horsewoman and to help her settle in, Władysław put enormous effort into all things equestrian. He loathed riding but, as long as he didn't have to sit on a horse himself, he did enjoy everything else connected with horses. Very soon they had an extremely successful award-winning stud farm. There was always a minimum of eighty horses, largely of Polish, Russian and Hungarian stock, some bred for racing, some for carriage driving but others also for the Army, which had very exacting standards.

My great-grandmother was involved at every level. She was often in the stables by 6 am. Before long there were horse auctions, dressage competitions, gymkhanas, carriage-driving events, and large races held in Vilnius, all eliciting widespread attention. By 1895, Władysław was so into it that to the delight of his wife he became Vice President of the Vilnius Horse Racing Association. As such, he made sure that racing events were followed by charity ones: dinners, receptions and other elegant social gatherings with the purpose of raising funds for some of his favourite causes – educating poor children, feeding beggars, providing medical treatments for the sick and homeless, running courses for peasants about agricultural practices and animal husbandry.

The stables in Lentvaris were magnificent and the manager was a retired cavalry officer called Weigert. There was a comprehensive staff, including of course a resident vet. There were indoor and outdoor manèges, the best possible equestrian surfaces and carefully chosen pasture grasses. An impressive collection of carriages was housed in a large building, horse drawn vehicles from the smallest to the largest – barouches, landaus, cabriolets, chaises, gigs, phaetons, broughams, breaks and sleighs. My grandmother Róża, always described her very favourite one, a two-wheeled trap from Sicily, extravagantly decorated with ostrich feathers, beads, tiny mirrors and handmade sequins. It twinkled and sparkled and dazzled, at times frightening other competing horses. Everyone wanted to be photographed with it even though in the black and white print of those days, much of the effect was lost.

There are countless references to the quality and scale of the whole set-up in Russian and Lithuanian National archives, including contemporary ones (eg, V. Drema LDK Miestai ir mmiesteliai. Is Vlado Dremos archyvy, Vilnius 2006, s369). Also in frequent press articles in newspapers and publications of the time like Kraj (in English: Country), Jeździec I Myśliwy (Rider and Hunter), Tygodnik Sportowy (Sporting Weekly).

In 1903, the Warsaw weekly, Tygodnik Sportowy, nr 28, wrote thus about my great-grandmother, 'Our sport has lady riders who not only excel at all things equestrian but also at tennis. We have record breakers, brave sportswomen with staying power, who can give most men a run for their money. One of them is unequivocally Countess Tyszkiewicz, Maria Krystyna née Princess Lubomirska, who a few days ago rode her horse from Lentvaris to Warsaw.' This was no mean feat as the distance is just under

400 km (approx 245 miles) but clearly Maryńcia's delicate frame belied her strength and drive.

The races attracted as much attention for the quality of the event and horses, as for the glamour, all silks and hats and high fashion. These are described in the press and in many letters from Lentvaris guests who gushed about everything not least: *'the perfect and charming hostess, at once a generous and relaxed lady of the house, and a superior and driven sportswoman'.*

Maryńcia's brothers rejoiced for their sister, sharing her all-consuming passion for horses. They'd earlier formed a partnership in Kruszyna and in 1885 Stefan Lubomirski had bought a mare called Barfleur in Austria which had been bred in England in 1881 *chez* Lord Strafford (maybe Stafford or Stratford. I don't entirely trust the spelling in the family archive). Barfleur marked the start of their long-term breeding of racehorses and in 1895 my great-grandmother's brother, Stanisław Lubomirski, got the first four full-blood English mares. In 1897, fifteen more arrived. Maryńcia and her brothers followed each other's equestrian activities closely, the Lubomirskis giving their sister every encouragement for her plans at Lentvaris.

Ever the energetic couple, Władysław and Maryńcia Tyszkiewicz, had very important events in 1893: the birth of their first child (Zofia) and... the building of a new town!

The nineteenth-century *Geographical Dictionary of the Kingdom of Poland and other Slav Countries* (Warsaw 1884 p.75) lists that in 1866, when Lentvaris still belonged to Władysław's father, Józef Tyszkiewicz, there were only one hundred and sixty-two people living in the area called Lentvaris which comprised a village, a grange and a lake. But by 1897, the National Historical Archives in Vilnius show that there were over one thousand inhabitants in Lentvaris. These were my great-grandparents' staff, tenant farmers and their families, plus those who had been enticed to live in their new town.

It was in 1893, with the agreement of the local Russian authorities, in the year of baby Zofia's birth, that Władysław and Maryńcia Tyszkiewicz built their new town. They called it New Lentvaris, to differentiate it from their estate. To transform a small settlement into a proper town, Władysław initially gave plots of land for free to people from certain listed professions:

policeman, fireman, doctor, chemist, tailor, blacksmith, cobbler etc. There was no shortage of willing applicants and within a few years the little town grew considerably (in 2020 it has 10,004 inhabitants).

The Tyszkiewicz were seen as welcoming, the area was green and beautiful, and the infrastructure kept improving in leaps and bounds: soon there were several doctors and a dentist, a vet, a notary public, a lawyer, barber, chemist shop, post office, other shops of various kinds run by Poles and Jews, good roads, easy access to Vilnius, good links with Warsaw and St Petersburg. The prices of food, and of houses and apartments to rent or buy were very reasonable and there were jobs aplenty, because of the rail links, factories and warehouses. Two brothers called Dowiałt opened a factory making metal files and other tools. By 1896 the nail factory created by Władysław's father Józef and by then leased to the brothers Frumkin, was employing three hundred and fifty-two people.

A risky and patriotic enterprise was the building of a school in Lentvaris. It had to be done under false pretences. Władysław and Maryńcia enticed a teacher from Warsaw who well knew what she was taking on: officially the school had to be registered as an establishment for the teaching of handiworks such as sewing, embroidery and other manual crafts. Secretly, however, and very much illegally (since the teaching of and in Polish was strictly forbidden by the Russian authorities), the children of the Lentvaris employees were taught Polish grammar, reading, writing, Maths and Geography. They never took books and copybooks home, and these were kept in a concealed cupboard built into the wall and covered by a painting. An informant always managed to warn the teacher when an inspector was about to come by and all evidence was swiftly hidden away. They somehow managed to conceal the real activities of the school right up to the First World War (1914–1918).

Unlike many people Władysław Tyszkiewicz welcomed Jews into his town, and he was to defend them vigorously in 1906 as the elected Warsaw envoy to the First Duma in St Petersburg. The very first doctors and lawyers in his town of New Lentvaris were of Jewish stock.

In order to avoid disorderly behaviour, taverns would not be allowed in my great-grandfather's town. In the hotel by the station, where there was a restaurant and a ballroom, alcoholic drinks were available but at a deliberately exorbitant price. By the avenue that led from New Lentvaris to the palace, Władysław created a little oasis, named Marywil in honour of his wife. He built several smart houses, each with a beautifully designed garden, high quality furniture and servants' quarters, excellent bedrooms and luxury bathrooms, all to encourage the more upmarket Poles from St Petersburg to rent them as summer holiday homes. (*Kraj*, issue nr 34,31-8-1894.)

There was a tennis court and a croquet lawn, separate gyms for adults and children, cycle races and athletic competitions. There were cards and chess and games with prizes and raffles. At weekends a band played. On hot days ice cream and orange juice were offered and fresh produce from Władysław's fields and orangery were available for sale. All the proceeds went into a fund for disadvantaged children from neighbouring farms.

One of the people who rented a holiday villa in Marywil for several years running was Dr Szereszewski from St Petersburg, assistant to the Tsar's personal physician. Apparently, his housekeeper made excellent tea and home-made jam. He became a good friend of my grandmother's parents, who not only had him to stay at the house but also went to visit him in St Petersburg.

Of course, over the years, before the First World War when friends came to stay in Lentvaris, the food and wine were exquisite, which many remarked on, but what they seemed to like best was the atmosphere created by Maryńcia and Władysław Tyszkiewicz. Apart from mealtimes, when everyone was expected to attend, guests were free to do what they liked: tennis, croquet, boating, riding, walks along the lakes. Carriages were available to them at any time if they wished to explore further afield.

Indoors, the library offered an extensive choice of books in various languages and also the services of a (paid) reader who read from requested books, recited poetry, gave summarised accounts from the newspapers and reported on aristocratic gossip from articles in the press.

Magical performances were given on the lake in Lentvaris on hot summer nights by all sorts of ensembles, concerts and plays with actors often brought from Italy. The children were allowed to watch the rehearsals (providing the plays were suitable for the young). 'The children' included not just my grandmother, her siblings, cousins and friends over the years, but also children of the staff and of local farmers whose horizons my great-grandparents were keen to expand.

The performances that most stuck in my grandmother's mind were by an eight-strong Neapolitan troupe who for several years running was engaged by her father for the whole season. They sang and danced in national costume on a floating stage made to look like St Mark's Square in Venice, lit up by lanterns. My grandmother's sister Zofia describes it in her memoirs. I was riveted by these images as a child and, with that dreaminess of an over-imaginative youngster, I pictured myself there with them in the early 1900s, before either of the two world wars.

In addition to the performances on the lake, many plays were put on in the theatre in New Lentvaris. They were often performed by professional actors stopping off en route between Warsaw and St Petersburg. People flocked and the locals were allowed to sit in the gallery. Sometimes shoemakers, seamstresses, tailors and other craftsmen were given extra tickets as an additional thank you for paid work done well. Amateur acting flourished there too, and my great-grandfather enjoyed it so much that he even had acting lessons in Paris with Benoît-Constant Coquelin from the Comédie Française, one of the greatest theatrical figures of the age.

At this point in the family history they could do pretty well anything they chose to. It was as near to paradise as could be found on earth. But all too soon that paradise would be lost to them for ever.

Lentvaris (Landwarów in Polish), home of Count Władysław Tyszkiewicz (1865–1936), his wife nèe Princess Maria Krystyna Lubomirska 'Maryńcia' (1871–1958) and their four children Zofia, Róża (my grandmother), Stefan (Stetysz) and Eugeniusz

CHAPTER THREE

A VERY SPECIAL GARDEN

THE CHERRY ON the cake. That is what the garden in Lentvaris was going to be. The year of 1894 had brought Władysław and Maryńcia a new baby, Stefan, and 1898 was a triple joy: the birth of my grandmother Róża, the finishing touches on the new house, and the massive undertaking that was the creation of the gardens and park in Lentvaris.

My great-grandfather wanted the best for Maryńcia and as garden designers go, Édouard André (1840–1911) was it. At the age of twenty he'd been apprenticed to Jean Charles Alphan and Baron Haussmann and, as Head Gardener of Paris, had overseen the planting in many public spaces including the Parc des Buttes Chaumont and the gardens of the Tuilleries. At twenty-six he won an international competition with his design for Sefton Park in Liverpool, and the world became his oyster. In *Traité Général de la Composition des Parcs et Jardins* (Masson, Paris 1879) he describes his projects: the Gardens of Monte Carlo, the Funchal Garden in Madeira, the public park in Cognac, Villa Borghese gardens in Rome, Luxembourg Castle, Montevideo, the Imperial gardens in Rio de Janeiro, the Tsar's gardens in St Petersburg and many more. In 1875, he collected thousands of specimens in South America including the *Anthurium andraeanum* and many Bromeliads and, in 1892, became Professor of Horticulture and Landscape Architecture at the French National School of Horticulture in Versailles.

The parks Édouard André designed for private clients, include four in Lithuania, all for my grandmother's family. Not only was my great-grandfather determined to give his wife a garden worthy of her status, but his two brothers and a cousin joined in and, with the help of his son René and the noted Belgian landscape architect Jules Buyssens (1872–1958), Édouard André embarked on his massive Lithuanian achievement:

- Lentvaris (*Landwarów in Polish*) – for Władysław Tyszkiewicz
- Užutrakis (*Zatrocze*) for Józef (Władysław's brother)
- Palanga (*Połąga*) for Feliks (brother)
- Trakų Vokė (*Waka*) for Jan (cousin)

Count Władysław Tyszkiewicz
(1865-1936)

Portrait of Édouard André (1840-1911) by
Édouard Debat Ponsan (1847-1913)
(By kind permission of Florence André)

Three of the estates were very close to each other, around 6 km away, with Palanga, much further, 400 or so km, on the Baltic coast. É. André wrote to his wife on the 21 June 1898: *'The park* (in Lentvaris) *is by the shores of a lake which makes it interesting'.* Two days later, he received a deposit of 6,215 rubles. According to an online inflation calculator, six thousand rubles in 1896 would have had an approximate value of £110,000 in 2017, not forgetting that an average worker in the late 1800s earned only about three hundred rubles a year.

My grandmother Róża, born in the same year as André's design for Lentvaris (1898), was too young to share in all the excitement but she certainly remembered her father telling her later that she and the garden were the same age and would grow together.

The terrain in Lentvaris was undulating. André re-shaped existing hillocks, scattered faux and real rocks, built grottos and channelled waterfalls. The considerable canalisation and heavy planting were largely carried out by soldiers and prisoners. Symbolic gardening was done by family members, whose names were attached to each sapling or shrub.

Around the parterre, architectural formality required columns, urns, small statues, a balustrade, and benches to enhance the structured planting where, amongst other flowers, were rare varieties of begonias imported from Belgium and France. Evergreens coloured winter views: avenues of oak, box hedges and Thujas. My great aunt, Zofia Potocka (1893–1989), describes the effect of the *rond point* with paths delineated by boxwood where beyond the central walkway lilac bushes concealed administrative buildings and stables, also providing a backdrop for the bust of a seventeenth-century Tyszkiewicz Bishop on a stone plinth. A path meandered through the park, much of it following the shore of the artificial lake, past unexpected vistas towards a waterfall, and small architectural structures (a shaded bower, a small chapel, a discreet pavilion). In an otherwise austere corner, you might find humour in a bench with artificial roots for legs, or mushroom-like stone stools. Whilst strolling through established native trees (lime, birch, maple, oak, pine, fir) around gentle bends you'd come across a striking foreign specimen, or small groupings of them when the artist's eye dictated: Douglas fir, European larch, Northern white-cedar or Eastern arborvitae (Thuja), broadleaf lime, European elder, silver maple, birch, willow, forsythia and elm (*Dendrological Studies of Lentvaris park* by Vaiva Deveikiené and Steponas Deveikis 2010–2011).

One area of the park became referred to as *'Riviera'* where in a secluded pine wood, my great-grandfather requested a tiny open-air chapel, with neither walls nor roof, just wooden benches on mock root legs and an image

Ст. Ландварово.—St. Landwarowo. № 67.
Видъ съ графской пристани.
„Café Riviera". Widok z przystani Hrabiovskiej.

View from Café Riviera across the lake, 1900s

31

of Our Lady of Częstochowa in a faux roots frame. An oil lamp burned night and day and anyone from the environs was welcome. In '*Switzerland*', where a stream flowed through a naturally wooded ravine, paths and steps on various levels tempted in different directions towards grottos, benches, small waterfalls. At the top of the ravine, a bower with a root-like fence and straw roof offered nesting for a stork, the symbol of good luck.

Since for Édouard André aesthetics should coexist with practicality, orchards, vegetables, herbs and flowers weren't walled off but separated by more natural evergreen hedges. Within these areas, there were countless roses but also cottage varieties: sweet peas, stock, poppies, snapdragons, mignonette and all the necessary plants for the resident herbalist's remedies.

The more I read about what Édouard André brought into my great-grandparents' garden and therefore into their life, the clearer the perfect balance: the formal and the natural, gentle transitions and sudden surprises, aesthetics and functionality. No wonder my great-grandfather rejoiced in showing off the garden and park every bit as much as strolling through them by himself in silence. André's design thrilled him: grandeur and intimacy, formality and freedom, vistas, hideaways and surprises, spaces that could be theatrical and natural, beautiful and useful, and where active outdoor fun could coexist with contemplation.

Władysław Tyszkiewicz was elated with Édouard André's vision and said so often. The garden became his pride, joy, comfort, the place he most longed for during his later exile in Italy; but that is in a further chapter...

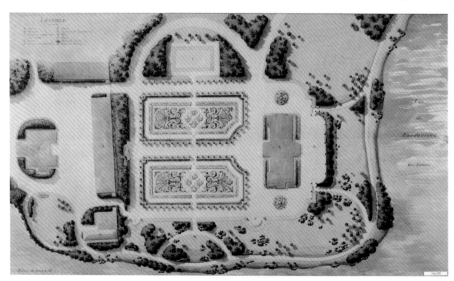

LENTVARIO PARKAS

EKSPLIKACIJA

1. Rūmai
2. Kumetynas
3. Kavinė "Riviera"
4. Vandens malūnas
5. Tvartas – karvidė
6. Svirnas – arklidė
7. Gyvenamasis namas
8. Arklidė – tarnų namas
9. Bokštas
10. Gyvenamasis namas

A Grota
B Didžioji kaskada
C Mažoji kaskada
D Uolos
E Belvederis
F Kriketo aikštelė
G Obeliskas
H Parteris
J Terasa

LEFT: *Édouard André's 1898 plan for the parterre in Lentvaris.* (By permission of Florence André and the Archives Départementales des Yvelines ref 141J279)

ABOVE: *The park in Lentvaris by kind permission of Vaiva Deveikienė (2007) based on old archives and the current layout. It shows how the parterre in the previous image fitted into the overall design*

(*errata:* F is labelled as a cricket pitch instead of croquet lawn. The tennis court to the right of the parterre on this picture isn't labelled, nor is the orangery, which is the building near the shore beyond the top left-hand corner of the parterre as on this drawing)

CHAPTER 4

BALLS, HOLIDAYS AND A
MOST UNUSUAL GIFT

THE ARISTOCRACY'S SOCIAL life in Vilnius and in Warsaw right up to the First World War was on as grand a scale as on the estates. In Vilnius there were many glamorous dances and parties, mostly during the season for racing, and agricultural shows with fairs of every kind during the day. The latter were a big attraction for the Tyszkiewicz children whose only participation in the balls was to watch their bejewelled mother glide down the stairs before a dance. The clothes and jewellery worn at these dances were indeed spectacular, the banquets lavish and much written about. There were balls several times a week during the season, in the grandest private houses, in the most elegant municipal buildings and in the best hotel.

Both my grandmother Róża and her older sister Zofia, described to me with relish their mother's earrings, brooches, necklaces, tiaras, chokers and rings. A Fabergé brooch my great-grandmother had been given by one of her brothers didn't enchant the girls nearly as much as a pair of long dangly earrings with diamonds of various sizes and emeralds in between. My grandmother was once allowed to gently make them swing with one finger when smiling a shy goodbye, before watching her parents get into their carriage for yet another glittering night out. She never forgot it as it was unusual for Maryńcia to permit such gestures from her children. Jewels were to be admired, not played with. These earrings shone brightly in Róża's memory forever as a magical symbol of her untouchable mother.

Maryńcia was not maternal. Screams, tantrums and stern reprimands often echoed around Lentvaris since my grandmother Róża was a nervous and difficult child, hyper-sensitive, prone to night terrors and panic attacks from an early age. She longed for her mother's attention, for some tenderness, for cuddles. Like all her siblings, she seldom got that from their mother. It was their father Władysław who, even though extremely busy and very often away from home, was totally present when with his children and made them feel he had all the time in the world. He was the one who gave them piggybacks, kissed and hugged them goodnight, sat on their beds for long chats and made them shriek with laughter with his pranks and sense of humour. His own father had been a strict disciplinarian, yet Władysław had a natural empathy with children. Sad for them that he was so often away...

Róża was the one that suffered most from their mother's coldness and pedagogical methods. Maryńcia believed that, like a horse, a child must be broken in. My poor grandmother's first and devastating feeling of bereavement came from this barbaric approach and it involved a doll.

On one of the forays into Vilnius with her beloved nanny (Paniunia), Róża saw a doll in a toyshop window that took her breath away. Her longing for that doll consumed her. She couldn't sleep and she begged daily to be given it for her birthday. Maryńcia told her that she'd have to wait a lot longer, until Christmas, and that then *maybe* the doll would be hers. For a small child, waiting for months was torture but finally Christmas came and Róża's joy at opening the parcel was such that she couldn't stop crying with emotion. She called the doll Belinda. A few days later her mother announced that she could have the doll for one more week and then she'd have to give it to the poor.

Róża begged Paniunia to run away from home with her so that she could keep Belinda forever and the three of them would live happily ever after in a secret place far away. When the doll was wrenched away from her on that fateful morning, her screams were heard by most of the staff. Paniunia cuddled the distressed child, sobbing with her, trying in vain to console. My great-grandfather was away at the time. There is no question that he would never have allowed such an act of cruelty. My grandmother never got over it. Something broke in her and made her even more sensitive and hysterical, thus further irritating her mother.

To many, Maryńcia was an excellent mother and, in a sense, she was. She made sure the children's education was top notch, their diet the healthiest possible, their clothes of the best quality, their manners impeccable. But horses and dogs were her passion. And although her strong feelings of *noblesse oblige* were amply demonstrated in her charitable work, and much praise was heaped on her regal standards of entertaining, there was also a recognition of her stiffness from some. When writing to his wife on 21st June 1898 about the designs for the park in Lentvaris, André says: '*The countess is a small dark-haired woman, not very communicative, with a very British manner and demeanour*' (*Les Lettres Ty*, red S Deveikis, Vilnius 2011 p.39).

From Dr L. Narkowicz's books about the Tyszkiewicz family, it is clear that the upbringing of the Tyszkiewicz children was like that of Polish aristocratic children in general, who spent much more time with their wet nurses, nannies, governesses and tutors than with their parents, often being left behind for weeks whilst the parents were away. By virtue of their positions at court and in politics the magnates in particular saw their chief responsibilities as lying outside the immediate family, dedicating their lives to their patriotic, political and social duties. They inculcated in their children the very same ideals which often resulted in producing remarkably brave and public-spirited people with an unwavering sense of duty, but at the expense of intimacy between parent and child.

Nothing much seemed to change from one generation to another. In her book *Piękna i Dobra*, Cholewianka-Kruszyńska describes the childhood of Countess Zofia Zamoyska (née Princess Czartoryska) as very lonely, being left with staff for months. Her father was Prince Adam Kazimierz Czartoryski, a candidate for the Polish throne, whilst her husband, Count Stanisław Zamoyski, was Marshall of the Polish Senate. Although warm towards her children herself, her father's position in society and that of her despotic husband, dictated the structure of the children's lives. In Sofka Zinovieff's book *The Red Princess* the writer mentions that Prince Peter Dalgorouky's parents *'tried to bring up their children the English way, with backbone and formal reserve'*. And Princess Maria Sapieha (born in 1910) writes that her earliest childhood memory is of intense distress at the departure of her beloved nanny. (*Moje Życie, Mój Czas*, 'My Life and my Times', written in 2006 and published in 2008 in Kraków).

Countless children of that milieu had their emotional needs fulfilled by their nannies, and Róża was lucky to have her adored Paniunia. Not all were so fortunate. Paniunia not only loved her but always tried to help her focus on the fun things around her: the fairs, the holidays, the beautiful bejewelled ladies sparkling in the candlelight. When occasionally Róża hid behind a screen to watch them process into the dining room, Paniunia never snitched.

As much as balls, dances, glorious clothes and jewels fascinated my grandmother Róża throughout her childhood, it was the holidays she told me about with real relish when I was little in Brazil. Whenever we went to Rio, Guarujá or Ilhabela, ('my' beach destinations) she'd sit under a parasol with an ice cream and tell me about 'hers'.

She loved holidays on the French Riviera and all over Italy, but Summer was often spent partly on her uncle Feliks's estate, Palanga, on the Baltic Coast (where Róża's grandfather Józef had built the famous pier). Feliks Tyszkiewicz had completed the building of his Neo Renaissance palace by 1897 and the architect was Franz Heinrich Schwechten (1841–1924) one of the best German architects of his time.

Grandma Róża's immediate family didn't stay in the main house in Palanga but in their own villa on the estate. It was large and square, with a verandah on each side, and two glass pavillions. The hordes of cousins were in and out of each other's houses and it felt like party time all the time.

The days on the beach were unforgettable, with men and women swimming separately, girls and ladies changing in wooden bathing huts on wheels, pulled by horses into the water. After swimming and making enormous sandcastles, there were huge lunches followed in the evenings by concerts and operatic performances in the park with singers and musicians from St Petersburg and Warsaw, performing in the open air late into the night. This was described in the 1902 issue 34 of the newspaper *Kraj*.

It wasn't suprising that for several holiday seasons, my great-grandfather Władysław, always keen to give access to a wider audience, suggested expanding the Saturday theatrical events in Palanga so that the public could also enjoy some of the performances. His brother Feliks put him in charge of setting his suggestions in motion and yet another idea was introduced, namely harvest festivals and flower shows. Władysław was in his element.

Autumn saw the Tyszkiewicz family heading for Warsaw where they went to as many concerts as they could at The Warswaw Philarmonic. The founders, in 1901, had been my great-grandfather Władysław Tyszkiewicz, two of Maryńcia's brothers (Stanisław and Stefan Lubomirski, with his wife Natalia) Tomasz Zamoyski, plus notable representatives of the music world. Architect Karol Kozłowski designed the institution's building in an eclectic style, modelling it on the Paris Opera and the inaugural concert, on 5 November 1901, included the world-famous pianist Jan Paderewski.

Warsaw's Opera was a great attraction too. It had an eight-month season, and in Russia, in 1901, the Tsar built the *Narodny Dom* (People's Palace), which contained the fourth Opera House in St Petersburg, plus theatres, concert halls and restaurants. The Tsar insisted on very low admission fees so that ordinary Russians would be able to have first class music and

Warsaw Philarmonic 1910

theatre. In fact, there was much to attract in Russia culturally for years: Pavlova and Nijinsky dazzled at the Imperial ballet; Rimsky-Korsakov was the conductor of St Petersburgh Conservatory and had students like Stravinsky and Prokoviev, whilst the likes of Rachmaninov, Horovitz, Efrem Zimbalist all trained in Imperial Russia; the Ballet Russe which in 1909 took the world by storm, was founded in Paris by Diaghilev for whom Stravinsky wrote fabulous ballet scores. Stanislavkis's Moscow Art Theatre showcased a new approach of naturalistic theatre, with Chekov producing plays that became world classics. All in all, between Warsaw, Vilnius, St Petersburg and Moscow, my great-grandparents were spoilt for choice.

When heading for Warsaw, they took with them the children's nannies, governess, teachers, several horses and extra staff. The resident workforce in the Warsaw house (on Ulica Warecka nr 11) wouldn't be enough: butler, footman, chef, two under chefs, valet, lady's maid, six chambermaids, four laundry maids, two coachmen, errand boy. Since at times there were as many as a hundred dinner guests, a large number of extra hands was taken on for the occasion and the atmosphere in the kitchen was apparently like before a battle. The Chef (Antoni Gwiazda) ruled with a rod of iron.

In Warsaw, my grandmother's family often walked in the Saski Gardens and the royal park at Łazienki with their beloved dogs (endless fox terriers and Boston, their bulldog), rode their horses in the park at the palace of

Wilanów, went to the races and other equestrian events. On Okólnik Street nr 5, there was an indoor manège (called Tattersal) run by a Mrs Maria Wodzyńska where my grandmother and her siblings had regular riding lessons. In fact it was there, in Warsaw, not in Lentvaris, that they all first sat on a horse as toddlers and only then, after a season with Mrs Wodzyńska, were they allowed to join their mother on more ambitious riding outings in the countryside.

In the Łazienki park there was a sports centre called 'Agrykola' – nothing to do with agriculture but with the name of a nineteenth-century engineer Karol Ludwik Agrykola. My great-grandmother and the children often went there for tennis tournaments which I assume were on indoor courts as it is unlikely to have had outdoor tennis competitions in winter. The tennis court at the Agrykola was the very first in Warsaw. My great-grandfather joined them when he could, although his times in Warsaw had to also accommodate his other duties including those linked to his position as Head of the Society for Advancement of Trade and Commerce in Warsaw (1903).

As winter drew in, skating and sledging became one of the children's favourite occupations; but the high point for them was their beloved uncle Stanisław Lubomirski's birthday party on the 23 November. Every year the children took great pains to find just the right presents for him. They derived huge pleasure from these themselves for years since the thoughtful uncle made a point of using the gifts whenever they met.

Decades later, looking at me with the intense eyes of a small child, my grandmother Róża told me that uncle Stanisław *always* wore the bow tie she'd chosen for him in 1905 when she was seven. *Always*. For *always* we must of course read *always when in her presence* but clearly Stanisław Lubomirski knew that the bow tie from that particular little girl was the most important gift, to be *seen* to be cherished *forever*. The buying of it had been frought with angst when her dithering in the shop had resulted in a fierce telling off by her mother. No wonder the bow tie glowed poignantly in her emotions and he knew it. She, the nervous and insecure one, the child most needing warmth and attention, lapped up the deep affection she received from the adored uncle who understood everything.

That very dear uncle Stanisław Lubomirski had no children and loved his siblings' offspring as his own. The toys he brought them from Austria and France were magical: glorious dolls with clothes for every occasion, furniture (including four poster beds), lacy bedlinen, diminutive plates and silver cutlery etc. Not to mention miniature carriages with toy stable boys, books with unforgettable illustrations, automata, the latest puzzles.

Stanisław Lubomirski's most unusual gift by far was one he brought from Egypt for his Lubomirski nephews Hieronim and Tomasz, who were his brother Stefan's (1862–1941) boys. They lived in Maryńcia's childhood home, the Castle of Kruszyna, and the gift was . . . A CAMEL! Tame and friendly, the creature not only allowed the children to cuddle and ride him but was also used for delivering post around the estate.

The camel came complete with an Arab groom and both were always taken to Warsaw for the winter with the family, where on Aleje Ujazdowskie nr 37, there was a large garden with stables and suitable accommodation. Much care was taken to provide extra heating for both human and animal, in view of the warm climate they had come from.

The sojourn in Warsaw would always be followed by Władysław and Maryńcia Tyszkiewicz heading for Milan, Berlin, Paris and Vienna for a spot of shopping. My great-grandfather loved helping his wife choose clothes. Her figure, even after four children, was perfect. Apart from the obvious (Hermés, Lanvin, Chanel etc), they loved going to Creed Boutique in Paris (a shop which has been in the same family from 1760 to this day). The Warsaw press often mentioned that '*Countess Tyszkiewicz is one of the best dressed ladies from her class*' (Dr L. Narkowicz, *Tyszkiewiczowie Rodem z Landwarowa*, 2013 p.214)

Alongside the sparkling social life my grandmother's family enjoyed, her parents never flagged in their dedication to charitable causes: in Lentvaris my great-grandfather decided to run summer holidays in log cabins, for children sick with TB so that they could combine having fun with the benefit of clean country

PHOTO-CRAYON VILNA

My great-grandmother Countess Tyszkiewicz née Princess Maria Krystyna Lubomirska ('Maryńcia')

air. Any medical treatment they needed during their stay was given at the Tyszkiewicz's own hospital at no cost to the patients. The twelve-bed hospital had been built by Władysław for those working on his estate, and also those not in his employ who were of meagre means and lived in the area. There was a full-time resident doctor (Dr Kazimierz Okulicz) who lived in a grace and favour lodge and a fully trained nurse and midwife, who had the help of two assistant nurses. In cases requiring surgery, patients were transported by carriage or train to the larger hospital in Vilnius, their treatment paid for by my great-grandfather.

In Vilnius, one of great-grandpa Władysław's projects was to create the very first Ambulance Service in 1902. After Kiev, Częstochowa, Łódź and Warsaw, the Tyszkiewicz Ambulance Service in Vilnius was the fifth. Władysław and Maryńcia mobilised a large number of people to help them in this enterprise: fellow aristocrats, priests, professionals from various walks of life and many doctors. They obtained permission from the Russian authorities to register the charity and set it up with their own funds. My grandmother's parents started by commissioning two horse-drawn ambulances abroad, made to order as copies of the ones used in Warsaw. The Vilnius Fire Brigade provided the horses. Władysław also donated a large quantity of medical supplies from bandages to medication and sent the ambulance teams to Warsaw for training. The newspaper *Kraj* wrote in issue 50, 1902:

A new philanthropic institution has been created for the city of Vilnius with the aim of bringing medical help in cases of street accidents and emergencies. It models itself on the now well known and successful Warsaw Ambulance Service. The very first Ambulance Service was created in Vienna, after the terrible fire at the Ring Theatre. In Warsaw a similar organisation was made possible by Counts Konstanty and Gustaw Przeździecki, and the founder of the newly formed Ambulance Service in Vilnius is Count Władysław Tyszkiewicz from Lentvaris.

On the 4 September 1902, my great-grandmother organised a big ball to raise money for this ambulance service. It was held at the Grand Hotel in Vilnius where she was to put on many regular fund-raising events for this cause over the years.

At the same time as Władysław purchased all the necessary surgical supplies for the hospital and the ambulance service he also ordered a vast quantity of ear trumpets (concerned as he was with the feeling of isolation suffered by the deaf). He distributed them to the poor all over Vilnius. Such empathy was also there for all to see in his attitude to mental illness. From 1901 to 1905 he was the Head Governor of the Neuropsychiatric Hospital in Tworki not far from Warsaw. The hospital is the birthplace of modern Polish psychiatry and had been founded in 1891. It was the largest of its kind on Polish soil and still exists today. My great-grandfather's empathy was apparent to all, in that he engaged with much more than just administration issues. He firmly believed that the most common cause of mental illness wasn't of a hereditary nature but the result of unemployment, poverty, family problems and the like. He maintained that patients shouldn't simply be treated with the latest methods available, but that they also needed to be *listened* to. He visited regularly and chatted to them at length, often introducing humour and normality into desperately sad situations. The patients loved him.

Władysław campaigned assiduously for and made big donations to the Children's Hospital in Vilnius which wasn't opened until 1906. This was way behind Lwów (1854), Kraków (1876) and Warsaw (1878). Maryńcia tirelessly organised many fundraising events (balls, races, lotteries etc) to raise money for this new cause.

In addition to spending vast sums of his own to fund and run his many charities, my great-grandfather combined his drive to raise additional money, with his love of the performing arts: he organised three theatrical performances in Vilnius in the summer of 1905, by inviting top actors from the Warsaw Variety Theatre. After paying the actors, who stayed in Lentvaris and went into Vilnius by train, considerable funds were pumped into his causes. This event had an additional and poignant significance: by his dogged efforts he somehow obtained permission for the actors to perform in Polish. This was of great import for the town since Vilnius at that stage had neither newspapers nor schoolbooks in the Polish language. (The main theatre in Vilnius only obtained a *permanent* license to stage plays in Polish several months later, in November 1905.)

1905 was also a very important year because Władysław finally succeeded in getting permission from the Russian authorities to build a Catholic Church in Lentvaris. He'd applied for the first time in 1897 and had received a resounding no. He kept asking repeatedly and the copious correspondence about the negotiations with the authorities is in the

Central National Lithuanian Archive in Vilnius. It took so long because of categorical refusals by the Russians who, at that time, were busy closing down Catholic convents and monasteries and converting existing Catholic churches into Eastern Orthodox ones. Allowing the actual building of an RC church was therefore totally against their grain. Countless interventions by personal friends in high places within the Russian administration and a petition with four thousand signatures were instrumental in finally bringing the go ahead, but only for a small and very low-key wooden structure.

There were fears of course that even though the plans for a chapel had finally been approved, there could still be a veto from St Petersburg, so the moment the permission was granted Władysław and Maryńcia Tyszkiewicz mobilised the locals who, with a superhuman effort and a shared sense of purpose put up a wooden church in ten days flat. This alone makes the *Church of the Annunciation of the Holy Mother of God*, a very special church for me as it represents the passionate fight for freedom to worship, such an integral part of the battle to cling to one's identity, both at a personal and national level. It was consecrated in 1906 by the Bishop of Vilnius, Edward von Ropp.

What the Russian authorities weren't aware of was that the humble outer appearance of the wooden chapel they'd allowed, belied the splendid interior: an ancient carved door, paintings brought over from the palace, and my great grandfather's beloved religious Italian sculptures; nor did they know that a couple of decades later he would be replacing the wooden structure with a large brick design in the style of the fifteenth century church Maria della Grazia in Milan (which houses Leonardo's *The Last Supper*).

Wooden church in Lentvaris, 1906

EXILE, ART AND WAR

IN 1904 MY great-grandfather Władysław Tyszkiewicz obtained the signatures of just under two hundred of the most important intellectuals in the country for a petition in support of one of his favourite causes, namely the battle for the abolition of restrictions against Poles in Lithuania. The demands were for basic national rights: the use of the Polish language in schools, law courts and administrative institutions and the development of autonomy at local government level, both in the cities and in the countryside, with the active involvement of every stratum of society. This memorandum was personally delivered by my great-grandfather to Premier Piotr Światopełk-Mirski in St Petersburg in December 1904 and was yet another reiteration of Władysław's views. Since 1897 he had repeatedly argued that peasants, artisans and labourers should be drawn into public life so that they could have an active political voice.

Not surprisingly the Petition was very badly received by the Russian authorities and in 1905 my great-grandfather only escaped deportation to Archangelsk due to the intervention of a few high ranking Russians who'd been his friends since their Law School days in St Petersburg. Thanks to them he managed to hurriedly board a train and flee to Milan.

Not a good year, 1905. In fact, it turned out to be a most important turning point in Russian history. Ever since serfdom had been abolished by Tsar Alexander II forty-four years previously, agricultural workers had flooded into the cities to toil in the industrial sector where the pay was miserable, the working conditions unsafe, the hours inhumanely long and exploitation by employers rife. On 22 January 1905, a young priest, Father Gapon, who had a complex relationship with the police and the worker's movement, led a march of workers and their families towards the Winter Palace, in St Petersburg. The intention was of handing the Tsar a petition urging him to save the Russian people from 'a despotic and irresponsible government' and 'capitalistic exploiters, crooks and robbers'. Thousands progressed peacefully towards the Winter Palace carrying icons and portraits of the Emperor, singing religious hymns and the Imperial anthem 'God Save the Tsar'.

Throughout the city, their way was blocked by infantry, Cossacks and

Hussars. Still not expecting violence, the processions continued calmly but the soldiers opened fire and it was carnage where men, women and children were mown down. Official figures quoted ninety-two dead and hundreds wounded. Robert K. Massie in his book *Nicholas and Alexandra* gives a vivid account of that appalling day and what followed. He estimates there must have been many more killed and injured. The day became known as Bloody Sunday and the cries of the people quickly became, 'The Tsar will not help us!' and 'We have no Tsar!' Gapon disappeared whilst other leaders started moving around the country circulating hugely inflated casualty figures. From his place of hiding, Gapon denounced the Tsar as having the blood of workers, their wives and children on his hands. Robert K. Massie writes: '*Abroad the clumsy action seemed like premeditated cruelty and Ramsay MacDonald, a future Labour Prime Minister of Britain, attacked the Tsar as a blood-stained creature and a common murderer.*' Bloody Sunday destroyed the long-standing image of the Tsar as the father figure, the protector, as one with his people.

Tsar Nicholas who hadn't even been at the Winter Palace on that fateful afternoon but was staying at Tsarskoe Selo, was appalled at what had happened. '*A painful day*' he wrote. '*Serious disorders took place in Petersburg. Lord how painful and sad this is.*' He invited thirty-four workers to Tsarskoe Selo to talk to them as a father to his sons, urging them to turn their backs on the advice of treacherous revolutionaries. When the delegation returned to St Petersburg they were laughed at, ignored or beaten up.

Five days after Bloody Sunday the Empress Alexandra wrote to her sister: '*My poor Nicky's cross is a heavy one to bear, all the more because he has nobody on whom he can thoroughly rely. . . . The bad are always close at hand. He remains brave and full of faith in God's mercy.*'

Three weeks later the Tsar's uncle, Grand Duke Serge, was blown up by a bomb and soon after a new worker's organisation arose, with Leon Trotsky as leader. The Tsar promised the formation of a series of 'Dumas' or representative assemblies to work towards reform. Internal tensions in Russia continued to build as radical socialist groups became stronger.

Notwithstanding my great-grandfather's departure to Italy in 1905, there is no question that his belief in his patriotic causes overrode his fears for personal safety. In his *Memorandum for the Minister of Internal Affairs in St Petersburg* he'd stated that he regarded serving his country to be his duty and so, with considerable courage, he returned to Poland from Milan in 1906 to take up an important appointment he'd been elected for in his absence, as representative of the Warsaw District at the First Duma in St Petersburg (Legislative body in the Russian Parliament). The newspaper *Kurier Warszawski* (1906 nr 121) wrote about him as follows:

'He is the embodiment of our striving and yearnings in this dark period. For all the years of his unstinting dedication, Count Władysław Tyszkiewicz is awarded the honour and great responsibility by Warsaw, our capital, of being nominated as the Warsaw representative at the first Duma in St Petersburg.' The same article described him as *'a person of outstanding calibre and values. There hasn't been a single important public issue (not only in Warsaw but in the whole country), that Count Władysław Tyszkiewicz hasn't been involved in.'*

My great-grandfather was safer for a while as he was less likely to be arrested whilst in his official appointment in the Russian Duma. Fearless as he was, his voice grew ever louder. As the head of the Polish Council in St Petersburg he renewed his fight for political autonomy for Vistula Land and submitted a memorandum to PM Stołypin demanding the cessation of pogroms against the Jews and granting them a full legal status.

When the Duma was dissolved after only ten weeks as too radical, the Russian authorities resumed their harsh interference in Poland's internal politics and social affairs. They were again extremely displeased with my great-grandfather as they saw him as not merely behaving like a representative for Warsaw but as an overly vociferous Polish patriot fomenting anti-Russian attitudes on a national scale.

This time he was again saved from deportation to Archangelsk by a combination of Russian friends in high places, money, knowledge of legal procedures and the fact that his father had been an officer in the Tsar's army. But it was a very close shave indeed on this occasion as he was already on a train bound for Moscow accompanied by Russian police, when he heard that exile had been granted after all instead of Archangelsk, providing he left the country once more and again without delay. He was taken off the train and he set off for Italy leaving Maryńcia to organise things in Lentvaris with the view of then joining him in Milan with the children. It was 1907 and he didn't know then that this second exile would last for seven years.

This flight for safety illustrates one of those on-going splits of identity and allegiances Poles had to live with. The Tyszkiewicz constantly rebelled against Russian domination yet they revered the Tsar of Russia as a person, sympathising with his position (the last thing Nicholas had wanted was to become Tsar). Although the Tsar's regime would have silenced my great-grandfather by deporting him to Archangelsk, my great-grandparents respected the Tsar and his family and admired his valiant attempts to be a good man. When some years earlier, in 1898, Nicholas II issued a dramatic appeal to all the governments in the world urging universal peace and disarmament, virtually the whole of Europe was astonished and dismissed the Tsar's plea in the same tone as the Prince of Wales who'd said it was 'the greatest nonsense and rubbish ever heard'.

My grandmother's family were appalled at such a world response, and they were visibly pleased when out of deference for the Tsar, a conference was organised in the Hague after all (in 1899). Needless to say the Tsar's suggestions of freezing armaments fell on deaf ears but at least rules of warfare were agreed, and a court of arbitration was set up. (Later, in 1914 just before the First World War started, Tsar Nicholas II begged the Kaiser to let the Hague settle the dispute between Austria and Serbia. He was ignored. Again, despite his vociferous opposition to the Russification of Poland and Lithuania, and of being himself constantly threatened by the Tsar's government, my great-grandfather empathised with the Tsar.

Soon after my great-grandfather's hurried departure to Milan in 1907, Maryńcia Tyszkiewicz, her four children and one maid, Marysia Plennik, followed to Italy by train. My grandmother Róża was heartbroken that Paniunia stayed behind but she was told that because she was nine years old, she didn't need a nanny. They went via Berlin where they stopped for three days at the 'Central' Hotel (later called 'The Adlon').

The children were taken to Berlin zoo, the amusement park, the wax museum and shopping for clothes. My grandmother told me years later how well she remembered the last evening at the hotel being spent in its 'Wintergarten' restaurant with magical lighting, delicious delicacies and a very smart waiter in tails tripping and just catching a cake with a flourish. Overleaf is an earlier photograph from the late 1800s. By 1907 there were many more tables. It was all great fun but of course the overriding joy for the children was that they'd soon be reunited with their father.

In Milan, the Tyszkiewicz lived for the first year on Via dell'Orso, in a large and sunny apartment behind La Scala, and later moved to a beautiful

Wintergarten in Central Hotel Berlin 1800s

and spacious villa a stone's throw from the gardens of Castello Sforzesco. Their local church was Santa Maria Delle Grazie, where, before and after the years of exile, my great-grandfather always began and finished each stay in Milan with a prayer in front Leonardo da Vinci's *Last Supper*.

In the beginning, only Władysław spoke Italian so Maryńcia and the children made extra efforts to pick up the language. My great-grandfather's butler, who was bilingual, helped with interpreting. A friendly Mademoiselle (Jeanne Port) was brought from France, a tutor called Zygmunt Dewar came from Maryńcia's childhood home Kruszyna, a local music teacher and a tutor of Italian were employed for the older children (Stetysz and Zofia) whilst my grandmother Róża and the youngest Eugeniusz were sent to school.

My poor vulnerable grandmother was miserably unhappy with the austere nuns but her older sister Zofia, clever and self assured, relished the many subjects taught by French and Italian teachers: Introduction to Chemistry and Physics, History of Art, Contemporary and Italian History, Classics, French History and Literature, Philosophy, Religious Studies, English, French and German. The only optional subject was singing.

There was terrific excitement that year when my grandmother's older brother Stefan (known as 'Stetysz') appeared in the newspaper *Corriere Della Serra* in Milan, as the youngest ever person to get a driving licence. It was 1907 and he was fourteen years old. The following year, however, brought terrible news: Władysław's first cousin Krystyna was widowed when her forty-seven-year-old husband, Count Andrzej Potocki, Austrian Viceroy of Galicia, was murdered by Ukranian student Mirosław Siczyński. In spite of his mortal wounds, Andrzej Potocki had time to confess his sins to a Catholic priest and say goodbye to his wife and nine children. My insecure ten-year-old grandmother Róża couldn't sleep for weeks, fearing someone would kill her Papa too... and to add to her night terrors, news came from Poland that fire had swept through the Lubomirski stables in Kruszyna killing many much loved horses...

A year and a half later a daring (or crazy) event took place on the occasion of the party for the fiftieth wedding anniversary of my great-grandmother's parents which was celebrated in Warsaw in 1909. As we know Władysław was exiled and it wasn't safe for him to be in Poland and yet there he is, on the family photo, second from the left.

He took a risk and zipped in and out of the country for the event which wasn't really a low key affair since the celebrations started with Mass and blessings by the Bishop of Warsaw, followed by lunch at the Hotel

Warsaw June 1909, fiftieth wedding anniversary of Prince Eugeniusz Lubomirski (1825–1911) and Princess Róża Lubomirska née Countess Zamoyska (1836–1915) parents of Maria Krystyna (Maryńcia) Tyszkiewicz third from the L in front of her husband Władysław. Seated on the floor, third from R to L, my grandmother Róża, eleven years old, wearing a scalloped white collar. I have the names of all those present.

Europejski, after which everyone moved on to the Lubomirski town house on Aleje Ujazdowskie 37. I don't know how he got away with it. But he did.

The year 1910 brought my great-grandparents great excitement with the news that my great-grandmother's brother, Prince Stanisław Lubomirski, had set up the Warsaw Air Association (Aviata) with the first flying school in Poland and an aeroplane manufacturing business. One can imagine just how thrilled my grandmother's brother Stetysz was. He was sixteen at the time and his uncle Stanisław Lubomirski's new venture was right up his street.

In 1911, Stetysz himself thrilled his parents and siblings again when at the age of seventeen he registered two patents for heating devices, one for cars, one for flying machines. Alas, Stanisław Lubomirski's excitement about the flying school and the aeroplane factory didn't last long: in 1912 the Tsar's government withdrew his licence and a few months later the army took over his business. One can see why the Tsar's government was so keen to steal this enterprise: in 1911 the Russian Navy had bought two aeroplanes after which, in eight months, Stanisław Lubomirski's aeroplane factory had produced ten aeroplanes (Farman-Aviata) and Blériot XI one of the first French flying machines. (*Kazimierz Sławiński, 'History of Polish Wings', Warsaw 1974, Andrzej Glass, Polish aircraft constructions 1893–1939, Warsaw 1976.*)

Weeks and months rolled on and my great-grandfather's passion for art kept him busy with the exciting antiques business which he'd set up in Milan. He called it 'Galleria Warowland' – anagram of Landwarów (the Polish for Lentvaris). He'd found a perfect setting for it in the Palace of Count Edouard Amman (today, Via Arrigo Boito 8) in the centre of Milan. Alongside his immersion in art, his ever-present philanthropic drive involved him also in the Milan Charity Society with Viscount and Viscountess di Modrone who became great friends and whose children often invited my grandmother and her siblings to Rimini on the Adriatic. Happy holidays were spent with many other Italian friends too: Visconti, Castelbarco, Gregorini-Bingham etc.

Galleria Warowland became a great success and soon needed larger premises, which my great-grandfather found on Via Allessandro Manzoni 10/Via Gerolamo Morone. He had eight large rooms there, filled with antiquities. He liaised with restorers, art historians and well-known antiquarians (like Gustavo Gagliardi and Alfredo Geri), organised auctions, sourced items for clients.

His business continued to develop; so much so that by 1913 he'd opened a second gallery in the resort of Salsomaggiore.

My grandmother and her siblings often came into the Milan gallery to feast their eyes.

Music and the performing arts figured large in their life in Milan: La Scala of course with an exciting season from Christmas to Easter, but also the many Milanese theatres: Teatro Manzoni for classical plays; Teatro Filodrammatico, with modern ones (apparently not suitable for young ladies); Theatro Lirico, for operettas and lighthearted entertainment; Teatro Giuseppe Verdi, popular with everyone not least school children, with historical plays and plenty of loud and exciting battle scenes.

The children were also taken further afield: Rome, Lido di Venezia, Burano, Pisa, Venice, Padua, Florence, Verona, and of course the lakes, Majjore, Lugano and Como. Władysław and Maryńcia were determined that they should get to know as much of Italy as possible during those years and, in spite of my great-grandfather's very busy life, he never grudged the time spent with his children, opening their minds to art and history. My great-aunt Zofia (later Potocka) always said that she owed her father the lifelong passion she developed for History of Art.

There is no doubt that such a long time (1907–1914) spent in Italy during formative years became ingrained into my grandmother's and her siblings' identity. Italy, more than France, Austria or Switzerland, got under their skin for ever. As for the language, my grandmother Róża, ending up in Argentina and Brazil after the Second World War, always made a total muddle of Spanish, Portuguese and Italian. Very fluent – but hilarious.

During the years in Italy, Maryńcia and the children went back to Lentvaris every so often so that she could keep an eye on the running of it. For Władysław the seven years ended when an amnesty was declared for political exiles. At this point my great-grandfather decided to have a sale of most of his art and return to his beloved Lentvaris with his family.

In 2015, Aisté Bimbirytè-Mackevičiené from the Lithuanian Cultural Research Institute, published a paper about my great-grandfather: '*Władysław*

Tyszkiewicz in Italy: 'Galleria Warowland' and his Milanese Collection'. In this paper she covers this major sale that my great-grandfather had on 3 to 6 February 1913 in St Moritz under the direction of M. Gustave Galiardi. The catalogue is archived at Fondazione Marco Besso in Rome.

The sale consisted of three hundred and twelve items, sculptures and paintings from between the fifteenth and the nineteenth centuries, amongst which were: El Greco, Bronzino, Pietro Longhi, Tiepolo, Titian, Corregio, Veronese, Justus Sustermans, Caravaggio, Bernardo Strozzi, Tintoretto, Parmigianino, Poussain, Canaletto, Ingres, Turner etc. The news about the collection spread outside Italy and Switzerland, and it was reported in the French, German and Spanish press. Individual examples of the collection also attracted special attention : the Spanish journal *Mundo Grafico* analysed *The Coronation of the Virgin* by El Greco, discussed its stylistic features, and based on those, dated it to the early period of the painter's oeuvre.

'The Coronation of the Virgin', El Greco (one of the 312 items in my great-grandfather's sale in St Moritz in 1913)
(By kind permission of the Fondazione Marco Besso in Rome)

I would love to know where all these items ended up… No question of claiming them back of course, as this was a legitimate sale, but it would be intriguing to see at least one of them in the flesh.

After the sale Władysław and Maryńcia Tyszkiewicz and the children returned home to Lentvaris. Their nineteen-year-old budding engineer son, Stetysz, set off to Oxford University to begin his undergraduate studies in Engineering. He was home for his very first break from Oxford when the First World War started in 1914 and he was never to return to the dreaming spires. My great-grandparents and their children hadn't been back in Lentvaris long when the war broke out. Stetysz was conscripted into the Russian Army in 1915 and his life took extraordinary turns from then on, not least landing right in the middle of the Romanov circle.

In those early days of the First World War, my great-grandparents opened their doors to a multitude of friends and extended family members who passed through Lentvaris en route to places deemed safer than their own homes. All were given shelter, clothes and food for the road ahead.

Every morning, my great-grandmother rearranged little flags on a map, marking troop movements – French, English, Russian and German, according to radio and press reports. Suddenly, everyone was placing their hope in the Russians, believing the Germans would never come that far. Having for years vociferously campaigned against the Russification of Poland and been twice exiled to escape the wrath of the Russian authorities, here was my great-grandfather, like everybody else, having to side with the opressor when faced with the then more immediate enemy, namely Germany. At one point a Russian dragoon cavalry regiment was stationed in Lentvaris under the command of Colonel Biskupski, of Polish ancestry, who actually ordered his men to behave in a civilised manner.

The officers ate at the same table as the Tyszkiewicz, enchanted by my great-grandmother's conversation and elegance. So accommodating were these Russians that in 1915 they dispatched most of the contents of Lentvaris into the depths of Russia to 'protect' them from the Germans just in case (!) whilst 'helping' to bury smaller items in the grounds. I don't need to tell you that none of it was ever seen again by my grandmother's family.

Not only was the Russian regiment stationed in Lentvaris for a while, but Władysław immediately offered his services to the Russian Red Cross and allotted several buildings in Lentvaris for a Red Cross Hospital of a hundred beds. The train station wasn't far and there were many horses that made the transportation of the wounded easier.

My great-grandfather and his brother-in-law, Prince Konstanty Lubomirski from Kruszyna, managed the hospital. Konstanty assisted during operations and my grandmother'sister, Zofia, helped the many nurses and doctors sent from Libava. She became a nurse overnight, not flinching at the appalling suffering of most under her care. She was just twenty-one.

My great-grandmother Maryńcia organised the kitchens with the aid of many local women but there were so many wounded that the whole extended family were involved in helping with whatever was needed: ferrying the patients, feeding and washing them, dressing wounds, writing letters to the families of the dying etc. My grandmother Róża, sixteen at the time, was of too fragile a disposition to go anywhere near the patients without having nightmares at the sight of their wounds, but helped as she could in the kitchens.

The Germans advanced ever closer and soon my great-grandfather had to move the hospital to St Petersburg (and later through the Caucasus to Persia (Iran) where he was appointed head of the local Russian Red Cross). As the hospital and the soldiers were leaving Lentvaris somehow my great-grandmother got wind of the fact that a Russian soldier had been ordered to stay behind to blow up the house as a parting gesture (thus to deny the

First World War Red Cross Hospital on Lentvaris estate. My great-grandfather Władysław Tyszkiewicz is the first man standing on the R. On his right stands his daughter, my great-aunt Zofia Tyszkiewicz (later Potocka by marriage). My great-grandmother Maryńcia sitting in the centre.

oncoming Germans access to such a suitable base). With neither husband nor eldest son Stetysz for support, Maryńcia showed enormous courage. She made a quick decision: having concealed a pony and trap in a copse, she used it to rush the young intoVilnius where she left them and the trap, and then rode her horse back galloping as fast as she could to Lentvaris. She then waited out of sight and confronted the soldier who was about to lay down the explosives. My great-grandmother bribed him with a fat wad of rubles and he disappeared into the night. I wonder if at any point it occurred to her that this little enounter might have had a very different outcome.

Before mounting her horse and heading back to her children in Vilnius, she placed a note in perfect German, addressed to the military commander whom she knew would soon be occupying Lentvaris. In it she appealed to his human decency, suggesting he and his men might respect the little that was left of the family possessions. She placed the note by a bust of herself, sculpted in 1905 by the well known Polish artist Mordasewicz.

I've indeed come to admire my great-grandmother immensely. The aloof woman who hadn't been great at cuddling her children, rose spectacularly to the occasion showing not only true grit in face of great difficulties but also, by all accounts, a new surge of warmth towards her offspring. Everything was on her slender shoulders, including suddenly, the educating of her children, since the resident tutors had left for their respective countries. The girls were teenagers so to supplement what she now had to teach them herself at home, they were taken, whenever possible, to secret private lessons held illegally in the Polish language. Lessons were held in different houses and the calibre was very high. (Some years later one of the masters became a University professor.)

The younguest child, Eugeniusz, was entirely taught by his mother. For Maryńcia a truly well-rounded education was paramount, which is what she'd had herself in her childhood home, Kruszyna. Unusually for that period, she'd been brought up to regard high level studies equally important for girls as for boys. Top of her list of essentials were manners, followed by a love of books, sport, foreign languages, history, European literature, piano, and a basic knowledge of philosophy, mathematics, physics and chemistry. She believed in training both the body and the mind. Although at times for my grandmother Róża this was too much, the others seemed to follow the leader, and she led by example as well as rules.

My great-grandmother stayed in Vilnius for the duration of the German occupation (1915–1918). At the very beginning, the Germans were fairly liberal towards the Poles in Vilnius and Maryńcia showed incredible diplomacy, expedience and negotiating talents in establishing as good a relationship as she could with the invader. She knew that they'd use Lentvaris as a base and indeed as their larder so she did her utmost to help them run the farms efficiently and produce as much food as possible, thus protecting the livelihood of her workforce, agricultural, administrative and in the estate factories. She made herself useful rather than a thorn in the Prussian side and gained their respect and goodwill. So much so that they gave her a stamped pass that allowed her to move freely between Lentvaris, Vilnius, Trakai and Užutrakis. Being a first-class horsewoman, she did so on her horse, keeping an eye on the management of the land not only in Lentvaris but the adjoining Tyszkiewicz estates.

Maryńcia went as far as entertaining high ranking Prussians for dinner in her mother-in-law's house in Vilnius on 11 Trocka street, where in a bubble of elegance and calm she spoke her mind on political matters without flinching. In a book about Vilnius during the German occupation, the writer A. Pukszto says of my great-grandmother that *'this petite and delicate looking woman showed no fear of the invader'.*

It goes without saying that the fact Maryńcia's first cousin Prince Zdzisław Lubomirski was in the Regency Council, proved a massive help as indeed did the fact that he'd been appointed Mayor of Warsaw by the military governor of the German-occupied part of the Polish lands, General Hans Hartwig von Beseler. Nevertheless, she knew how to oil the cogs. She achieved much using her extensive contacts to save many from persecution.

During the German ocupation of Vilnius (1915–1918) my great-grandmother avoided taking the children to Lentvaris so as to reduce their distress at seeing the state their beloved home was in. In a later letter to his sister, Władysław's first cousin, Jan Tyszkiewicz from Trakų Vokė, described his feelings when going there: *'One feels like an uninvited guest amongst the mangy quarantined horses grazing on the lawns and crowding the stables, countless Germans everywhere and their Russian prisoners staggering about in every part of the house.'* She could shield the children from that, but she couldn't prevent them from seeing what went on in Vilnius where there was no shortage of wounded Germans and Poles. Nor indeed could she cover their ears when conversations all around were about the horror of the trenches, the carnage of battles on both fronts, the thousands of people abandoning their homes and fleeing to the forests, or to overcrowded villages and towns, only to find further hardship and devastation. Malaria, cholera and dysentery raged.

Scores of local volunteers of every social class moved heaven and earth to set up more hospital facilities in Vilnius and my great aunt Zofia joined a large group of women as a nursing assistant, doing whatever was needed however unsavoury or heart rending. What her mother Maryńcia didn't know was that Zofia was working mainly with typhoid and dysentery patients putting her own health at serious risk.

Throughout this period, each in a different part of the globe, both Władysław and Maryńcia Tyszkiewicz worried desperately about their son, my great-uncle Stetysz who was part of the close Tsarist circle. In 1917, two revolutions swept through Russia. It was to be the ending of centuries of imperial rule and the onset of political and social changes. Growing civil unrest and serious food shortages, brought about open revolt. Tsar Nicholas II was forced to abdicate, unaware that the following year, on 17 July 1918, he, his wife Tsarina Alexandra and their five children (Olga, Tatiana, Maria, Anastasia and Alexei) would be shot, bayoneted and clubbed to death in Yekaterinburg. Throughout all this, my great-grandparents only received snippets of information about Stetysz. It must have been hell.

I do need to devote quite a few pages to my great-uncle Stetysz and his involvement with the Romanovs but first, without delving into the massive, heroic, many faceted and devastating course of the First World War, I'll leapfrog to its very end. In 1918, miles West from Lentvaris, the vital Greater Poland Uprising against the Prussians took place and Poland was victorious. Its territorial gains were confirmed by the Treaty of Versailles in January 1920 (a most important of peace treaties because it brought The First World War to an end). The Russian Red Cross was closed down on Persian soil, and my great-grandfather Władysław Tyszkiewicz returned home.

～～

My grandmother Róża might have fallen apart completely during the First World War. But she didn't. The hyper-sensitivity of her childhood became less raw, inspite of the horrors and dangers witnessed and endured. Maybe because her mother Maryńcia had become more protective of her and at last Róża felt loved. Maybe because Róża, sixteen when the war started and twenty when it ended, could not fail but admire her mother's courage in face of the enemy and see that this was the moment when Maryńcia excelled in protecting the three children she had under her wing. The one Maryńcia worried most about was Stetysz because since 1914 he wasn't there with her, but in the jaws of war.

CHAPTER SIX

STEFAN TYSZKIEWICZ AND THE ROMANOVS: LOVE, DEATH AND ESCAPE

THIS IS HOW Princess Maria Lubomirska née Branicka (1873–1934) describes my great-uncle Stetysz in her memoirs:

'Big ears, huge black eyes, ugly, kind' and yet... *'Of all the dancers Stefan Tyszkiewicz is the most attractive due to his height and youthful charm. When he dances, he lowers his head above the young lady like a bird of prey and seems to possess all of her as he glides in a waltz.'*

My great-uncle Big-Ears really wasn't run-of-the-mill. Second child and first son of Władysław and Maryńcia Tyszkiewicz, he was christened Stefan after one of his mother's brothers, Eugeniusz after his maternal grandfather and, wait for it, Maria after the mother of Jesus. In those days men were often given names of female saints as middle names. My own father was christened Józef Adam Maria Teresa Mycielski. My son should be jolly grateful I didn't call him Bernadette.

I'm not quite sure at which point Stefan Tyszkiewicz became Stetysz (the first syllables of name and surname put together) but this was the name he was known by all of his adult life.

Stetysz showed a remarkable aptitude for technology from an early age. As mentioned earlier, he obtained a driver's licence in Milan as a fourteen year old and was a patented inventor at seventeen (in 1911) with two heating systems, one for cars, one for what were then called flying-machines. When he was forced to abandon his Engineering studies at Oxford University on his very first holiday back home (with the start of the First World War) he was very sad. He was never to return to the dreaming spires but he knew where his duty lay and immediately volunteered for the Russian branch of the International Red Cross. For conspicuous bravery in saving, under fire, seven gravely injured soldiers, he was awarded the (Russian) Cross of St George.

There are many accounts of his bravery during that time, one of them in an obituary in *Wiadomości* nr 1584 published on 8 August 1976 in London.

The writer describes the events which led to Stetysz being awarded the St George's Cross by the Russians:

'The offensive of the German army (Nov 1914) had reached Łowicz where a battle raged. Stetysz (twenty years old) hearing that in a besieged village (Maluszyce) several wounded people were trapped in a burning house, set off towards them on his own in a car. He rescued them, put them all in the car and brought them to safety under enemy fire. His car was damaged by bullets, but no one received further injuries. He was recommended for the Cross of Saint George by two Colonels and the people of Łowicz. This was most unusual since he was not in the army, merely a young volunteer in the Red Cross.'

In 1915, Stetysz was conscripted into the Russian Army. He joined as an officer and fought first on the Volhynian then on the Lithuanian front. He took part in the front line in the cavalry and was later in the trenches. From late 1916 he was adjutant to the 6ft 7in tall Gen. Grand Duke Nicholas Nicholaievich, 'Nikolasha' (born 1856 died 1929), then the Commander-in-Chief on the Caucasian Front. His Imperial Highness Grand Duke Nicholas Nicholaievich had been one of the most important men in Russia, so much so that in 1915 the Duma had been stormed by his vociferous supporters who begged him to take power. He refused out of loyalty to the Tsar. Having been recalled from his command of the Russian armies, he became Viceroy of the Caucasus and commander on the anti-Turkish front.

As his adjutant Stetysz met the Grand Duke's step-daughter, Princess Helena Leuchtenberg, and soon after, when Stetysz was 23 and Helena 25, they married in Yalta, on the 5 July 1917. (I have a copy of their marriage certificate.)

Her mother was Princess Anastasia ('Stana') one of the daughters of the King of Montenegro. One of her aunts was Queen of Serbia, another was Queen of Italy (wife of Victor Emanuel III). Through her father (Georgi Beauharnais, 6th Duke of Leuchtenberg) Helena was great-granddaughter of Tsar Nicholas I, great-great-granddaughter of King Frederick III of Prussia and great-great-granddaughter of Napoleon's Josephine through her first marriage to Alexandre Beauharnais.

On her father's side Helena was:

Stetysz's wife, Princess Helena Leuchtenberg, granddaughter of the King of Montenegro, and her father George/Jerzy/Georgi Maximilianovich, 6th Duke of Leuchtenberg

– granddaughter of Tsar Alexander II's sister (Grand Duchess Maria Nicholaievna)

– great-great-granddaughter of Tsar Peter III and Catherine the Great.

– great-granddaughter of Napoleon's Josephine through Josephine's first marriage to Alexandra Beauharnais.

And so on. You can see how, Lord help him, my great-uncle Stetysz became part of the closest Tsarist circle. I suppose he was lucky not to have been in that milieu a few years earlier, when in 1905 his (then future) mother-in-law 'Stana', with her sister Militsa, introduced the legendary self-styled mystic Rasputin, to the Tsarina. The two Montenegrin sisters were known as *'The Black Princesses'*, the *'Black Crows'* or even *'The Black Peril'* due to their interest in Rasputin and his occult and weird mystic practices. The Tsar's mother, the Dowager Empress Marie Feodorovna, loathed the two Montenegrin princesses to such an extent that she called them *'The Cockroaches'*!

After meeting Rasputin, the Tsar referred to him in his diary as '*a man of God*' and a year or so later he wrote: '*Militsa and Stana dined with us. They talked about Gregory (Rasputin) all evening*'. The Tsar and his wife were completely taken with Rasputin and hugely grateful to the Montenegrin sisters for introducing him.

The Tsarina with her children and Rasputin plus unknown woman circa 1910 (Alamy)

Rasputin not only looked quite alarming but he was said to have BO and far worse personal habits and desires. The serious issue though was that having convinced the Tsar and Tsarina that he was holy and the only person who could make their beloved haemophiliac son Alexei better, he manoeuvred himself into all sorts of political scenarios and many, including the Dowager, would say he played a considerable part in the Tsar's downfall.

Rasputin became so powerful that when Tsar Nicholas II took personal command of his forces in the First World War in September 1915, he left his wife Tsarina Alexandra in charge of Russia's internal affairs with Rasputin as her adviser. It was downhill all the way from then.

By the time Stetysz married Helena (5 July 1917), Rasputin had been murdered (December 1916) and the Tsar had abdicated (March 1917). By various accounts Rasputin took some murdering: the poisoned cake he was given had no effect at all, the shots fired at him didn't kill him either and he had to be pushed into a freezing river before he gave up the ghost. Anyway, by the time Stetysz and Helena got married, the 'Mad Monk' was no more and both Stetysz's mother-in-law Stana and her sister Militsa, who'd introduced him to the Tsarina years before, had come to their senses and saw Rasputin for the dangerous fraud he was. They fell out of favour with the Tsar and Tsarina when they tried to warn them against him.

Stetysz and Helena were married in a Roman Catholic church and then, with special permission, in an Orthodox one, since Helena's family had converted to the Russian Orthodox religion when they moved to Russia from Bavaria in the nineteenth century and linked their lives to the Romanovs. This double ceremony was most unusual in those pre-ecumenical times.

Yalta 5 July 1917 Wedding of Stefan Tyszkiewicz ('Stetysz') to Helena Leuchtenberg daughter of 6th Duke of Leuchtenberg. Standing is Helena's step-father, Grand Duke Nicholas Nicholaevich, the Tsar's cousin (Nikolasha) who commanded the Russian Army in the First World War, and Helena's mother Anastasia, known as 'Stana', daughter of the King of Montenegro

Married bliss didn't last long for Stetysz as when the Bolsheviks came to power in October 1917, only three months after his wedding to Helena, many Romanovs gathered in the Crimea at Villa Ai Todor. In February

1918, this group was split and the more important Romanovs, including the Tsar's mother, were detained in Grand Duke Nikolasha's Dulber Palace. They were in danger of being either slaughtered or deported as were Stetysz and Helena.

Eventually this group of survivors were saved by the British Battleship HMS *Marlborough*, sent by King George V and Prime Minister Lloyd George and sailed to safety from Yalta on 11 April 1919 (having boarded over the 7th, 8th and 9th).

Alas, the Tsar, Tsarina and their five children, imprisoned in Yekaterinburg, almost 3,000 km from Yalta, had remained at the mercy of the Bolsheviks. On 17 July 1918, almost a year before HMS *Marlborough* took its passengers to safety, the Tsar and his family were bayonetted, shot and clubbed to death, at orders from Lenin. Several of their very close relations were thrown down a mineshaft in Alapaevsk the next day. I hope the perpetrators, who heard them singing hymns below ground as they awaited their deaths, were

Tsar Nicholas II, Tsarina Alexandra and their five children (Wikipedia.org)

haunted by it forever. Four other Romanovs were shot in Petrograd on the 28 January 1919 and hurled into a common grave.

My great-uncle Stetysz and the surviving Romanovs were lucky to get out when they did but there is no doubt that the gratitude towards King George V for sending HMS *Marlborough* was tainted by sadness that his Prime Minister Lloyd George had objected to earlier suggestions of saving the Tsar and his family. Apparently the fear had been that this could have sparked a revolution in England.

Overleaf is the passenger list of those on HMS *Marlborough* in Yalta on the 9 April 1919. Stetysz and Helena are on the second page (see pages 66 and 67).

The passenger list doesn't show the pet dogs that came too: Mutzi, Toby, Bobi, Chi Foo and Soon (the latter two being the Dowager Empress's Pekingese). Stetysz recounted that the Romanovs were hugely grateful to the British officers for being kind not only to them but also to their beloved dogs.

Vice Admiral Sir Francis Pridham (First Lieutenant at the time of the evacuation) writes in *Close of a Dynasty* about the extraordinary fortitude shown by the passengers, and their clear efforts to cause as little inconvenience as possible. He marvels at the courage of these people, who for months had been in constant danger of assassination, who were leaving their country forever and whose final destination was unclear. He adds:

'They expressed repeatedly their gratitude for the little we were able to do in providing for their comfort, while declaring that they had been prepared to be satisfied with much less.'

The boarding of HMS *Marlborough* had been distressing to watch: The Dowager Empress, regal in the eerie fog that enveloped all, kissed one of the ponies that had pulled her landau before walking towards the beach. Pridham writes at the time: *'It is dreadful to see them, dazed and heartbroken, except for the children who fortunately don't realise what is happening'.* The Dowager herself later described her feelings. *'What grief and desperation...'* She was appalled and helpless at the sight of distraught people on the shore trying to save themselves and their families, begging to be allowed on board of this ship, any ship. Pridham writes: *'...Her Majesty was frequently greatly distressed by the pathetically urgent pleas which she was unable to meet.'*

APPENDIX VII

List of Those Embarked on Board H.M.S. Marlborough at Yalta, Crimea, on the 7th, 8th and 9th April 1919

Her Imperial Majesty THE EMPRESS MARIE FEODOROVNA OF RUSSIA.

Her Imperial Highness The Grand Duchess XENIA ALEXANDROVNA, sister of the Emperor and wife of The Grand Duke Alexander Mikhailovitch.

*His Imperial Highness The Grand Duke NICHOLAS NICHOLAIEVITCH, cousin of The Emperor.

*His Imperial Highness The Grand Duke PETER NICHOLAIEVITCH, brother of Grand Duke Nicholas.

*Her Imperial Highness The Grand Duchess ANASTASIA, wife of the Grand Duke Nicholas.

*Her Imperial Highness The Grand Duchess MILITSA, wife of the Grand Duke Peter

Their Highnesses Prince FEODOR, Prince NIKITA, Prince DMITRI, Prince ROSTISLAV and Prince VASSILI, sons of the Grand Duchess Xenia.

*Their Highnesses Princess MARINA and Prince ROMAN, children of the Grand Duke Peter

Princess OLGA ORLOFF, mother of:

Prince NICHOLAS ORLOFF. His wife Princess NADEISGDA ORLOFF, younger daughter of Grand Duke Peter. Their daughter, aged one year, Princess IRINA ORLOFF.

Prince YOUSSOUPOFF (senior). His wife Princess ZINAIDA.

Prince FELIX YOUSSOUPOFF, son of the above. His wife Princess IRINA, daughter of the Grand Duchess Xenia. Their daughter Princess IRINA, aged five years.

Princess OLGA PETROVNA DOLGOROUKI, mother of:

Prince SERGE DOLGOROUKI, Marshall of Her Majesty's Household. His daughter Princess OLGA, and his niece Princess SOPHIA DOLDOROUKI.

Princess OBOLENSKY, Her Majesty's first Lady in Waiting.

Page 1 of 2 of the passenger-list on HMS Marlborough *in April 1919 – Appendix VII of 'Close of a Dynasty' by Vice-Admiral Sir Francis Pridham KBE, CB published by Allan Wingate, London Copyright 1956. NB Sir Francis Pridham was himself on HMS* Marlborough *in 1919 as its First Lieutenant*

Admiral Prince VIASSEMSKY, Admiral of the Imperial Yachts. His wife
   Princess MARGARET VIASSEMSKY.
The Countess ZINAIDA MENGDEN, Lady in Waiting.
Madame SOPHIA EVREINOVA, Lady in Waiting to Grand Duchess Xenia.
Colonel Prince ORBELIANI, on the Staff of the Grand Duke Alexander.
*The Count and Countess TYSZKIEWICH, daughter of the Grand Duchess
   Nicholas by her first husband.
*The Baron and Baroness STAAL, and daughter Baroness MARIE STAAL.
General and Madame CHATELAIN and daughter aged six years.
*Count FERSEN, M. BOLDYREFF and Dr MALAMA.
General FOGUEL, on the Staff of the Grand Duke Alexander.
Governesses: Miss COSTER, Miss TURK, Miss KING and Miss HENTON.
Nurses, Maids and Men servants:

With Her Majesty.	Mlle GREENVELD.
	Maids: VASSIELIEFF and OLGA VASSILIEFF.
	Man servant: VIGISS.
	Cossack Guards: YASTCHIK and POLIAKOFF.
*With the Grand Duke Nicholas.	Men: SMIRNOFF and TATAVEROFF.
	Maids: MICHAELONKA, MICHAELONKA and GRUSSBERG.
*With the Grand Duke Peter.	Man: FROLOFF.
	Maids: YOUPKOVA, MORAT, KOUPTSOVA, PESAREVSKY and FROLOFF.
With the Grand Duchess Xenia.	Man: KOLOMINOFF.
	Maids: PAVLOVA, BALOUSIEVA, AFFANASIEVA, PAVLOVA and SEBOLEFF.
With Princess Orloff.	Maids: ANTONOVA, SAVILINA and PRAKFIEVA.
With Prince Youssoupoff.	Men: TESSFAY, TROPIN and LATT
	Maids: JOVRAVLOFF and LATA.
With Ladies in Waiting.	Maids: APSE, OZER and ADELE.
With Prince Dolgorouki.	Man: CHOURILOFF.
	Maids: RETKIN and LOUISE.

Of the above those marked * disembarked at Constantinople and
transferred to H.M.S. *Lord Nelson*, all the remainder remained onboard
until the ship arrived in Malta.

L

Page 2 of 2 of the passenger-list on the Marlborough in April 1919 – Appendix VII of
'Close of a Dynasty' by Vice-Admiral Sir Francis Pridham KBE, CB published by Allan
Wingate, London Copyright 1956. Great-uncle Stetysz is at the top (the first asterisk)

Pridham also mentions the kindness of the royals towards their servants and one of his examples is Princess Marina's generosity of spirit towards her maid. The Princess was the daughter of Nikolasha's brother, Grand Duke Peter, and of Grand Duchess Militsa (Stetysz's mother-in-law's sister). She had a small one-berth cabin for herself and her maid. The latter was meant to sleep on a mattress on the deck.

Princess Marina insisted the servant had both mattresses, one on top of the other, whilst she herself would sleep on the deck with a blanket. That proved unnecessary because First Lieutenant Francis Pridham found an extra mattress but he noted the kindness in his diary. The Princess had explained that *'her maid suffered from rheumatism and needed a soft bed, whereas she herself was used to roughing it, having been in the Caucasus campaign for many months as a hospital nurse'*. He says this was but one example of the thoughtfulness of the Imperial family towards their employees and bemoans that these were *'the very people who had for years been accused of being pitiless tyrants,'* concluding: *'In those days we had not yet learned to suspect or recognise the insidiousness of Leftist propaganda.'*

Six days after sailing, HMS *Marlborough* docked in Constantinople. I've tracked down an interesting little document in one of Stetysz's files: a certificate from the Italian High Commission in Turkey, dated 17 April 1919 and signed in Constantinople by the High Commissioner, Count Carlo Sforza. It allows entry into Italy to a number of passengers. The first six people are given pseudonyms in order to travel incognito. They were to be the family Borisoff.

1. S. A. I. Il Granduca Nicola (His Imperial Highness Grand Duke Nicholas Nicholaevich 'Nikolasha'), ie Stetysz's wife Helena's step-father.
   Signor Nicola Borisoff

2. S.A.I. La Granduchessa Anastasia (Her Imperial Highness Grand Duchess Anastasia), ie 'Stana', daughter of the King of Montenegro, Stetysz's mother-in-law.
   Signora Anastasia Borisoff

3. S.A.I. Il Granduca Pietro (His Imperial Highness Grand Duke Peter Nikolaevich), brother of 'Nikolasha'.
   Signor Pietro Borisoff

4. S.A.I. La Granduchessa Miliza (Her Imperial Highness Grand Duchess Militsa/Miliza) wife of Grand Duke Peter, daughter of the King of Montenegro, Stana's sister. Peter was Nikolasha's brother. So two sisters were married to two brothers.
   Signora Miliza Borisoff

5. S.A.I Il Principe Roman (His Highness Prince Roman, son of Grand Duke Peter).
   Signor Roman Borisoff.

6. S.A. La Principessa Marina (Her Highness Princess Marina, daughter of Grand Duke Peter).
   Signorina Marina Borisoff.

The next two names are those of Conte Stefano Tyszkievich (*sic*) and Contessa Elena Tyszkievich (Stetysz and Helena but with an Italian/Russian spelling), followed by seven names of those allowed to enter Italy in their company, plus their servants (whose names don't appear on the certificate).

The invitation to Italy came about because the Queen of Italy, yet another Montenegrin princess, was Stetysz's mother-in-law's sister Elena.

One can see at the bottom of the HMS *Marlborough* passenger list a few pages back, that the names marked with an asterisk were transferred from HMS *Marlborough* to HMS *Lord Nelson* in Constantinople. As we know, the Dowager Empress, detested Their Imperial Highnesses Dukes Nikolasha and Peter (brothers) and their wives, *the cockroaches* Stana and Militsa (the Montenegrin sisters). She could never forgive them for having introduced Rasputin to the Tsarina and that grudge remained forever, even after the Montenegrins changed their stance and warned the Tsarina against the 'Man of God'. The Dowager was very keen indeed to have them, plus Stetysz and Helena, put on another boat and was delighted when this part of her extended family was transferred to HMS *Lord Nelson* and taken to Genoa.

After a brief stay in Italy, Stetysz felt compelled to return to Lentvaris. The Polish Soviet war had started in February 1919, before his escape on HMS *Marlborough* and, as soon as he was back, he volunteered for the cavalry in the Vilnius region, joining Lieutenant General Jerzy Dąbrowski's army as a volunteer.

ALTO COMMISSARIATO
ITALIANO

Italian High Commissioner in Turkey

L'Alto Commissario Italiano in Turchia

CONTE CARLO SFORZA

certifica

che :

S. A. I. il Granduca NICOLA

S. A. I. la Granduchessa ANASTASIA

S. A. I. il Granduca PIETRO

S. A. I. la Granduchessa MILIZA

S. A. il Principe ROMAN

S. A. la Principessa MARINA

(che, per viaggiare o rimanere in incognito, useranno i nomi, rispettivamente, di Signor Nicola BORISOFF, Signora Anastasia BORISOFF, Signor Pietro BORISOFF, Signora Miliza BORISOFF, Signor Roman BORISOFF e Signorina Marina BORISOFF);

il Conte Stefano TYSZKIEVICH,

la Contessa Elena TYSZKIEVICH,

recansi in Italia e con Loro sono autorizzati ad entra_ re nel Regno :

il Barone Alessio DE STAEL

la Baronessa Elena DE STAEL

la Baronessa Maria DE STAEL

il Signor Artemi BOLDAREFF

il Signor Boris MALAMA

il Conte Paolo FERZEN

il Conte Alessandro FERZEN

e dodici domestici.

Costantinopoli, 17 Aprile 1919.

L' ALTO COMMISSARIO

Certificate from the Italian High Commission in Turkey, dated 17 April 1919 and signed in Constantinople by the High Commissioner, Count Carlo Sforza

He fought until 1921 when, as a delegate of the Chief-of-Staff of the Polish Army, he took part in the League of Nations commission charged with defining the new Polish Lithuanian border. Following the birth of his daughter Natalia, Stetysz with his wife and baby left for Paris to resume his academic studies, interrupted seven years earlier at Oxford. In 1921 he was admitted to the École des Sciences Politiques for a politics degree and simultaneously attended lectures at the École Centrale des Arts et Manufactures on automotive technology.

CHAPTER SEVEN

CRYSTAL BALLS, LOVE AND THE POPE'S PINEAPPLE

THE FIRST WORLD War was over, and people longed for an intimation of what was to come. For some, this future clearly lay in predicting it: one way of earning some money involved getting yourself a crystal ball, a pack of tarot cards and some exotic attire. A few notches up from that and you advertised yourself as a highly educated professor, a gentleman from high society with superior fortune-telling powers. Apparently vast numbers of women from all social classes flocked to such people. My grandmother Róża and her sister Zofia were no exception.

Maybe the alacrity of so many came from more than just playful curiosity and had something to do with hoping for better days, golden surprises, a big prize from fate to recompense for tragedy and loss. Whatever it was, Róża and Zofia first trotted off to a certain Tatar woman who peered into her glass ball with great concentration. My great-aunt Zofia was told that she'd soon be married to a tall and handsome young man with a dimple in his chin. This much turned out to be true: Count Klemens Potocki, her future husband, did have a cleft chin. Zofia giggled, explaining that this facial characteristic was a sign of power and that in Persian literature, the 'chin dimple' was referred to as a well into which a lover falls and is trapped!

The next consultation took place in a very elegant apartment where the fortune teller was a distinguished looking white-haired gentleman, known as 'The Professor'. His shelves, heavy with tomes, and the walls covered with expensively framed certificates lent gravitas to the proceedings. He inspired complete confidence and took great pains to explain that his every word was based on solid scientific research. Zofia was told that she'd already been on this planet four times, and that in one of her incarnations she'd murdered her husband in Egypt. In her diaries, Zofia writes that she had enormous fun, which would indicate she didn't take any of it seriously, yet she didn't wince at the hefty consultation fee, returning several times for more.

The last appointment she and my grandmother attended was in a dingy hotel where a scruffy looking couple received the clients. The wife explained she was a medium and whilst she prepared for the séance her husband grilled my grandmother and her sister as to their surname, their parents' status even asking point blank whether any family jewellery had survived the war! I imagine at this point, if Maryńcia had known what her girls were up to, she'd have put a swift stop to it, but there was much else to concentrate on. Of course, everything had changed since the war, but one had to find a new *modus vivendi* and remind oneself that Poland was free again.

The First World War and the agrarian reforms that followed it, had left the Lentvaris estate dilapidated and Władysław and Maryńcia recoiled from spending money on maintenance and renovations for fear of another conflict. The plumbing was in a terrible state, the electrical supply severely damaged, most of the contents gone. They moved into the former estate manager's house and only used a few rooms in the main house, spending more and more time in Warsaw. These consequences of the First World War were not the only thing that had ravaged their estate and finances. The other disaster had been a huge betrayal; in 1922 my great-grandfather owned 36,052 acres in the Vilnius area but the totally trusted person who had full power of attorney for managing most of their assets in their absence, disposed of quite a few acres without their knowledge over the years and finally even sold their large Warsaw house! Needless to say after that last sleight of hand he promptly disappeared without trace. I know his name and rather unusual surname, but I imagine some of his descendants might well still live in that area. I shall spare them. Sins of the father...

In the 1920s my great-grandfather revived his antique business in Milan. In spite of having closed Galleria Warowland he continued to pursue his passion for art with a salon in his friend Count Gian Giacommo Gallaratti Scotti's palace. This brought him a welcome income. He came and went between Warsaw, Milan and Lentvaris.

One of Count Gallaratti Scotti's sons had lost a hand in the Italian-Abyssinian War and was very withdrawn. My great-grandfather took him under his wing and brought him (plus two friends and a man servant) to Lentvaris for the summer. Dilapidated as Lentvaris was, with a lifestyle no longer glorious as in the past, Władysław and Maryńcia were nevertheless determined to give the young man a wonderful holiday amongst people his own age. My grandmother and her siblings involved him in everything, took him on visits to countless relations, paying no attention whatsoever to his physical disability and bringing him out of his shell. He loved it.

This was but one example of the fact that notwithstanding the sadness of a ruined estate and home, my great-grandparents were set on providing a welcoming place in Lentvaris. Friends and family still came in droves for the summer months, cramming into accommodation that was basic by comparison to past life in the main house, but the atmosphere was one of fun and conviviality. Stetysz and his wife and daughter, based in France, visited too.

The active social life kept picking up for the aristocracy after the war. Ladies met and bonded over tea in each other's houses or hotels and in the countless tearooms and cafés reopening in Warsaw and Vilnius. From 1920 onwards, many elegant balls were given. There were again two carnivals a year (Winter and Summer), fairs, racing, birthdays, weddings and christenings. Nevertheless, my great-grandparents' life in Lentvaris became increasingly low key. For them, gone were the days of luxurious foreign travel, visits to galleries, the opera and the theatre, clothes shopping all over Europe, sharing their art collection in Lentvaris with many visitors.

My grandmother Róża hated dances anyway. Before the war she had associated them with longing and envy because she was then too young to attend and her older sister Zofia rejoiced in telling her all about the dresses, food and the dancing (to music from the BEST orchestra, namely Józef Karasiński's). Pretty and full of sparkle, Zofia tormented her shy, younger sister with lavish accounts of endless dances not least of the best ball of all, *chez* the Potockis on one of the most prestigious streets in Warsaw, Krakowskie Przedmieście nr 15. And boy did she rub it in: how the Potocki sons, Roman and Józio were the most gallant young hosts! How many flowers she'd been given and by whom. What amazing dancers Tomasz ('The Lion') Zamoyski and Zdzisław Lubomirski were! Nobody could lead the old Polish *mazurka* quite like those two. And no, Róża couldn't have any of the party favours that Zofia, and every guest, had received: a tiny basket, a miniature shepherdess, a fan, all in navy blue and gold, the colours of the Potocki crest. *'One day you'll get your own, if you stop being so shy.'* Róża never did altogether stop being shy. Zofia was the shining star, the dancing light; Róża the bird with a broken wing and a fragile heart.

In the inter-war period there were weddings galore and Róża did enjoy those. These were the roaring twenties, when young people in Poland and Lithuania, having regained their countries' independence now hoped for stability. Zofia's marriage to the very charming Count Klemens Potocki with the chin dimple, was one such happy occasion, and took place in

Lentvaris in 1922. It was a small event because they couldn't entertain in the great house, but a hugely happy one due to the sparkling love of the young couple. They adored each other even though Klemens did have a roving eye and was an incorrigible charmer and flirt throughout his life. Zofia forgave him everything and I remember them many decades later, in the 1960s, in a poky little flat in Communist Poland, giggling in corners like lovestruck teenagers.

My great-grandparents were thrilled when Zofia had a baby in 1923, a year after her wedding to Klemens Potocki. Their boy, called Maurycy (known as Moryś) was to become my (as yet unborn) father's very favourite first cousin. More about him and his ghastly and brave young death later. In 1923, it was his life that was being celebrated and his christening was yet another wonderful occasion for a party.

The joy was compounded by a great surprise: it was at one of those countless social events that Władysław and Maryńcia's younger daughter, my grandmother Róża Tyszkiewicz, met Władysław Mycielski from Kobylopole. (I shall refer to him as Władzio, so as not to confuse him with my grandmother's father Władysław Tyszkiewicz).

Władysław and Maryńcia had been on the verge of taking their younger daughter to a convent in Kraków to become a nun and she was quite amenable to the idea, but lo-and-behold, the shy unassuming girl got her beau. It was the talk of the town. Grandma Róża told me decades later, that not only had she believed that no man could possibly ever fall in love with her but, inspite of having a loving father she'd always felt threatened by men, however charming. She was also very pious. No doubt the aura around her sent them the message that she was unavailable, so the unlikely news of her engagement spread like wildfire.

Władzio Mycielski, my paternal grandfather, came from a noble family from Western Poland, first mentioned in 1470 when his great-(times twelve) grandfather, Florian Mycielski was a courtier with a seat in the Senate and a counsellor of King Kazimierz Jagiełło. Although Róża would have married Władzio anyway, due to his great gentleness, kind eyes and subtly protective demeanour, the fact that through the centuries his forebears showed enormous courage, resonated well with her parents.

Just one of countless examples of Mycielski bravery are the military achievements of Władzio's great-grandfather Ludwik and Ludwik's twin, General Michał, described by Janusz Staszewski in great detail in

Biographies of Distinguished Poles from the Eighteenth and Nineteenth Centuries (published in 1930 by Poznań University). The part played by them in the 1830 November Uprising, including Ludwik's heroic death at the age of thirty-five, was imortalised in a painting from 1887–1888, (Olszynka Grochowska), by the renowned Polish Painter Wojciech Kossak. To this day there is a street in Warsaw, Ulica Ludwika Mycielskiego, which means Ludwik Mycielski's street.

Impressive also was the fact that in the 1812 campaign of the Napoleonic wars, Michał Mycielski aged only sixteen, was awarded the Virtuti Military, the highest Polish military decoration for outstanding combat merit, on a par with the Victoria Cross. Ludwik's and Michał's mother Anna Mycielska, although vociferously anti-Prussian, was nevertheless a personal friend of the future king Frederyk Wilhelm IV and she replied thus to his letter of condolences: *'La patrie a été genéreuse envers moi. Je lui ai donné cinque fils, elle m'en a rendu deux.'* ('The mother country has been generous towards me: I gave her five sons and she gave me back two.') In the 1970s their correspondence was in the Hohenzollern Museum in Berlin. I assume it still is. Two more of Anna Mycielska's sons were also awarded the Virtuti Militari.

My grandmother Róża might not have known every detail of the bravery of her fiancé's family over generations but she knew that Władzio was no wimp. When Archduke Franz Ferdinand's assassination unleashed the First World War, Władzio, aged twenty, was on the French front and in 1918, as second lieutenant, he took part in the Greater Poland Uprising against the Prussians (a vital insurrection in which Poland was victorious. Its territorial gains were confirmed by the Treaty of Versailles, a most important of peace treaties as it brought the First World War to an end).

He then fought against the other bogeyman, namely Russia, as adjutant to General Kazimierz Raszewski during the Bolshevik war. After attacks and counter attacks, when the loss of Warsaw seemed certain, the Polish forces achieved a decisive victory at the Battle of Warsaw and the war ended with a ceasefire in October 1920. At this point, after the Peace of Riga was signed (1921) the disputed territories were divided between Poland and Soviet Russia and Poland regained a territory of around 200 km East. My grandfather Władzio was awarded the Krzyż Walecznych (Polish military decoration for an individual 'who has demonstrated deeds of valour and courage in battle'). He was twenty-seven. With the fighting over, this sweet, intellectual, kind and gentle man was glad to at last turn to his studies. His subjects were History and Philosophy at Poznań University. He also did a course in Estate Management. And then, in 1923, he met my grandmother.

Róża could barely breathe when he asked her to marry him. It was unbelievable. When they had first met, she couldn't quite understand why someone so special would notice her. How did he know that underneath her shyness and anxieties there was a sense of humour and a deep desire to be good and kind and loving?

She remembered for ever the very first time she had made him laugh. They were sitting in the orangery in Lentvaris, and she was bemoaning the fact that there were no longer any pineapples growing there. The glazed roof was leaky, there weren't enough people to look after the tropical fruit that had been cultivated there before the war, but nothing would change the fact that every time Róża pushed the squeaky glass doors and padded inside she didn't see the missing panes, the meagre plants clinging to life, or the rotting wooden shelves, but was instantly transported into the aromatic and warm tropical microcosm of her childhood, where precious pineapples lorded it over the profusion of oranges, lemons, tangerines and figs.

Throughout her childhood, children had seldom been allowed a slice of pineapple, reserved as these were for dinner parties and special guests. As she sat with Władzio on a rusty metal bench which she'd covered with a rug, she recounted an amusing occasion in 1919, barely a year after the end of the Second World War. A distinguished visitor was coming for the weekend and although the orangery was bare, Róża's mother Maryńcia had somehow sourced one pineapple, not particularly large but precious, to be protected at all costs from the jolly band of very young members of her extended family. In just one short musical sentence repeated over and over, the youngsters were protesting against not being allowed to share in the exotic fruit, reserved only for the adults and their distinguished visitor.

The children thought it hilarious as they ran around the table faster and faster singing: '*Ananas nie dla nas tylko dla biskupa*', which means '*The pineapple is not for us but for the bishop*'! As Róża told Władzio about this little event of four years before, she made him laugh heartily by urging him to sing the ditty again and again trying out absurd rythms and descants. She was taken aback by the ease with which she could let her guard down with Władzio and make a fool of herself without embarrassment. They called their 'song' *The Pope's Pineapple* because the guest in question was Monsignor A. Ratti, the Papal Nuncio. I'm sure he consumed his pineapple with gusto! In 1922, one year before Róża and Władzio met and her sister Zofia married Count Klemens Potocki, Monsignor Ratti was anointed Pope (as Pius XI).

Róża and Władzio were married in April 1924. Wedding bells pealed louder than any others in Róża's heart. For years she'd heard her mother say that she'd be 'hard to place', that she was too anxious, too shy, too delicate; that she'd never find a husband. And yet she'd found a man, the best of all, the kindest and most caring. Or rather he'd found *her*. She knew she'd adore him forever. And she did; but as the bells rang out a thousand Allelujahs on that sunny wedding day, neither of them knew that their 'forever' wouldn't be very long.

CHAPTER EIGHT

CHURCHES, NAUGHTY CHILDREN AND A FABULOUS CAR

RÓŻA, NO LONGER Tyszkiewicz, thrilled to now be Róża Mycielska, was sad to leave Lentvaris but gloriously happy not to be going to a convent but to her own new home with her own new husband, even if it was almost 800 km from Lentvaris, just on the outskirts of Poznań. She knew she could see her parents and her sister when they came to Warsaw for the winter and that was much nearer, 300 or so km away.

One year later, the youngest of my grandmother's siblings, Eugeniusz, married a young and charming Russian widow, Olga Strukow (whose first husband had been murdered in a forest by his estate manager). Eugeniusz adopted Olga's daughter (from her first marriage) and loved her as his own. They had four more girls and a son. I met great-aunt Olga only once decades later and I remember her as a beautiful and enchanting *grande dame*. She radiated optimism, humour and warmth.

There was much joy for Władysław and Maryńcia in 1925, with their youngest son Eugeniusz's wedding to Olga, but no happiness for my grandmother Róża who in the same year gave birth to my father Józef Mycielski and a year later to her second child Krystyna (Kika). What should have been events surrounded by pure joy became the beginning of a difficult and very sad time. Róża suffered from what is now known as post-natal depression and my saintly and empathetic grandfather Władzio did whatever he could to help. He was out of his depth and my grandmother's mental problems continued, with sleepless nights and bouts of agoraphobia for years.

Due to Róża's mental state, it was impossible for her and her husband to travel to Lentvaris in 1926 for the consecration of the brick church Władysław and Maryńcia were finally able to build. The small wooden chapel the Russian authorities had allowed them to erect in 1905 was demolished and the new church was designed in the style of the fifteenth century church Maria della Grazia in Milan.

The walls of the Tyszkiewicz church in Lentvaris were painted in 'sgrafitto', the technique where layers of different coloured plaster were

Church of the Annunciation of the Holy Mother of God, Lentvaris (family photo)

applied, and then scratched off, thus creating patterns and shapes that emerged from the lower colours. Murals cover the walls of the church almost entirely to this day and current publications state that this church is one of the biggest and most impressive examples of monumental painting from the beginning of the twentieth century to be found in Lithuania.

According to my great-aunt Zofia Potocka's memoirs, in 1926 Pope Pius XI sent the seventeenth-century crucifix seen in the photograph on the right on the main altar, as a precious gift to my great-grandparents on the occasion of the consecration of their new church. Rev Gintaras Petronis believes my great-grandfather bought the crucifix and the Pope blessed it. Whatever the case, it is a special treasure.

Although sad not to have been in Lentvaris for the consecration of his parents-in-law's church, Władzio was glad to be near his widowed mother, Zofia Mycielska who lived in his childhood home Kobylopole, near Poznań. My grandmother loved her mother-in-law. Like her son Władzio, Zofia Mycielska had empathy and kindness and not only was she a source of warmth and understanding for my grandmother, but she provided my father, Józef Mycielski, and his sister Kika with a haven in Kobylopole as they were growing up.

On Róża's better days, when her agoraphobia was more manageable,

Interior of Church of the Annunciation of the Holy Mother of God, Lentvaris
(Photo by kind permission of the Vicar of Lentavris Church, Rev Gintaras Petronis)

Kobylopole nr Poznań, built in the 1840s on the site of a previous house

Władzio managed to coax his wife out of the house, often just as far as the garden. One day, to everyone's surprise, she asked him to take her to the Mycielski church in Gostyń, on Święta Góra (Holy Hill). This was most unexpected because Gostyń was an hour and a half away. Both my grandmother's husband and her mother-in-law hesitated, seeing this as good news but simultaneously being filled with foreboding: what if halfway there Róża had one of her panic attacks?

Their attempts to dissuade her failed when weeping in her husband's arms my grandmother blurted out that she *had* to go because only the miraculous image of Our Lady in the church on Holy Hill would be able to help cure her mind. Her guilt at not having been able to travel to Lentvaris for the consecration of the Tyszkiewicz church permeated her every word. The courage Róża showed on that journey to the Mycielski church was heart-rending. She clung to Władzio's hand, putting every effort into stopping her short breaths from escalating into hyperventilation, asking him how much further, how much longer, how soon, reaching for her rosary, wiping her tears.

When they arrived, the Abbott received them with the usual respect and protocol he always used for any member of the founders' family. He clearly enjoyed prolonging his welcoming greetings but on this occasion he saw the priority lay elsewhere and he diplomatically faded into the background, leaving Róża kneeling in front of the holy image, flanked by her husband and mother-in-law, both holding her hands, both joining in her prayers.

On the way back Róża slept all the way. Władzio let his mother settle her for the night whilst he joined the nanny in overseeing the children's bedtime. I'm so very grateful that he often shared many details of their life with his sister-in-law, Zofia, who could both write and talk about it decades later.

Basilica of Święta Góra (Holy Hill), Gostyń, Poznań, built by Konarzewskis and Mycielskis in the seventeenth and eighteenth centuries

'The naughtiest and best-looking children for miles', was the opinion many had of my father Józef and his sister Kika, the blue-eyed Mycielski siblings, inseparable partners in crime who went through countless nannies, governesses and live-in tutors. *'I'd rather starve than have a death on my conscience,'* one disgruntled young woman announced as she handed in her notice. No amount of pleading for her to reconsider, no promises of a salary increase could induce her to stay: Józef had (again) pushed Kika's pram into the pond and whilst the nanny braved the cold waters to prevent a drowning, he took all his clothes off and climbed a tree. Since Kika was still being wheeled in a perambulator, my father can't have been more than three or four at the time. I can't say I blame the wretched woman for heading for the hills.

My father Józef Mycielski and his sister, Kika, 1929

Other nannies came and went and as the children developed, so did their tactics for getting rid of staff. My father, Józef, was hell bent on trying to fly so he repeatedly jumped from high places with open umbrellas or flapping capes breaking limbs on two occasions, bitterly disappointed that he'd failed to take to the skies...

He and Kika were also very keen to walk around the world and they set off more than once with a favourite toy and provisions, convinced that if they followed the sun, they'd end up back in the same spot. The police were called on more than one occasion, and yet another employee of the Mycielskis couldn't pack her bags fast enough. They never went to school and were taught at home.

My grandfather Władzio did his utmost to be father and mother rolled into one. Róża adored her husband, but her insecurities, foibles and mental health issues continued to figure large. My father Józef and Kika never forgot sad occasions like their mother sitting on the lawn in Kobylopole, eyes fixed on the house, in great fear that the building was about to disappear. And yet, inspite of their mother's mental instability, Józef and Kika had a happy childhood. They always felt loved and didn't dwell on the dilapidation of the family estates. They still had great memories of weeks spent at home, with grandma Zofia in Kobylopole, in Lentvaris, in Kretynga, which belonged to their great uncle Alexander (Oleś) Tyszkiewicz, and in Kruszyna, their grandmother Maryńcia's childhood home.

Even with their dilapidation after the First World War, all these houses had nooks and crannies, favourite secret places and, outside, parks, ponds, grottoes, lakes, ancient trees, ponies, dogs. And, of course, 'upstairs-downstairs' intrigues. Józef and Kika loved lurking below the railings of the servants' veranda on the staffs' evenings off, to eavesdrop on their conversations. At one time Kika was particularly riveted by the gossip about the unrequited love of the butler for the lady's maid. Like the best TV soap of today, the plot's twists and turns seemed to go on forever. The children did their utmost not to miss too many episodes.

Above all, in those inter-war years, there was a large extended family who enjoyed spending time together and in spite of everything, managed to retain their sense of fun. Maybe it was for the children, maybe because the grown-ups knew that once humour is snuffed out, hope goes too.

My grandmother Róża's parents, Władysław and Maryńcia Tyszkiewicz, were glad all four children had married but there was sadness not only about Róża's mental state. Their son Stetysz's union with Helena had turned out not to be a bed of roses either. She had an all-consuming mania for hygiene and tormented all and sundry with it, even her poor fox terrier. He lived mainly indoors, was bathed at least once a day and, on the rare occasions that he was allowed outside, had to walk on a lead along paths that had been thoroughly swept and washed. Helena changed her shoes before and after going into a bathroom, sat on only some chairs but not others and was never seen without a wide brimmed hat so that neither sun nor dust would touch her face. Her eccentricity had more lurid manifestations too: in later years, wherever Stetysz and Helena stayed, she took with her several little caskets containing the mortal remains of her miscarried babies. They were placed on the bedside table, next to a glass of water, a rosary and, quite possibly, a bottle of Lysol!

Hardly surprising that Stetysz and Helena's only daughter Natalia was also unusual. She kept to her room when in Lentvaris for the summer, avoided her cousins and, unrealistically aspiring to become a famous singer, manically brushed her teeth (presumably because when you sing you have to open your mouth and others can see them). Thank goodness Stetysz was hugely absorbed in his many ideas during the period between the two world wars. And remarkable they were too. 1924 was a fabulous year for him as he began working on a project to design a car with the idea of expanding motorised road transport in Poland. He founded a partnership for the purpose in the Paris suburb of Boulogne-Billancourt. He named it 'Automobiles Ralf Stetysz' (a contraction of his name with the acronym in Polish of: **R**olniczo **A**utomobilowo-**L**otnicza **F**abryka **S**tefana *Tyszkiewicza*, translating as: the 'Agricultural-Aero-Automotive Factory of Stefan Tyszkiewicz').

His prototype vehicle used an American engine of the Continental Motors Company. The aim was to construct an all-terrain passenger carrier adapted to a very poor road infrastructure and easy to maintain and repair. In 1925 he succeeded in producing two models:

- The model TC with a 6-cylinder engine of 2760 cm^3 capacity and 42 horsepower
- The model TA with a 4-cylinder engine of 1500 cm^3 capacity and 20 horsepower.

Publicity poster for the Stetysz car

The car was exhibited at both the 1926 and 1927 *International Paris Car Show*, where it gained the reputation of a good quality 'Colonial' car. In 1928 production was transferred to Warsaw, to an existing factory, 'K. Rudzki & S-ka'. The Stetysz car met with success at Polish sporting and trial events.

The car-bodies were manufactured by the aero specialist, Plage & Laskiewicz of Lublin. In moving the operation to Poland, Stetysz had to place a considerable amount as collateral. In support, his wife Helena parted with her own family heirloom, an eighty-six carat emerald brooch, which according to family archives had once belonged to her great-great-grandmother Catherine the Great. Perfectly possible. I don't know what happened to this brooch in the end. If someone had sold it at auction with the provable provenance, I might have been able to trace it through the auction houses. But which auction houses and in what country? Maybe it was pawned and not redeemed. I shudder to think what such a brooch would fetch today.

The initial batch of cars of both models proved durable and their sales looked promising. They were featured at the Poznań International Fair and marketed as 'the first Polish made car' and as a 'a vehicle for rough roads'.

Stetysz Car 1928

The Stetysz car participated in the *1929 Eighth Monte Carlo Rally* when it won recognition and a prize for comfort and its adaptability for long-distance travel. Alas, inspite of being the first to arrive in Paris, the co-driver was taken ill near Lyons and had to be admitted to hospital, which cost so much time that the car was obliged to drop out of the race.

Monte Carlo International Auto Rally 10 January 1929 – prize giving ceremony. Stetysz coming down the steps holding his hat. Prince Pierre de Polignac of Monaco (father of Prince Rainier III) top centre with a cane

So much talent, such success and promise. And then... disaster! On 11 February 1929 the Stetysz Warsaw factory was totally gutted by fire. Six completed cars were lost and 27 nearing completion. Two hundred had been ordered. One or two were saved. There were rumours of arson by competitors, but nothing was ever proven. Stetysz was devastated. He wasn't a financially savvy man, hadn't insured his factory and most of his wife's jewellery had gone. Understandably she didn't offer what was left.

With his usual courage and determination, he did his utmost to rebuild the factory, planning to do so in Lentvaris, but the move was blocked by shareholders of K. Rudzki & S-ka, a firm specialising primarily in bridge construction. Eventually, Stetysz had to resign himself to discontinuing his own brand and focused instead on importing and producing Fiat and

Mercedes models under licence. He distributed Chrisler, Voisin and Lancia vehicles for 'Auto Expert' in Warsaw. In 1936, he represented Daimler-Benz in Poland. This can't possibly have filled the hole left in his life by his wonderful Ralf-Stetysz car... I just wonder whether there might still be one somewhere, rusting in some barn or distant field....

CHAPTER NINE

THE SECOND WORLD WAR, SIBERIA AND BEYOND

MY GREAT-GRANDFATHER Władysław Tyszkiewicz was heartbroken about the state of his beloved Lentvaris and he knew the world would never be the same again. The Great Depression that followed the roaring twenties didn't help but Maryńcia showed what she was really made of, telling her family they should all be grateful for being alive and concentrating on her husband. She had mellowed very visibly and showed her affection much more readily.

Keeping her husband happy became increasingly difficult. He was sweet, and he adored her, but he never got over what had happened to his country, his life's work and the loss of all his treasures which he'd been forced to send to Russia 'for safekeeping' in 1915. As the post-war years rolled by his humour, *joie de vivre* and sparkle left him, and he became sadder by the day. The fact that his now adult children had flown the nest and only came to see him in the summer made him very lonely.

For as long as his health allowed, he went for solitary walks along the lake several times a day. In 1932, Władysław developed Multiple Sclerosis and before long he was bedridden. Maryńcia and my great-grandfather's devoted old man servant, Bolesław Lelewski, shared the difficult task of looking after him and they did so with total dedication. He died in Lentvaris on the 21 September 1936. I'm glad he left this planet before the Second World War as he was at least spared the final and permanent banishment from the land that was so much part of his identity.

My grandmother Róża was inconsolable with her father's death, walking side by side again with her old foe, guilt. Guilt for being unwell, guilt for not having visited her father as often as he deserved, guilt for being a burden.

Many came to my great-grandfather's funeral. My great-aunt Zofia Potocka wrote: '*We took him along the beautiful lakeside path he so loved, and there were many of us. All the locals came, even the rabbi, heading several Jewish delegations. We buried him in his church for which he'd had to fight against the Tsar's authorities for so hard and for so long.*'

In the midst of so many Catholics, Maryńcia was particularly touched by the Jewish contingent, there to pay their respects to one who'd fought so actively for their rights.

My father's and Kika's carefree childhood vanished overnight when the Germans invaded Poland in September 1939. Since the Mycielski houses were very near the border with Germany, Józef, Kika and their parents sped East towards Lentvaris. My great-grandmother Maryńcia had already taken flight so my Mycielski grandparents and their children sought shelter instead with uncle Alexander (Oleś) Tyszkiewicz in Kretynga where they arrived on 28 September 1939.

My great-grandmother Maryńcia Tyszkiewicz, three years after her husband's death, just before leaving Lentvaris for the last time in 1939

After the Bolsheviks entered Lithuania in June 1940, the Mycielskis tried to leave Kretynga on 20 July but turned back when they saw the hordes of terrified displaced people fleeing in various directions. Via a roundabout route they eventually reached Vilnius by lorry and paused in the Tyszkiewicz apartment on Trocka Street. They knew full well they'd gone from the German frying pan into the Russian fire and that it was only a matter of time before they were found by the NKVD (which later became the KGB).

To keep as low a profile as possible, they moved out of the family apartment and stayed in a rented hovel in the backstreets of Vilnius for nearly a year. My fifteen-year-old father and his father Władzio earned a meagre living by painting walls. Kika, fourteen years old, got a job with a third-rate ceramics company. The irony of her role in that establishment never escaped her and made her laugh even at the time: all day long she painted kitsch figurines of none other than Stalin!

My grandmother Róża stayed indoors most of the time because of her agoraphobia. Maybe she also feared being recognised. She knew her family's days were numbered, and the intelligenzia and aristocracy would be hunted down first. She arranged and rearranged her *nécessaire*, incessantly handling the bottles and pots, rubbing the gilt monogrammed tops against her sleeve. That small valise and its contents were all that was left of her world.

When my aunt Kika came back one evening, after a day of painting rows and rows of plaster Stalins, her mother was sitting on the floor, blacking out the coronet on the thick linen cover of her *nécessaire*, tears streaming down her face.

The *nécessaire* (marked G. Keller, Paris) had clearly been given to my grandmother before she was married (1924) as the initials were the maiden RT rather than RM for Róża Mycielska.

Photos from the 1990s after this necessaire found its way from Lithuania to England having been kept safe for decades by an old family retainer

I assume my grandparents had no idea where the rest of the family were at this point. In fact, my grandmother's mother Maryńcia, sister Zofia and the latter's son, Moryś, were in German-occupied Warsaw. Zofia's husband Klemens, in a German prisoner of war camp, was never again to see his son, as the teenage Moryś was soon to be taken to Auschwitz. Moryś was but one of the oft forgotten hundreds of thousands Catholic Poles that suffered and died in German concentration camps. This beloved only son of Klemens and Zofia Potocki was a brave boy indeed. The moment the war broke out he volunteered for the AK, the Polish underground resistance, and Zofia later found out that under interrogation in Auschwitz he never revealed the names of other young members of the underground. Moryś wrote to his mother from Auschwitz, not once bemoaning his fate, but asking her to check on the mother of one of his fellow inmates who didn't have enough to eat. Moryś Potocki was murdered in block twenty-five on the 15 October 1943. He was nineteen. The prisoner number tattooed on his arm was 31 252.

My grandmother Róża's youngest brother, Eugeniusz, with his wife and six children were much luckier in that they were given shelter by the King of Sweden, Gustav V, cousin of Stetysz's wife Helena. The king met Eugeniusz in Stockholm in person and installed them in a comfortable three-room hotel suite.

Eugeniusz Tyszkiewicz was no slouch though. He soon got himself sorted and worked every hour of the day to support his family, starting by rearing hens and selling eggs, whilst his elegant and determined wife Olga set up a fashion atelier. He and his family were to stay in Sweden after the war until, some years later, the children disbanded to Spain, the US and the UK. Only Eugeniusz, Olga and her daughter (Irena Nakó) remained in Sweden.

My grandmother Róża Mycielska née Tyszkiewicz

As for my great-uncle Stetysz, the outbreak of war in 1939 found him and his family on the territory of the Lithuanian republic, where he was involved in converting petrol engines into gas-powered ones, owing to the petrol shortage. Thanks to his contacts with the Italian delegation in Lithuania, he helped many Poles escape the conflict. His wife Helena and eighteen-year-old daughter Natalia were evacuated to Italy having been given 'safe conduct' through occupied Poland and Germany thanks to the intervention of the Italian government. After the annexation of Lithuania by the Soviet Union in June 1940, Stetysz was arrested and taken to Moscow to the notorious Butyrki prison. His first interrogation was to be remembered by him with humour for the rest of his life:

Q *Surname?*
A *Tyszkiewicz.*
Q *Count?*
A *Yes. Count.*
Q *Mother's name?*
A *Lubomirska.*
Q *Princess?*
A *Yes. Princess.*
Q *Wife's name?*
A *Helena*
Q *Maiden name?*
A *Leuchtenberg*
Q *Her father's name?*
A *Jerzy (Georgi). Deceased*
Q *Her mother's name?*
A *Anastasia Montenegro. Deceased*
Q *Where is your wife?*
A *In Italy*
Q *Why?*
A *She is staying with her family*
Q *What family?*
A *Her aunt. Her mother's sister*
Q *I see. She's with her auntie. And what's this auntie's name?*
A *Elena di Savoia*
Q *Who is this auntie's husband?*

A *Victor Emanuel III*

Q **I understand his name is Victor. Is Emanuel his surname? And why the third? What does this Victor do?**

A *He is the King of Italy*

This bit of information clearly threw the official completely and he rushed out, presumably to consult his superiors on what to do next. He returned after a while, sat down and said something like this: '*Well, I understand that your wife's aunt is the Queen of Italy and that her husband is the King. But in all that confusion I forgot to ask you: What is the patronimic of this Victor Emanuel III?*'

Stetysz barely concealing his laughter answered: '*Humbertovich!*' which was of course carefully and slowly written down on the form by the official. (A patronimic is a name derived from the father's name so for example: Ivan Nicholaevich means 'Ivan, son of Nicholai'. The question above was absurd and funny because in Italy patronimics were not used like in Russia but since King Victor Emanuel III's father was King Humberto I, Stetysz thought on his feet with his answer and said 'Humbertovich'!)

After this delightful exchange, Stetysz was moved to the Lubianka prison where he was to spend several months. In February 1941, he was called to the main prison office. There, waiting for him, was a smartly dressed representative from the Russian Ministry of Foreign Affairs. He addressed Stetysz respectfully as Count Tyszkiewicz, announcing that Stetysz would be released the following day and allowed to join his wife and daughter in Italy. He'd be provided with all the necessary clothing etc by the kind and generous Soviet Government! There had to be a catch and there was. The condition for such a release was:

1 that Stetysz would sign a statement as to his excellent treatment in jail
2 that he'd sign another statement promising to obey what orders might be given to him abroad by agents of the NKVD (the secret police, equivalent of the KGB as it later became)

Needless to say, Stetysz declined and he remained in Lubianka until the Soviet Polish agreement which opened the doors of the prisons releasing what Poles were still alive. This was when the Russians became allies against the Germans.

He was released from Lubianka Prison on the 5 October 1941 due to the intervention of General Georgi Zhukov (after a request by General Anders), and made his way to General Anders' army which was being formed in preparation for a mass exodus from the USSR. He was appointed officer-in-charge of the motorised unit of the Polish II Corps.

Having traversed into Persia (now Iran), thence to Palestine and Egypt, as a captain in the 1st Krechowce Uhlan Regiment and as communications officer and personal adjutant to General Anders, he was especially useful in 1944 liaising with Italian units fighting on the Allied side. He was liaison officer to General Utili in his dealings with Badoglio and King Victor Emanuel III.

Stetysz set up the Polish Red Cross in Italy. He had to start from scratch, so it was an enormous job requiring a lot of initiative. In due course that branch of the Red Cross was comprised of one thousand six hundred uniformed Poles and vast numbers of volunteers. He was responsible not only for hospitals but also for shelters for the soldiers of the Polish II Corps

After the battle of Monte Cassino, L to R: General Anders, Cavalry Captain Stefan Tyszkiewicz (Stetysz), Prince Umberto of Italy, General Zygmunt Bohusz-Szyszko, Lieutenant Eugeniusz Lubomirski (By kind permission of Prince Jan Lubomirski)

and their families. Stetysz had to find materials which were scarce eg ice for the hospitals (as the Germans had destroyed the ice factories), so he started his own ice production. During the build-up to the Battle of Monte Cassino, he invented a mechanism for discovering and destroying non-magnetic anti-personnel mines. This invention was used by the British and must have saved many lives.

After the Battle of Monte Cassino (17 January–18 May 1944) Stetysz again joined the Red Cross at the request of General Anders. At the end of the Campaign, when Anders' army was moved to England followed by demobilisation, Stetysz's role with the Red Cross ended automatically.

On the 14 June 1941, my grandparents Władzio and Róża Mycielski with their children Józef and Kika, were arrested in Vilnius by the NKVD and loaded into cattle trains to Siberia the following day. My father was sixteen and Kika fifteen. Władzio was put on another train with a different destination. Józef and Kika never forgot their father's arm being brutally twisted behind his back and his eyes looking deep into theirs for the very last time as the heavy carriage door slid shut. They never saw him again.

I don't know how much my father and his sister understood of what exactly had happened politically. My grandmother knew full well that after the Germans invaded Poland from the West, the Russians invaded it from the East and Poland ceased to exist. Both Germany and Russia set about destroying Polish heritage and culture, burning books in the Polish language, closing cultural institutions, schools, universities, museum and theatres. The Catholic religion, one of the pillars of Poland as a Nation, was also targeted, and both Soviets and Germans persecuted Polish Catholic organisations and clergy. Germany and Russia made a pact (the Nazi-Soviet Pact against Poland), with the Soviet Union acquiring over half of the territory of the Second Polish Republic. This was about 201,000 square kilometres (78,000 sq mi) inhabited by over 13,200,000 people. Within months the Soviets deported a total of more than 1,200,000 Poles in four waves of mass deportations from the Soviet-occupied Polish territories. My father Józef, his sister Kika and their parents were in the fourth wave, in 1941.

When Róża found herself as the only parent, without her beloved Władzio to take care of them all, she was well aware that they were most unlikely to ever see him again. Suddenly, from the depths of her helplessness, she managed to summon an extraordinary resilience. She'd now have to protect her children, Józef and Kika, fledglings under her wings.

As the journey wore on, babies fell quiet and died. Mostly the guards threw the dead babies out of the air vent. When adults breathed their last, they placed the bodies on a platform by the engine, to be pushed off when the train stopped or slowed. Kika recalled mothers burying their babies with their bare hands when the train stopped along the way in the middle of nowhere in the Russian steppes. A particular occasion returned to haunt her and my father more than any other: the train had stopped, the prisoners had been told it would be there for several hours, but it suddenly moved off and a tiny girl was left behind in the open wilderness. Kika never forgot the mother's screams as the train gathered speed.

My father Józef had been given an Atlas by his great uncle Oleś Tyszkiewicz in Kretynga in 1940 in which, unbeknownst to his mother, he painstakingly traced their trajectory during the train journey to the depths of Russia. This was a teenager's madness since a fellow deportee (Mr Górnicki) was shot for doing exactly the same. Below is my translation of the explanation my father wrote in the Atlas in Rio de Janeiro in 1947:

'This Atlas was with me during our whole stay in Siberia. One of my fellow deportees to the depths of Russia, Mr Górnicki, traced our deportation route on a piece of paper. He was executed for this reason. I succeeded in concealing this Atlas and eventually bringing it out of Russia.'

The labour camp didn't need to be surrounded by barbed wire as it was in such a remote place that that there was nowhere to run to. My father Józef, Kika and their mother lived in wooden shacks like all the prisoners. My grandmother and Kika pulled thistles all day and were forbidden to protect their hands with strips of cloth. My father did maintenance work on buildings. One of the guards was particularly beastly and as soon as the work was done, he made the prisoners undo it in order to do it again. Once a week there was music and compulsory dancing. Those who had no strength to dance were threatened with guard dogs.

When it was a question of life and death and protecting her children, my mentally fragile grandmother shed all her foibles and phobias and fought for them like a tiger, stealing vegetables and old bread, taking big risks and receiving severe punishments in the process.

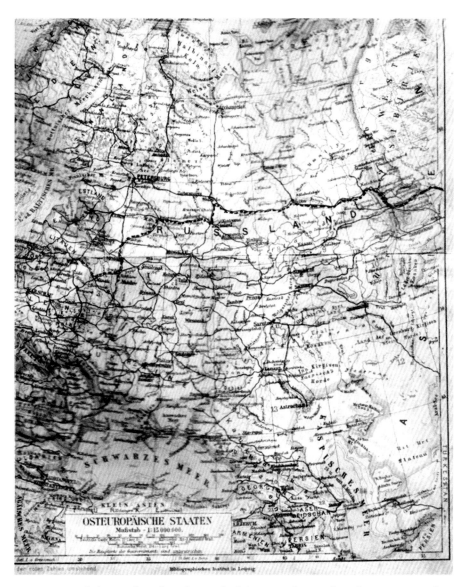

Page in my father's atlas where he marked the route during their deportation to the labour camp in Siberia

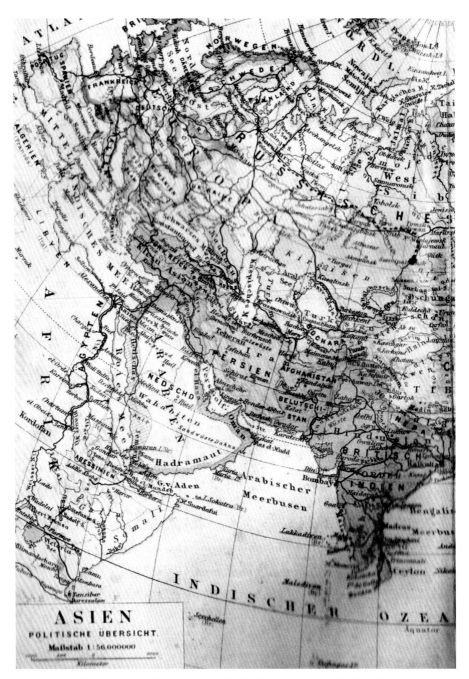

Continuation of the route to the Gulags from my father's atlas

Freedom came when, after having invaded Poland in 1939, Germany marched into the Soviet Union (on 22 June 1941), and suddenly Russia and Britain had a common enemy. Due to British mediation and pressure, the Soviet Union and the Polish government-in-exile (then based in London) re-established Polish-Soviet diplomatic relations in July 1941. This resulted in the Soviet Union agreeing to release tens of thousands of Polish prisoners from Soviet camps. The Polish General, Władysław Anders, just out from the Russian Lubianka Prison, began creating a Polish Army having been made its Commander. Eventually well over one hundred and ten thousand Poles including thirty-six thousand women and children managed to leave the Soviet Union with General Anders' Army.

When it came to the Poles, their rescue wasn't immediate so having been deported on the 14 June 1941 (merely a month or so before the agreement to free Polish prisoners) it wasn't until 10 October that the Mycielskis were released from the camp; and it was only the following year, on 7 April 1942 that they arrived in Tehran. In June 1942 they joined the Polish Army.

It took so long because nobody knew then how many Poles had been deported nor exactly where to, so finding them wasn't easy. In many cases the prisoners were simply told they were free, but they had no idea where to go, where their army was, where to sleep, what to eat. Crippling hunger, severe thirst, dysentery and typhoid contributed to the fact that more died during the long trek than in the camps. It was very lucky that my grandmother and her children survived.

At the beginning of their journey, Róża and her children had heard that there were good apples in Samarkand. A juicy golden apple figured large in my father's fitful nights and although they never did get to those orchards, the fruit forever awoke in him a beckoning image of hope. Years later he wrote a poem about it: *The Golden Apple of Samarkand*. I don't know why it isn't one of the poems in his published book of verse and alas the pencilled text is no more. A heart-rending poem that did survive is *The Doctor*, about a certain unassuming humble man who left an indelible mark on Józef, Kika and their mother. My father dedicated it *In memory of our 'doctor' from the winter of 1941–42 in the steppes of Khazakhstan*. I can't translate it as a poem because I'm not a poet, so below is my best attempt at conveying it in prose. I tried to end up with what my father did achieve: poignancy, zero syrup or cliché. I feel I owe it to him and to the man he wrote it for but I'm not at all sure I've succeeded.

'There was a man amongst us in those days in the steppes, small, thin and fidgety. He scuttled over the hard ground, long nose pointing out every corpse, pointing it out to Mother Earth as if it were her fault. A wolfish yellow tooth protruded from his thick lip, yet the kindest human smile hovered behind it. Snow-white cold wrapped itself around his bony feet. He scurried along the hard, impenetrable soil, among the yellow corpses, blackening like scabs on the bare ground. Grey shaggy sheep, unkempt clumps of life, dotted the steppes whilst the wind sniggered and chuckled from its hideaways.

Deep within the breast of his tattered clothes he gripped a small metal spoon. It was his talisman. He knew its power, its promise of a sequel, its message of hope. Gently he approached each one still breathing, lowered the spoon into dry and empty mouths, lifted stiffened tongues and, with a doctor's gravitas, brought meaning to the torment. With this one tiny piece of cutlery he conjured up images in half-lucid minds of delicacies of long ago. He kept alive their hope that there'd be a day when they would eat again.

He didn't remonstrate when they called him 'doctor'. The sick dream of health, they'd rather live than rot. So, on he went, wearing his doctor's mantle, his title without certificate, a role invented by fate so that they could once again experience what it means to live.

And then his own day came: he left the night's embrace with a new dawn, in search of those to help, as every day. No longer man, more reed now, bending in the wind, spoon held tight against his chest. The steppe, with uncouth harshness, vomited snow at the staggering form, until death saw fit to lounge and sprawl upon the land. Small tufts of being dotted the landscape: the same old sheep, grey and shaggy as before. The ground bared its scabs to the rejoicing howls of a delighted wind. All by themselves, tiny flecks of snow gathered into a burial mound.

The giant thistles reached out.'

Weeks after my father, Kika and their mother were released, dreams of Samarkand apples long gone, one day they came across a railway line. Their thoughts were not about what the name of the station might be, or whether the next train would stop there, or what direction it would be travelling in. The next train represented freedom from suffering, yes, but it was because they'd decided to throw themselves under its wheels.

What saved them at that moment was the sight of a Red Cross flag fluttering on the locomotive. Although they didn't realise it at the time, Róża's brother, their own uncle Stefan Tyszkiewicz (Stetysz) was involved in organising the sending of Red Cross trains deep into Siberia, in search of the desperate groups of released prisoners, to bring them to safety.

Kika lightened her accounts of those dreadful times with vignettes of humour. One example was when she was taken short on the Red Cross train that had saved their lives. When staggering through the steppes, in rags, covered in lice and sores, weak from hunger and diarrhoea like everybody else, there was no room for self-consciousness. But once on a train, surrounded by smartly uniformed soldiers, embarrassment set in with a vengeance. Kika was mortified when she became increasingly desperate for a loo and shyly asked a soldier how far they were from the next station. The kind officer, understanding her predicament, ordered the train to stop and led her outside.

A barrel was ceremoniously brought for her to sit on, and not only did the soldiers form a circle around her, but they faced out. She could only see their backs and hear their strong voices in a rousing patriotic hymn! A long while later, a soldier saluted, placed the barrel on his shoulder, saluted again and marched off as if this were part of a perfectly normal dignified everyday military routine.

Other humiliations awaited them though: by the time they reached Persia (now Iran) in April 1942, via Kazakhstan and Turkestan, they knew that their uncle Stetysz was in Tehran with the Red Cross. My father tried to get into the smart hotel where Red Cross and military personnel were staying but he was shooed away by the doorman and had to sit in front of the hotel for hours until Stetysz returned for the night. The moment he finally saw his uncle and felt his strong arms around him he knew that some sort of light was beginning to flicker on the horizon. His knees buckled.

The kindness they received from ordinary people in Tehran was never forgotten by my grandmother and her children. It was overwhelming after the horrors of the very recent past.

They were lucky. They were alive. Their father Władzio was dead, so was their uncle Wojtek and they didn't yet know that in 1943 their first cousin Moryś Potocki, would be killed in Auschwitz.

In March 1942 my father writes in his diary, that news reached them of their father's death five months before: *'Our Father died on the 6th October 1941 at 8 in the evening, in Siewurałłag 10, odt 47 Łagomandirowka. The*

My father Józef (seventeen) and his sister Kika (sixteen) in 1942 after being deloused and given clothes by the Red Cross

last train station was Gary, then 180 km by boat along the river Sośwa, and finally 17 km on foot to the labour camp.' He was forty-six.

Below is the translation of a letter sent to my aunt Kika by a Mr Zygmunt Horodecki from an address in Florida. It is dated 21 July 1982. Mr Horodecki was in the same camp as my grandfather Władzio Mycielski but survived.

Dear Madam,

I enclose a few memories I have of your father. We were deported to Siberia from Vilnius in June 1941 and were taken to the same labour camp in the Northern Urals. I met your father in the camp when we were placed in the same labour group. His behaviour, his demeanour and, above all, his eyes radiated warmth, peace and enormous goodness which, in those particular circumstances, made a tremendous and unforgettable impact. He had a deep faith which undoubtedly gave him strength.

There is one incident which sticks most vividly in my mind. It happened towards the end of our work together. It was autumn and we were felling trees. I remember the golden leaves on the branches and the shrubs. Your father and another prisoner were sent for some water to a brook nearby. As they didn't return for a while, I and another prisoner were sent to look for them. I saw your father by the brook, and I was struck by the expression on his face. His companion, at his feet, was gutting a rabbit.

When I asked what was going on your father told me that whilst he was working, he'd felt very hungry and weak. He prayed for food and strength, and then, just as he and the other prisoner were approaching the brook, a large bird of prey took flight and dropped a dead rabbit at your father's feet. He believed this was God's answer to his prayer and that God had sent them food. Indeed, on that day, instead of an infusion of grass and herbs, he had rabbit broth which he shared with others.

Soon afterwards we were separated and placed in different work groups. It wasn't long before I heard that he had died of exhaustion and of some form of infection caused by the bites of the horrid insects that tormented us in the woods.

After an eventful life, with the passage of time and my advanced age, I cannot alas, recall many more details. You probably don't remember, but I waved you goodbye when you left England for Argentina. We cannot complain about the ground we've covered since being chased from our country.

I enclose my best wishes to you and your mother.

Z. Horodecki

In June 1942 my father Józef, aged seventeen, joined the Polish Army, Airforce Division. His diary for 1943 is filled with places like Tehran, Kirkuk, Basra, Baghdad, Khanaqin, Hamadam, Ismailia, Tell-el-Kebin and many others. He mentions that on the 12 December 1943 he stopped near Cairo, at his uncle Stefan Tyszkiewicz's villa at the foot of Cheop's pyramid (where Stetysz was placed in the service of the Red Cross).

My father Józef Mycielski, aged seventeen, Tehran 1942

My aunt Krystyna Mycielska 'Kika', aged sixteen, Tehran 1942

In Tehran, Kika, at just sixteen years old, did a crash course in Nursing and registered for a placement in Palestine, ending up in Egypt with general Anders' army. Kika's nursing in the Desert Hospital involved caring not just for weak or injured men, but for countless malnourished children and babies, and then washing many of them for burial.

Here is the translation of a note written to her by one of the men she looked after: '*God gave us hell but then came heaven, an angel stood beside me with God's grace in her eyes. May He bless you for ever, Sister Kika, my blue-eyed angel. You're not just a nurse, you're a miracle in my desert.*' He died a few days later.

When the war ended (August 1945) Róża, Józef and Kika found themselves in London. They had nothing to go back to in Poland and, like many other Poles, they feared another war. There was also the deep sense of betrayal, impossible to minimise: with the First World War Poland had had the support of the Allies in post-war negotiations. She didn't lose her sovereignty or her borders. Alas, the same didn't happen after the Second World War when the Americans and the British agreed the Russians could keep the lands they'd taken. The last step in this injustice was the Yalta agreement which allowed the Soviets carte blanche to fully occupy Poland. My father was wounded to the quick by this, then and forever. My aunt Kika was more understanding and argued later that without American support in those post-war dealings, Churchill's hands were tied.

What will never be understandable though is the Poles not being allowed to take part in the Victory parade, having to watch from the sides, in spite of the irrefutable fact that they'd shown immense bravery and had played a crucial role in Germany's defeat.

Air Chief Marshall Sir Hugh Dowding, head of RAF Fighter Command wrote: '*Had it not been for the magnificent material contributed by the Polish squadrons and their unsurpassed gallantry I hesitate to say that the outcome of the Battle of Britain would have been the same.*'

There were fourteen thousand Polish airmen in fifteen RAF squadrons or with the US Army Airforce; No. 303 Squadron claimed the highest number of 'kills' (one hundred and twenty-six) of all the squadrons engaged in the skies over Britain; four thousand Polish seamen served with the Royal Navy; the Poles worked six years to crack the Enigma code; forty-three per cent of all reports the British secret service received from Continental Europe was from the AK (Polish underground). The Polish underground resistance was the largest in all of occupied Europe, covering both German and Soviet zones of occupation and, in addition to providing vital military intelligence to the British, they disrupted German supply lines to the Eastern Front and saved more Jews in the Holocaust than any other Western Allied organisation or government. On land Polish ground forces, allied to the British (General Anders' Army), or serving under British command, numbered one hundred and forty-two thousand by the war's end. A further two hundred thousand were recruited by the Soviets to fight against the Germans under their command; Polish ground forces took part in key battles: Warsaw (1939), France (1940), Narvik (1940), Tobruk (1941), Normandy (1944), Monte Cassino (1944), Arnhem (1944), Berlin (1945).

More than 18 per cent of Poland's population were killed, 38 per cent of national assets lost. (Britain lost 0.8 per cent and France 1.5 per cent). Nobody questioned the Polish contribution to the Germans' defeat, yet in Yalta, in February 1945, five years of Nazi slavery were replaced by Soviet slavery for decades. Poland as a country was herself lost until the fall of Communism in 1989. Not surprisingly my family, like countless other Poles, wanted to be as far from Europe as possible.

For the Mycielskis the 'New World' beckoned in the shape of South America. My twenty-two year old father, his sister Kika and their mother Róża boarded the ship *Jamaique* in le Havre on the 4 February 1947 and arrived in Rio de Janeiro on the 25th. They sailed into the bright spectacular beauty of this Brazilian landscape, and amazingly, improbably, unbearably, they did so to the sound of one of the most haunting Polish military songs of all time, drifting towards them from the adjoining cabin. *Czerwone Maki na Monte Cassino,* or in English 'The Red Poppies on Monte Cassino'. Red because they'd been nourished by Polish blood.

The move to Brazil was about to bring a new member into the family, like them exiled by war, like them hoping for peace and a new beginning: my mother.

CHAPTER TEN

A CHILD'S TORMENT, THE SECOND WORLD WAR AND ESCAPING THE NAZIS

A LOVE CHILD, conceived in illicit passion, my mother Wanda (pronounced Vanda) was born in 1925 in Warsaw. She was my grandmother Grażyna's second daughter, very much a planned baby but planned not with Grażyna's husband Zygmunt Karpiński, but with her lover, Antoni Dygat.

What had possessed my grandmother Grażyna to marry Zygmunt? She wasn't on the shelf, was bright and attractive, and I cannot believe that she could have been in love with him. Not that he wasn't suitable. He was. Extremely. A brilliant economist on the Board of the Bank of Poland, a pillar of the establishment, a man with total integrity and an unwavering sense of duty. And he adored her. But he was shy, serious, with not much humour, and heavy going. Boring in fact. Poor Zygmunt. My heart goes out to him because it wasn't long after their wedding that the affair started between his wife and his first cousin, Antoni Dygat. Until his death, Zygmunt pretended not to know that my mother wasn't his daughter. She was the spitting image of her biological father. People noticed. But Zygmunt never let on.

For my grandmother it wasn't even a case of *entre les deux mon coeur balance*. Between solid Zygmunt and the colourful, artistic, partly French architect Antoni, Grażyna's choice wasn't a matter of measured decisions, let alone of a dutiful rejection of temptation. Passion flared and reason flew out of the window for both her and her lover, eventually bringing tragedy to two families. Antoni had two children and a very loving wife who, like Zygmunt, never got over it.

To the casual observer, Grażyna and Zygmunt Karpiński had a very good marriage. With her wit and bright intelligence, my maternal grandmother was the perfect wife for a man in his position, running their Warsaw house impeccably, from organising the staff to being a huge asset during business dinner parties. She was also an informal and delightful mother to her two girls. My Mama always remembered intimate fun moments like burrowing under the bedclothes of her mother's bed, jumping on it as if it were a trampoline, watching Grażyna smile at her child's antics whilst the studious older Eva got on with something useful like writing study plans.

In my mother's memoirs (written in the 1990s, when she was in her mid-sixties), she recalled a wonderful childhood, and some of her most magical memories were of winter holidays spent in Rabka, year in, year out. Until one day the place became synonymous with grief as her world came crashing down.

To understand my mother Wanda the adult, the woman my father Józef Mycielski married, it is helpful to acquaint oneself with her early life, starting with the traumas of her childhood and the two extremes of what Rabka represented to her.

Rabka was a small resort in South Eastern Poland, an hour or so from Kraków. Instead of having the same apartments at the Palace Hotel in St Moritz every year, Grażyna (once she'd had children) preferred instead to have the same rooms reserved every winter in the cosy Hotel Primavera in Rabka, which sat comfortably on the brow of a hill.

There was no railway station in Rabka. The sleeper train from Warsaw arrived in the slightly bigger nearby village of Chabówka where two sleighs awaited, one for the trunks, one for the passengers. In my mother's memoirs she describes these arrivals thus:

'Smothered under a prodigious number of sheepskins with a giant moon and millions of stars above, the jingling of bells and the snorting of horses in my ears, it was a fairytale. The shadow of each sleigh silhouetted on the snow added to the magic. The journey always felt too short.'

Drawing up to Hotel Primavera in darkness they were welcomed by the manager with hot chocolate and, after a token brushing of teeth, my mother and her sister Eva would fall asleep under huge feather eiderdowns. In the happy years, as a small child, Wanda was adamant that there were no sprites in St Moritz, only in Rabka, where they slept under the snow and fairies skated on frozen streams.

Mornings were spent skiing, tobogganing, and messing about in the snow, whereas afternoons were devoted to an occupation their mother Grażyna called 'verandeering'. A sacred ritual, it was non-negotiable. On the verandah of Hotel Primavera, wrapped in multiple layers of woollen underwear, long johns and various pairs of socks, sweaters, shawls and sheepskin jackets, my mother and Eva were manoeuvred into giant fur-lined sacks reaching up to their chins and then helped onto deckchairs, also fur-lined. Faces smeared with thick sun cream, with a final sheepskin placed on the top like a lid, the children spent two hours in suspended animation at –20ºc. This treat was supposed to be good for your lungs and general wellbeing. Grażyna told her daughters it was good for the soul too. And it was. Rabka and magic were synonymous.

And then one day, Rabka, became also and forever a symbol of despair. The years of agony and ecstasy for Grażyna and stark torment for Zygmunt ended in divorce in 1933. The fact that my mother wasn't Zygmunt Karpiński's daughter was an open secret that nobody talked about, except Grażyna with her parents.

My mother was eight. She knew nothing of their suffering. She'd lived her daily life in Warsaw undisturbed: school, piano lessons, birthday parties, visits to the dressmaker, walks in the park with her mother, botanical gardens with her Grandpa, summer holidays at the seaside.

And then one day she found herself very near Hotel Primavera, in front of a brand new building. She was told by her mother this was St Thérèse School for girls and that it had a modern sport centre, tennis courts and a swimming pool. Ah and vast verandas where at least ten girls could 'verandeer' on each. Wanda was to remember forever the nasty smell of fresh paint everywhere and the puzzlement of having it all being pointed out to her. After all she loved her school in Warsaw and this place had nothing to do with her.

The following year, after Christmas, she was thrown to the lions. She was the youngest child in the school in Rabka and the only pupil in her form. A nondescript woman gave her lessons in a classroom with too many windows and full of empty desks. Meals were served in a high-ceilinged refectory, ten girls to each table. My mother sat facing the windows and the light hurt her eyes. The food tasted of nothing; the table was too high.

She slept in a dormitory with five other girls. Before going to bed she pretended to take the obligatory shower in a cold cubicle because when the tap was turned on, the water rushed from high above scalding or freezing. She never managed to set it right, so she solved the problem by standing aside splashing the towel. Personal hygiene was not her priority. After lights out she wrapped herself around Monsieur Liné, her beloved monkey, and lay with him in the centre of the bed, her head under the bedclothes. *'I wiped my sodden eyes and face with Monsieur Liné's green robe'*, she writes in her memoir and I shall draw on her words.

Letters from home were handed out after breakfast by the headmistress. She sometimes asked 'permission' to read them and this felt like an assault, but Wanda didn't have the guts to refuse. She raged inside against the headmistress and against herself and kissed her mother's letters limp. They spent the days in her pocket, slept under her pillow and were read and reread countless times.

'I longed for my mother, longed for her bed. Mama's bed, the bed I had been born in, was the heart of our house. When I lay in that bed with Mama, at the age of two, three, four, five, six, seven, pressing my body into her side, the smoothness, warmth and scent were paradise. Sometimes we talked, sometimes we played word games that made us laugh. Sometimes Mama read to me, sometimes she read her own book. Whatever it was, it was bliss. I wanted Mama and her bed. Not just her letters under my pillow.'

Letters home had to be handed in unsealed. The headmistress might well have thrown many away as she wouldn't have approved of the genre of Wanda's missives home: *'Dear Mummy, dear Daddy, Grandma, Grandpa. Take me away from here, take me away from here, please take me away from here. I promise to be good. Take me away from here.'* Wanda wrote them every day; two or three pages or more on really bad days. Eventually the moment came when her body gave out. All she remembered was coming round in a comfortable bed with Monsieur Liné by her side. A nurse patted her head and urged her to go to sleep. She was later told she had slept for ten days.

Several times a day she was vaguely aware of being propped up and coaxed to swallow spoonfuls of sugar soaked with lemon juice and sips of water. Finally one morning Wanda awoke and didn't want to go back to sleep. She asked for something to read and from then on, her days were divided between *The Waverley* novels and sleeping. How much of Walter Scott she took in at the age of nine is anybody's guess. Suffice it to say that she was able to enjoy it.

Zygmunt came and went. *'Why Daddy?, I wondered. The headmistress visited every morning. She wasn't welcome. One afternoon she announced with a smile that I'd be going home in five days' time. One word burst into my head: Mummy!!'*

When the day came for Wanda to be delivered home, a school representative accompanied her to Warsaw by train. Something was wrong. There were two people waiting at the station, neither of whom was her mother.

'Daddy took me by the hand, and Eva put her arm around me. I allowed them both to kiss me, but I didn't want them there. Daddy carried me up the drive. We sat in a row on the sofa. My head was blank. "Mummy has found another man and left us" Daddy's voice broke and there were tears on his cheeks. I cringed. Indecent exposure. I want to go to bed, I said.

Grandma and Grandpa were waiting in my bedroom. I must have sobbed in Grandma's arms to the point of exhaustion. I only remember waking in the early morning with Monsieur Liné by my side and Grandma sitting next to my bed.'

Wanda's grandmother came every morning and left late afternoon. Wanda was to see her mother as soon as she was strong enough. At last the day came. She threw herself into Grażyna's arms and they hugged, crying together.

After the divorce, the rules of engagement were not harsh but clear and strict: Grażyna never crossed Zygmunt's threshold, Wanda and Eva never crossed hers. Most weekends were spent at Grażyna's mother's. The girls had all their holidays, summer and winter, with Grażyna. Their Grandma came too as a guarantee that there wouldn't be some impromptu visit by Grażyna's new husband Antoni, *'the Hippo, ugly and stupid. From time to time he met Mummy well away from where we were. This infuriated me. He was robbing me of Mummy's presence for a whole day. I decided to put a stop to this outrage, and I wrote him a letter:*

Jastrzębia Góra, 6th August 1936
Dear Sir,
This is a request. Please do not disturb our holidays. You have my mother all the year round. I only have her during the holidays. She was mine before she was yours.
Yours faithfully
Wanda Karpińska

Antoni sent a short answer: a promise to do as asked and a question why such a formal letter. *'Stupid man! I loathed him. How else did he expect me to address him?'*

Not long after this exchange, bad news came from Warsaw: war was imminent. Zygmunt was sending a car to collect them. Wanda and Eva were taken back to him, and Grażyna to Antoni.

A few days later Zygmunt and the girls were ordered out of the house by the authorities. Their street had been declared the last line of defence from the advancing German army. Zygmunt deposited Eva and Wanda at their grandmother's, nearer the centre of town. For a few days the air raid sirens sounded, and the radio blared out patriotic themes. The mayor of Warsaw assured its inhabitants that they were united, strong and ready to face the enemy.

On the 10 September 1939, Wanda and Eva said goodbye to Zygmunt who handed his mother-in-law a wad of banknotes and asked Eva and Wanda whether they wanted to come with him or to stay with Grażyna. He must have known what the girls' answer would be, but I think it was very noble of him to give the children the choice. He left in a convoy of cars, some armoured, with military escort. They were heading for Romania hoping to save the Polish bullion reserves from falling into German hands.

'Mummy was waiting for us in Grandma's drawing room, ergo the world was still standing. But then a tall man with the face of a handsome fox walked through the door. He came from the inside of the apartment therefore he was there before us. I knew instantly who he was. Mummy's husband, the hippo, the monster in person, who had kidnapped her and taken her away from me when I was eight. I was now thirteen. Grandma had allowed him into her home. My world was thrown off kilter.'

The bombing was fierce. In addition to Grażyna and her daughters, there was a bizarre assortment of people in Grażyna's mother's cellar not least Antoni's pernickety half-sister Totta with her cigarette-rolling contraption. She ignored everyone's polite request to poo in the furthest corner of the cellar arguing that it was quite unnecessary because her poos were minute! Then there was a spinster cousin of Grażyna's, clutching a bag full of summer dresses in one hand and fingering her rosary beads with the other. Wanda's grandmother, calm and practical, marvelled at the uselessness of elegant summer dresses in a city under siege. A former maid came with her baby and Wanda had her beloved dog Smyk who clung to her like a limpet. Antoni scanned the beams and architectural structure with his professional eye for the safest place, since the explosion that had sent them scurrying to the cellar was rapidly followed by others. Wanda buried her face in Grażyna's lap, with her mother's fingers in her ears. Smyk shivered between them.

After three days a man rushed in shouting that the roof was on fire. They stood in the street as the house was destroyed by flames. Grażyna's mother was glad her husband hadn't lived long enough to see such devastation. They set off in thick smoke, with houses burning on both sides of the street, and people covered in blood with limbs missing. They were taken in by a family of complete strangers who shared their house and food with them all.

When one day everything went quiet and they emerged from their saviours' house, they stared in disbelief: it was the only building standing in the street. All around smoking walls stuck out from mounds of rubble and the square was swarming with dazed people picking their way through the ruins. Suddenly the eerie silence was broken by the whirr of very low-flying aeroplanes with black crosses under their wings. Wanda was petrified. These were German planes, flying as low as they dared to make people cower, flaunting the might of the conqueror. She recorded in her memoir:

'Mummy took a good look at them and said: "Today is the first day of the German occupation of Poland." It was the 27th September 1939. She was to live through five long years of it and not even she could have foreseen its full horror.'

As if by instinct, small groups of people walked towards a church. The door was gone, the walls showed huge cracks, windows were blown out. Fragments of stained glass crunched underfoot but the spire still pointed to the sky. In no time the church was packed. Even to the thriteen-year-old Wanda the familiar unchanging ritual of the Mass felt like an assurance and a show of defiance. There was no homily and only those at the front could see the priest, but once the service was over, the crowd spontaneously burst into the hymn *Boże Coś Polskę* – the second National Anthem so to speak, sung for centuries at all solemn occasions or after High Mass. It needs to be quoted in its entirety to understand the poignancy of that moment in the shattered church:

Through countless ages, through Thy loving power
Thou gavest us glory and Thou gavest us might
Saved by Thy shield in Poland's bleakest hour
Within our darkness shone Thy glorious light
Here at Thy altars we pray in accord
Our country's freedom bless today Oh Lord

This was the version known by 'the lucky generation' born in an independent Poland between the two World Wars. But on that day the last sentence of the hymn, sung in that ruined church, was like a stab in the heart. They sang not *Our country's freedom bless today oh Lord,* but *Our country's freedom **give us back** oh Lord*. The teenage Wanda understood why grown ups were moved to tears every time *Boże Coś Polskę* was sung. '*Now my generation was as one with the grown ups. We could all cry together.*'

After the surrender, trying to find their way home was a bizarre obstacle course, with many detours through smoking mountains of rubble and pools of mud created by water spurting from broken mains. Wanda burst into tears at the sight of a young woman wailing in what had been the threshold

Warsaw destroyed by the Germans

of her house. They turned another corner and Zygmunt's house, the girls' home with 'Daddy', stood whole, unscathed and with the contents intact thanks to the housekeeper (who'd insisted on staying due to the charms of a young soldier stationed down the road).

A few days after their homecoming, Wanda ventured out to see whether the local grocer's shop was still there. As she turned the corner, she heard the rhythmic sound of boots on cobbles. A detachment of eight men abreast was marching down the narrow street. She stopped dead, flattening herself against the wall.

She writes in her memoir:

'I watched them pass like a well-oiled machine. I choked with fury. These people were invading MY street, MY city, MY country. I was thirteen so the word rape did not spring to mind. Decades later, however, I can find no other word to describe the outrage I felt.'

The following day an officer of the Wermacht and two subalterns arrived to search the house asking where Herr Doctor Karpiński might be. Grażyna told him, truthfully, that she didn't know. They spent hours in Zygmunt's study rifling through his papers and checking every room in the house. Grażyna's mother suddenly stopped following them around and sat for the remaining duration of the search, motionless on the sofa. The reason was revealed only after they left.

'When the soldiers had arrived and were walking up our drive, Grandma had pounced on her necessaire and hurriedly transferred small bags of gold sovereigns, dollars, rubles and precious stones from the necessaire into her famously long pockets. As she wandered through the house watching the soldiers' every move, the already sagging pockets began to come apart at the seams. Maybe the simple act of sitting down and staying put, saved not only a substantial amount of cash but quite possibly even avoided deportation. That very night, when the moon hid behind a cloud, the mini sacks were buried under the cherry tree.'

A few days later all secondary schools were closed, and teaching went underground: clandestine classes were established all over Warsaw. The children gathered in private houses in groups of five or six plus a teacher, never twice in the same house, never arriving all together, always at irregular intervals. All through the German occupation primary, secondary and higher education thrived due to great bravery. If discovered, teachers and pupils were sent to concentration camps or shot there and then. The long list of the activities punishable by death was very clear in the constitution for the territories of the 'Ex State of Poland' proclaimed by the General Governor Hans Frank. The obsessive repetition of the last five words in each sentence left no margin for error: **wird mit dem tode bestrafen** (*will be punished by death*).

Wanda's sister Eva joined the underground girl guides and was introduced to the skills of sabotage, top secret of course. Not even Grażyna was told of any such activity by her older daughter, but she suspected it and she too had her secret plans.

Every evening for an hour or so the wireless was on, broadcasting interminable Red Cross lists of names of people who'd found themselves catapulted abroad after the fall of Poland. 'Mrs so and so in Rome, Mr such and such in Romania etc' and one day finally, 'Zygmunt Karpiński in Paris'. *'Daddy was alive,'* Wanda relates. *'Eva turned away to wipe a tear and Mummy said five words which punched me in the stomach: You must join him. My reaction was instantaneous: I don't want to.'*

For the next three months my grandmother Grażyna fought on two hostile fronts: German officials and stubborn daughters. She procured certificates, permits, warrants, visas, shivered for hours in endless queues, sat in airless waiting rooms, confronted stony-faced officers at the Gestapo headquarters. This was the beginning of the occupation. A few weeks later such negotiations would have been impossible. Just before Christmas 1939 a wad of documents stamped with a swastika arrived in the post with two one-way tickets to Rome. This had been thanks to a childhood friend of Grażyna's, the wife of the Italian consul in Warsaw, by then in German allied Italy. She sent Eva and Wanda an invitation for the duration of the war.

On the morning of 6 January 1940, my mother and Eva boarded a train for Rome.

'My eyes were so swollen from crying that I could hardly see the step.

Eva climbed on to the train, I stumbled behind. As the train moved slowly away, I put my head out of the window. Mummy stood rigid on the receding platform. Suddenly she leant against a column. Inside the moving train I lurched forward in a futile attempt to reach her. My umbilical cord had just been ripped off.'

<center>~~~</center>

Although it was January when the girls arrived in Rome the city was bathed in translucent light and the air was warm. In the gardens of Pincio, bonnetted babies sailed in prams like Spanish galleons, their nannies uniformed captains at the helm. Their older siblings pushed wooden hoops or cuddled frilly dolls. It could have been a spring day in the park in Warsaw, aeons before the war.

Mussolini had signed a full defensive alliance with Nazi Germany a few months before, but he hadn't yet declared war on Britain and France. The sisters, Eva (eighteen) and my mother Wanda (fourteen), were very briefly lulled into a war-free state of mind. With the aplomb of a seasoned traveller Eva made sure to cram the maximum number of sights into the three-day stay in Rome. Wanda obediently followed her guide, absorbing the treasures of Rome as far as her numbed brain would allow.

The grandeur of St Peter's square amazed and dwarfed her, the Vatican failed to fire her imagination, the Castle of Sant'Angelo gave her the creeps, and the Coliseum, in spite of her pious efforts to imagine the early Christians being devoured by wild beasts without a word of complaint, didn't make her heart go out to them. However, the Fontana di Trevi was love at first sight. Its waters springing from some invisible source somewhere in the bowels of the grand building behind it, cascading into a large shallow dish-like basin with mythical figures she knew well, was thrilling. There were Tritons, sea horses and Neptune himself and the whole wonderful thing almost filled the tiny piazza where it sat. This was magic.

Three days later, Eva and Wanda took the train to Zurich. Zygmunt was already there on Bank business and met them at the station. *'As the Simplon Express rushed into the 19 km long tunnel at the Italian end at Domodossola, I wondered what the point of all these experiences was if I couldn't share them with Mummy.'*

Twenty-four hours on and they were on a train again, this time with Zygmunt, bound for Paris where the Bank of Poland and the Polish

Government in exile had established a base for the duration of the war (or so they thought). The boarding house where they had taken rooms was called 'Bon Acceuil' and it lived up to its name. Their rooms occupied the two top floors of a five-storey building in the Boulevard Raspail.

As soon as Eva and Wanda met the Bank staff already installed at the 'Bon Acceuil' they stepped into a grown-up world hitherto unknown to the fourteen-year-old Wanda but of which, to her surprise, she was a welcome member. These were a group of civilised people, thrown together by circumstances and willing to make the best of it. Social life, somewhat stripped of its many rituals, found a new expression. More often than not they dined in somebody's kitchen or in small groups in the local bistro. At weekends they walked in the Bois de Boulogne, watched children sail their toy boats on the pond of the Jardin du Luxembourg, visited museums. It suited Wanda to the ground.

France did not feel like a foreign country to my fourteen-year-old mother. She knew its history and was fluent in their language, had read French children's classics, knew their nursery rhymes. She was happy to be placed in the Institut Normal Catholique d'Adèline Désir (or Cours Désir for the initiated), where some twenty years earlier Simonne de Beauvoir had been a pupil. This was nothing like Wanda's experience in the lion's den that had been St Thérèse Boarding School for Girls in Rabka when she was eight.

The stay in Paris proved to be a turning point for Wanda who actively decided that she would not give in to the frequent bouts of desperately missing her mother, so she was game for every outing and every activity available. Judging by the entries in her diary, she coped:

'*7th February 1940 – Ash Wednesday: We had our foreheads sprinkled with ashes. Thou art dust and to dust thou will return. Think on that old girl!*'

'*Mummy writes that it is so cold in Warsaw that people freeze to death. Why am I not there with them? Is it really true that there was such a day when I left Poland? After supper I locked myself in the bathroom and blubbed for hours.*'

'*15th February 1940: Mlle Tibier said she was very pleased with me. A hardworking girl, she said. That's me! Ha ha ha!*'

'*I read in a Polish paper that the Germans (may they all perish) put*' up gallows in the Square of the Redeemer in Warsaw, right in front of the church where I was baptized. What is happening to the world?'

'*18th February 1940*: *Mass at the Madeleine. It's a church with a long tradition of brilliant preachers. Today's preacher broke that tradition with a bang!*'

'*20th February 1940*: *Chamberlain said something about Norway and Neutrality. I must find out what he meant. Gorgeous weather. How can ghastly things happen under such a blue sky?*'

'*24th February 1940*: *We went to see Aida. Phenomenally wonderful. I nearly clapped my hands off.*'

On the 11 June 1940 at 9 am six Bank of Poland cars and the armoured vehicle containing the Polish bullion reserves left Paris. Wanda and Eva were surprised to be driving through such empty streets. Many shops were closed. Several had large notices with *Fermé jusqu'a la Victoire* in bold defiant letters. As they approached the outskirts of Paris the scene changed completely. Masses of cars, all driving in the same direction, soon formed a monumental traffic jam of vehicles trapped bumper to bumper. Every now and again they advanced a few yards only to come to another long halt. Many overheating cars had to be pushed aside, often into a ditch.

The party finally reached a splendid chateau near the village of Bourg d'Iré where for a few days Wanda and Eva played ball on the lawn and lay on the grass whilst Zygmunt and the big Bank bosses sat glued to the wireless with worried faces. On the 14 June 1940 Paris fell. Wanda wrote in her diary:

'*Paris has fallen. What now? After supper, on the cool stone steps, I played patriotic songs on my mouth organ. I got huge applause and after my "concert" we listened to the English Queen speaking on the radio in French to the women of France. When night fell, Mr W. who likes a bit of fun, stood me in a sleeping bag on the balustrade with a lit torch in my mouth. I was supposed to be a ghost, so I duly produced ghostly moans. It was very jolly. What a pity the war will chase us out of here, probably tomorrow. I don't see this as inappropriate frivolity but the undaunted human spirit at work.*'

On the 19 June the group left the village of Bourg d'Iré for Libourne where it was decided that the bullion and the Polish Government in Exile were to head South with the hope of crossing the border into Spain, whilst the three Directors of the Bank of Poland and their families (which included Zygmunt Karpiński, my mother Wanda and her sister Eva) would head for Pointe de Graves with highly sensitive Bank archives packed in three containers: a file, a case and a metal box which Zygmunt held on to at all times. (See appendix 2)

As the cars drove between woods and the sea, more and more people joined them, a motley crowd of soldiers and civilians, French and foreign, on foot or bicycles, scuttling like rabbits into ditches and hollows whilst German aeroplanes strafed them. Wanda wasn't frightened although to her dismay she had no authority over her legs and Eva had to drag her. She didn't mind the idea of dying. She just didn't want to die without seeing her mother again.

Finally, on Saturday 22 June 1940, France signed the armistice with Germany and two cargo boats sailed into view, flying the blue ensign. One of them was the *Clan Ferguson*.

'As Daddy, Eva and I with three other people were being rowed to the ship the aeroplanes returned. Their unnerving whine accompanied our frantic scramble up the circus-like rope ladder which dangled with the sea as safety net. We made it to the deck drenched by huge sprays, courtesy of two bombs. Mercifully they only hit the water. Another hour or so the beach was empty. We were packed into the Clan Ferguson *like sardines. The sea was rough, the wind and rain unrelenting. The only two cabins were temporarily transformed into delivery rooms where two French women gave birth to two boys, within an hour of each other.'*

At 6 am on 25 June 1940 the *Clan Ferguson* docked in Liverpool harbour. A few hours later the car sent by the Bank of England to take them to the hotel (which was to be their home for a week) stopped at a fashion shop where Zygmunt bought Eva and Wanda a skirt and a jacket each. *'The charming assistant was not surprised when asked to place our own garments in the bin.'*

At Euston station they were met by officials from the Bank of Poland who took them to the Kingsley Hotel in Holborn. After three days they moved to a comfortable flat in St John's Wood.

The Blitz started on the 7 September 1940. On two or three occasions when the Luftwaffe ran amok over their heads, they fled back to the Kingsley Hotel where it felt safer under the billiard table in the basement than on the 5th floor at home.

At the St John's Wood flat, Zygmunt did his best to entertain the girls. To take their minds off bombs he taught them bridge and they played far into the night at a table in the windowless hall out of reach of flying glass. Sometimes they slept on platforms at tube stations, the best possible shelters underground, and daily life continued regardless. Wanda relished her bond with the friendly Londoners. Like them she and Eva shopped in battered half-gutted shops with defiant notices of 'Business as Usual'; they lunched in Lyons Corner Houses, went to the pictures and walks in Hyde Park. They danced every day and if the Luftwaffe were too noisy, the orchestra played louder. When bombs fell too close, they dived under tables only to emerge with more zest for dancing. Courage manifested in this way had perforce to co-exist with the blocking of one's mind to the horrors of what the bombs that had just missed them had caused to others.

Wanda recalls in her memoirs:

'Never in the field of human conflict did so many owe so much to so few. I was elated by Churchill's words. This sense of elation was further increased by the delivery of a piano that Daddy finally agreed to rent for me. On the day it arrived I wrote in my diary: "I thanked Daddy very very much and I ought to feel grateful, but I don't. I must be a monster not to feel any closeness to my own father." Little did I know then the true source of such feelings.'

Before 1940 was out, the nearly fifteen-year-old Wanda was sent to boarding school in Scotland to be near Eva who was reading Mathematics at Glasgow University. The school (Laurel Bank) had been moved to Auchterarder House which the owners, who had departed to America, had leased out for the duration of the war. Wanda was very happy there and devoured all the classics not least Shakespeare which drove her to improve her English as much and as soon as possible so that she could savour the bard's *oeuvre* fully.

In 1943, back in London, Wanda and Zygmunt had the narrowest of escapes from a doodle bug. They had been sitting in the house in Redcliffe Square (which the Bank of England was renting for them). Seconds after both got up to get something to eat, the windows were blown out by an explosion which caused countless shards of glass to embed themselves in the sofa they had just left.

Wanda studied for the London Matric, did courses at the Polytechnic, resumed her advanced piano studies, whilst Zygmunt continued working towards the restitution of the Polish bullion (by then in America). Eva soon fell in love with a fellow Pole and got married. Then, finally, in 1945, aged twenty, after five years of not seeing her mother at all, suddenly, whilst brushing her hair, Wanda looked at herself in the mirror and the penny dropped: she was Antoni's daughter, not Zygmunt's. The realisation brought her instant relief as it explained her lack of closeness with Zygmunt, the 'Daddy' who'd always been beyond reproach, always undeserving of her feelings of distance and irritation which had in turn brought her permanent feelings of guilt. She wasn't Karpińska. She was Dygat. Grażyna and Antoni were in Paris and that is where she had to go to confront them.

'I left Daddy standing on the platform at Victoria, a lonely figure. He waved, I waved back. The wad of dollar bills weighed heavy in my handbag. I did not deserve his generosity. As the train gathered speed I relaxed into my seat. The crossing from Dover to Calais seemed to go on forever. At last we were docking.'

On arrival in Paris she burst into Grażyna and Antoni's apartment and leant her back against the door. Even before hugging her mother she asked for the truth. They hadn't expected that. Stunned, her biological parents, confirmed it. The erstwhile monster, the horrible Hippo was no more. Before she realised how she got there she was in her parents' arms, Mummy and Papa, her father, her REAL father. He was so tall!

'I wanted to talk about us, us three, our new life together as it should have always been. As for Mummy, she was the unchanged, unchangeable Mummy, her unique scent mine again.'

Wanda was in a state of bliss, a child again but a happy one.

'Papa uncovered before my eyes the Paris of his youth. The Paris of the Café Concert, of Yvette Guilbert, the great Sarah Bernhardt. Montmartre, the Quartier Latin, the bateaux mouches on the Seine, the École des Beaux Arts where he had studied architecture. I saw the world around me through the eyes of this captivating man at my side. My Father, my Real Father. He was warm, he was gentle, he was tender. He was perfect. I sprouted wings.'

It is not surprising that when the Cortot School of Music in Paris offered Wanda a place, saying she had every chance of becoming a concert pianist, she turned it down and decided to go to Brazil with her parents.

CHAPTER ELEVEN

WEDDING BELLS, MANGY DOGS AND MAGIC SPELLS

IT WAS AT Prince Roman Sanguszko's house in São Paulo that my parents, Józef Mycielski and Wanda Karpińska met in 1947. They were both twenty-two. The Prince was a friend of the Tyszkiewicz and of my mother's parents before the war and he was able to stretch out a helping hand and immediately bring them into his European and Brazilian circles. He'd had the presence of mind (when the war started in 1939), to load up many lorries with his priceless possessions from the palace of Podhorce (or 'Pidhirsti' in Ukrainian) and flee through Romania. He emigrated to Brazil after the war with his treasures.

My mother's biological father, Antoni, had been a leading architect in Poland. As an émigré in Brazil, with Prince Roman Sanguszko's help he got a job with a well-known Brazilian firm, albeit as one of many draughtsmen. My mother's parentage was an open secret for decades, until Zygmunt Karpiński's death, and my mother's official maiden surname remained as Karpińska.

Wanda had so many nicknames that in order not to confuse you I will stick to her Christian name but not without explaining that it is only in English that Wanda is pronounced with the W as in wand. My mother hated that version and always asked English speakers to pronounce it as it should be pronounced: Vanda.

In her 1990s memoir, that I shall be drawing on, my mother writes:

'I remember sailing into Guanabara Bay, a young single woman with her parents, dazzled by the sun, smitten by the heat, struck dumb by the scale of the landscape. Leaning over the rail with the smell of sea in my nostrils, the cool breeze on my skin, I let myself be drawn into the aura of this unknown enticing country in which I was coming to live, not by my own choice but some shrewd and welcome fate.'

When my parents met in São Paulo in 1947 my mother slipped into their relationship like sliding into a pair of comfortable old shoes. He was

Polish; he was delightful; he made her feel closer to her roots. As for my father she was solace and he'd tell her repeatedly: 'You're a poultice for my soul', certainly not the most romantic of expressions but an accurate one. His personal experience of Stalin's Gulag and the unimaginable suffering of his fellow deportees and his own were an open sore. She somehow soothed him.

Passion wasn't the main ingredient in their marriage. I imagine that if they hadn't been thrown together by the traumas of war and exile, they wouldn't have married, but would have been great friends who scintillated at each other's dinner parties. What they did have together though was the joy of a shared love of literature, poetry, philosophy, Eastern religions, Art. My parents were multilingual, had an acute sense of humour and of the absurd, invented crazy languages, smoked endless cigarettes and howled with laughter. They were married in February 1948.

Wedding of Józef Mycielski to Wanda Karpińska, São Paulo 1948

Józef and Wanda spent their honeymoon night in a ramshackle fisherman's cottage on a soft sandy beach, lapped by the warm Atlantic. Not a living soul in sight. *'Leaves rustled in the tropical breeze, which prompted Józef to hum into my neck, in an exaggerated Maurice Chevalier accent: "Every little breeze seems to whisper Louise…". He called me Louise after that for days.'*

On that honeymoon night events took an unusual turn with a mighty clap of thunder followed by torrential rain pouring down on them through gaps in the roof. My parents in turn giggled and read the *Bhagavad Ghita* under a parasol tied to the bedpost to protect them from the elements. Raindrops against buckets and saucepans dotted around the floor, turned the metal utensils into soothing percussion instruments to the delight of the newlyweds.

'The next morning, drunk with the marine air and lethargic after a night of little sleep, I watched him turn cartwheels on the beach, all long legs and golden hair.'

In 1949, when Wanda was pregnant with me and, just as she'd come to feel that Brazil was under her skin forever, my father decided they should leave for Argentina. Greener grass… His mother Róża and Kika, his sister, were already there and he had it all worked out: his mother could run a boarding house, Wanda would look after the baby, he'd become a translator and Kika already had a job. They'd be a fabulous team!

'His eyes, which moments before had been pools of dejection, burned bright with hope. "To new beginnings! Eat, my darling," he urged me. A new Russian neighbour had taken to leaving samples of her cooking on the doorstep. "Aren't we lucky to have such a kind person a few doors down?" I looked at my husband over the chicken Kiev with warmth and puzzlement. What have I done? Why have I married this man?'

Kika did indeed have a job. She'd been offered training and work as a theatre nurse in a prestigious hospital in Buenos Aires, as a result of a chance meeting in the Argentinian capital. A Polish doctor, who, like her, had been attached to General Anders' army seven years earlier, had first seen her in 1942, as a sixteen-year-old nurse in the Desert Hospital in Egypt. He'd been struck not only by her beauty but by the kind and sensitive aura around her. This Polish doctor barely believed his eyes when he saw her again in

Buenos Aires, in 1949. He instantly realised that his offer of a job meant Kika and her mother would no longer need to live on bread, bananas, cheap sweets and occasional delicacies swiped from silver trays at smart cocktail parties at various embassies or at the Polo Club. In fact, that was where the doctor had bumped into her, at a Polo match she'd been invited to by some Argentinian Adonis who, unlike the doctor, hadn't noticed Kika stealing food. Her stomach, and her mother's, shrunken from hunger in the war and during the impecunious years that followed, couldn't cope with much. Hiding morsels in pockets and handbags for later, had become second nature and an art.

Having decided that a move to Argentina was a must, my father bounced around his wife looking for the city plan of Buenos Aires so that he could decide where *exactly* they should live. They'd have to be within easy reach of the capital but not in it. His child would need space, fresh air and contact with nature. He was thrilled that the railway between BA and surrounding areas was wonderful and Kika would have no problem commuting to work.

On the 10 July 1949, whilst Józef chirped around the house rearranging pamphlets about Buenos Aires and the Argentinian song *Chacarera* blared from his radio, Antoni died suddenly of a heart attack. He was sixty-three. For Wanda the death of the father she'd discovered only four years before was as devastating and as cruel as for her mother. The usually strong and resourceful Grażyna, in a state of uncomprehending shock, lay next to his body for several hours until my mother told her that the undertakers would be coming soon and that they needed to dress him for burial. My mother, pregnant with me, nearly miscarried as a result.

In Brazil, funerals usually take place within twenty-four hours of death. Grażyna and Wanda had no choice but to summon their resilience and within days the plans for a move to Argentina gathered momentum. The trip was only a few weeks away.

And so it was that Józef and Wanda Mycielski prepared for departure. There were crates of books, of course, and clothes: everything from hand-me-downs donated by the Polish Church in São Paulo, to party gowns made by my mother from discarded curtains, and an array of Savile Row suits and dinner jackets given to my father by a relation who'd escaped from Europe with most of his riches just before the Second World War. Lucky Józef: the relation in question had the same size feet as him so countless pairs of pre-war leather shoes (black, brown, two-tone) filled a huge battered leather suitcase to the brim. All had wooden shoe trees and flannel shoe bags with suede tassels. Good footwear was essential. My father tenderly attended to a barely perceptible scuff mark as if it were a scratch on a newborn's skin.

The packing was left to my mother because my father couldn't possibly travel until he found exactly the right tones of shoe polish for every pair, and the correct brushes and cloths. My mother knew full well there was no point whatsoever in suggesting these purchases could be made in Argentina. She just hoped that the little bit of extra money she'd given him to buy groceries wouldn't be spent on yet one more different shade of shoe wax.

Józef returned from the first day of searching, minus the shoe polish and groceries but with a cut class vase from an antique shop. The vase reminded him of 'Napoleon's glass', a goblet on which Bonaparte had scratched an N with his diamond ring. The occasion had been an ancestor's christening which Napoleon had attended. The baby had been called Constance Victoire in his honour and she'd been held at the font by Napoleon's general Massena to whom my Mycielski great-great-great-great-grandfather had been aide-de-camp. Józef was thrilled and gave an excited lecture to my mother explaining that this kind of glass had a concentration of lead oxide between 24 and 30 per cent and could therefore be worked with any etching technique!

'It took three more shopping trips for Józef to decide he finally had all he needed to travel. He returned from the last one with a huge smile, a bunch of Hibiscus pinched en route from somebody's garden, and yet another book about Matisse. That evening we ate our Russian neighbour's rollmops, listened to Chopin's Nocturne in C sharp minor, and belly laughed as Józef impersonated an imaginary French official pompously addressing the residents of a piddly little town on the occasion of the inauguration of a new bridge.'

Laughter and sudden bouts of weeping came at the most unexpected moments for both Wanda and Grażyna, as of course is the case for all bereaved people. For Wanda though, the fact that she had only known her father for four years was particularly distressing.

Grażyna despaired at the young couple's decision to whizz off to Argentina, not because she didn't want to be left behind but because she could well envisage what sort of chaotic life her daughter was about to take on. Her son-in-law's suggestion that she should make the permanent move too, just as soon as the baby was born, filled her with horror. She missed her husband terribly, but she'd be fine where she was, in São Paulo, working as a *dame-de-compagnie* to a rich French woman (with the charm of a rattle snake but a generous purse) and had no wish to start all over again in yet another country. She'd come, but only to meet the baby. God Almighty, a grandchild was on the way. The announcement of *any* baby's birth invariably made her sigh with pity. A child's death on the other hand, whilst causing her to genuinely empathise with the parents' loss, elicited expressions of relief (not always under her breath) that the infant had been spared. One more little angel in heaven. *Deo Gratias.* The fact remained that she'd soon have a grandchild, she'd have to meet it and of course she would love it.

When Grażyna waved the young couple off she was filled with foreboding. Her enchanting and dementing son-in-law was a walking existential ache, her daughter a heroine and a fool. But she'd do what she could to help. And she wouldn't lose her sense of humour. A few days later she gleefully related to Wanda in a letter, that as she walked home, some youth slowed right down on his motorbike, making appreciative remarks about her bottom. *'I told the idiot not to waste his time and to go home because I'm fifty-one not twenty! You should have seen his face when I turned around!'*

Wanda would miss her mother and she knew full well that just like her, Grażyna would be living with tears, laughter and Antoni's absence for years to come but she knew also that her mother had many devoted friends and neighbours who would all rally round.

My mother couldn't wait to meet Józef's mother and sister. Before arriving in Argentina she'd had only a mental picture of Róża and Kika from their funny letters and Józef's description, plus two passport shots taken in Tehran after their release from the Siberian labour camp. In those photographs they were two beggar women, thin lipped, blotchy and swollen with vacant eyes. There was a third, later photograph, where the same women stood by a fountain in Buenos Aires: Kika, a beautiful girl in a nurse's uniform, with her middle-aged mother wearing a jaunty hat.

My mother and Kika bonded at first sight, finding a friendship of rare quality and an unspoken pact of mutual support established itself between the sisters-in-law for the rest of their lives. In those first hours after meeting Kika for the very first time, Wanda knew that she'd never have secrets from her. They would always be able to talk about anything. For now, they'd concentrate on Jozef's idea of a boarding house, which was about to materialise, against all odds.

What kind of genie, lover of whimsy, led Róża to a 'suitable' villa for a boarding house cum restaurant, in Tigre, a fashionable weekend town an hour's train ride from Buenos Aires? Deportation, deprivation, starvation, homelessness, bereavement... nothing had altered the grandeur of my grandmother Róża's vision. From the marble steps, the balustrade and bevelled windowpanes, to exotic shrubs down to the rowing boat moored at a tiny private pier, their pocket-sized home had the air of a Lilliput palazzo. On closer inspection the gap between skirting and floor was a good three inches, flakes of stucco rained on their heads, wallpaper puckered. Flowering scented creepers pushed their tendrils under tiles, tangled with electric wires, competed with rot, both wet and dry, whilst armies of tiny beetles and weevils munched merrily through the fabric of the building. But there was a chandelier! Józef was ecstatic.

The house had been bought by my grandmother Róża with their demob payouts, plus money given to her in London in 1946 by a Polish lawyer from New York. He'd been one of several bright children of very poor peasant stock, that Róża's Mycielski brother-in-law had searched for in remote rural areas all over Greater Poland in the 1910s so that he could pay for their education. By 1946, the man was a young lawyer in America and he'd moved heaven and earth to track down my family through the Red Cross and army records. He was very sad to hear his benefactor had died in Siberia but glad to be able to help my grandmother and her children.

Grandma Róża and my father were thrilled with the idea of a boarding house, whilst Kika and my mother viewed the situation with a mixture of humour and foreboding.

'On our very first evening together, having met only hours before, Kika and I sat in complete harmony on the verandah watching fireflies, when the magic was suddenly broken by our uncontrollable giggles as we conjured up images of guests being electrocuted due to the faulty wiring or groaning in their beds from indigestion' (as a result of Róża's abysmal cooking).

'...The next day, Józef was far too busy to help with the unpacking and immediately started painting a beautiful sign for the gate: Pensión de la Luna. *He spent days trying out different fonts and buying paints*

with money I'd been putting aside for our baby's birth. I swiftly took matters into my own hands and through a few well-placed contacts, found rich private students of English, all over BA. I hid every penny I earned in a washbag under the sink.'

Customers did come to *Pensión de la Luna,* but they left in droves too, often without paying, having developed coughs and wheezes from the strangely beautiful spores that proliferated in their bedrooms overnight. Amazingly, several guests did return. Some came to woo Kika who regarded them all with amused detachment. Others were dreamers and barstool philosophers. Drawn to discussions with my father about the universe, the impressionists or Sartre, they lolled in a communal alcoholic haze by the canal, as he twirled a tiny paintbrush, perfecting perfection, adding golden lettering to the abominable menu. 'Presentation is vital,' he repeated, ignoring his sister's suggestions that he might try to get a job.

Unsurprisingly, it wasn't long before *Pensión de la Luna* closed its doors. My father made two announcements: that he'd become a bookbinder and that he couldn't live without a dog. He went out to look for a bookbinding course and came back with two malnourished English Setters he'd bought from a gipsy by the church. He called them Martha and Charles.

Within days, my mother caught the mange from the dogs, which amused my father no end; not due to the fact that, like them, she couldn't stop scratching, but because in his opinion the red patterns on Wanda's pregnant stomach made it look like a globe.

'How could I be cross with him when he was so funny? Look! Here's Australia. And India is just over there! He made me squirm and giggle as he searched for Poland and France. A kind vet gave me a huge discount, maybe because he could tell funds were meagre and that I'd be using the dogs' mange cream on myself too.'

In January 1950 I was born. Years later, Kika's description of the event was so vivid that I can see it now in my mind's eye: the obstetrician wearing a bespattered apron over an ill-fitting suit, stubbing out a cigarette on his way into the delivery room; a nurse turning up the volume on the radio to drown the sounds of their patient's agony; Eva Perón's voice mingling with my mother's screams (one addressing her people from the balcony at the Casa

Rosada, the other trying in vain to push her baby out). According to Kika, when I finally emerged, my head looked like a zeppelin. 'You've deformed my child,' my father yelled. Kika did what she could to calm him down, telling him that, given time, my head would shrink to a normal shape.

When my mother and I were wheeled into a room, my grandmother Róża stroked her barely conscious daughter-in-law's head with infinite tenderness. Wanda had been so brave having this baby, in this world now by the finest thread of fate: I wouldn't have been there at all, had they all perished in Siberia, like my paternal grandfather Władzio Mycielski. I can well imagine that on that morning, my grandmother's eyes, limpid blue and childlike, allowed a fleeting glow of hope to wash over their permanent look of bewilderment. That day was a special day. And in her pockets, solace. In one, as always, her rosary and a picture of Saint Joseph of Cupertino. In the other, I have no doubt, something to eat. Maybe a morsel slipped off a salver at a neighbour's buffet lunch? She never lost the fear of being hungry.

Wanda could feel that Kika was just as overwhelmed with love for me as she was. And she had no doubt about what her own mother Grażyna would think about my birth: that I was to be pitied, not for the shape of my head but for being born at all. As for my father, I heard from Kika that in that hospital room he could ill conceal his state of mind. She knew him so well, better than anyone, ever since they were little. Nothing about him escaped her. Hurriedly pecking his wife on the cheek, he cracked a joke about the shape of their daughter's head, and he was gone. Kika knew full well that instead of going home, he'd be veering off to the nearest tavern.

Later, when Kika arrived back, she found him sitting by the canal, writing a poem. One look at his face told her that the image he couldn't banish from his mind was that of a dead baby, a baby being thrown out of the cattle train by a Russian soldier during the long journey to the Siberian labour camp.

With the moon slipping behind the tangle of jasmine and bougainvillea that fought for control of the veranda, she cradled him in silence. So bespattered was the paper with his tears that they couldn't read the poem when the sun brought in a new day.

At this point I need to tell you that I am terribly important. Like the Queen I have two birthdays. I was born on the 26 January but my birth certificate and all official documents say the 30th. My father was unaware that in the times of Peron the law required you to register your baby on the day of its birth. When he arrived on the 30th, he was told he would have to pay a fine. Outraged, he hot-footed back to the hospital, where the accommodating doctor tore up my birth certificate and issued a false one with January 30th as the official date.

———⚬⚬⚬———

Within days of my birth my maternal grandmother, Grażyna, arrived from Brazil complete with food parcels and a determined gait. She was greeted by Ramona, a neighbour of the Mycielskis, who prided herself in having magic spells for every occasion, not least the arrival of a new baby, distant travel, problems with sleep, warts and troublesome neighbours. She also sold magic powders, one of which was in great demand amongst the spinsters of the parish and was called 'husband-catching powder'. Although my grandmother Róża had herself bought the latter for Kika, in this case Ramona's offers of help were so overwhelming that Róża worried herself sick that if rejected, Ramona would cast some curse on the entire family. She'd been known to do just that in the neighbourhood.

Grandma Grażyna paid no attention to such superstitions but taking one look at the general situation she made a decision: reminding herself, in no uncertain terms, that honesty without tact is cruelty, Grażyna informed her family of her resolve. She'd speed back to Brazil and resume her work as *dame-de-compagnie* to Madame Rattlesnake to save enough for a ticket for my mother and me to join her as soon as possible. She assured everyone she'd send on more tickets so that the rest of the family, including the dogs Martha and Charles, could join us in due course. She kept her promise. Within a few months we were all in Brazil.

———⚬⚬⚬———

CHAPTER TWELVE

THE HOURGLASS

THE HOUSE IN Tigre hadn't been sold for much, so my parents, Kika and I moved in with grandma Grażyna, whereas Róża found a grim little cottage in a rough part of São Paulo, in an area infested by mosquitos and prone to floods. She was surprisingly chirpy when my father and Kika transported her and her clobber in the banana seller's van to her new abode. The banana man was an affable soul and didn't mind lending my father his vehicle. He liked Wanda's mother Grażyna and was happy to help.

After hours of choreographing the chaotic unpacking of their mother's sad belongings, Józef and Kika made for home. They stopped en route in a little tavern and sat in silence exhausted, holding hands like they'd done many times as children in Poland before the war. So often had they huddled in the orchard, making wild plans to follow the sun around the world, until it brought them back to the same spot. Maybe by then their mother's agoraphobia would be better. Maybe by then their adored father Władzio would no longer need to hug her until her fear of shadows subsided, or coax her into coming out into the garden, just one step or two over the threshold. They never forgot occasions when Róża slumped on the grass, with her head in her beloved husband's lap. He'd gently stroke her hair, hoping she'd close her eyes, but she fixed them on the house, fearful that the building would disappear. Józef and Kika were a team since then and for the rest of time.

As they sat in the tavern on that evening in 1950, worn out after moving their mother into her new home, Kika knew that this new beginning in Brazil wouldn't be a walk in the park, but she couldn't have foreseen the relentless demands life would place upon her in the decades to come. Nor could she envisage the extent to which, like with their father, her fragile physical health would belie her vast resources of inner strength. She did know, however, that she had three powerful allies: faith, humour and her sister-in-law.

That evening in the tavern was to remain in Kika's memory for ever. She was visibly emotional when recounting it to me years later. This was not Samarkand, no golden apples yet that she could see, but it was another new beginning. The image of her brother leaving the tavern never paled:

as they walked out into the night, Józef giggled, leapt into the air and clicked his heels. His gangly shape seemed to her to hang in the beam of the streetlight, as if frozen in time.

———⁂———

Róża settled into her ghastly little house, as much as settling anywhere was possible for her. Ever since the devastation of her world, and in spite of her fragility, she somehow adapted. She no longer suffered from agoraphobia. Her *modus vivendi* became one of scurrying between her home and ours, the church, food halls, street markets, and bric-a-brac shops where she scoured for cheap imitations of grand jewellery and endless kid-skin gloves. The latter were always bought from the same stall, made not out of some unfortunate young goat but of 'GENUINE Nylon', as the vendor proudly advertised.

Every flat surface in my grandmother's house was invisible, covered as it was by an extraordinary array of belongings: hair nets and bananas, missals and rosaries, boxes of corn plasters, nail polish, eye drops, lotions and potions, holy pictures and figurines, elastic bands and pencil sharpeners, paper clips, jelly babies, matches, tissues, nail clippers, coins, countless square tins of various sizes and shapes.... From a distance you could be excused for thinking you were looking at a maquette of a densely populated metropolis. Stacks of French magazines towered in every corner, books teetered on rickety chairs, half empty chocolate boxes protruded from drawers.

One of the highlights of my grandmother Róża's life was coming to see me, her baby granddaughter. She fussed over me, blessed me, kissed my toes, lit candles to encourage my fate to be kind. Her other passion was the long-suffering curate, Padre Atanázio. I don't think he had ever suspected what the Almighty had in store for him. Padre Atanázio's domain was Igreja do Calvário, on Rua Cardeal Arcoverde, the church on the top of a hill in São Paulo. His own personal calvary was dealing with my grandmother. Róża blushed and giggled when she saw him, brought him coconut balls and other sweetmeats, set about every polishable thing in the church with endless flannels brought by her from home (much better than the ones in the sacristy), checked candles, dusted kneelers. She went to confession at every opportunity. Poor Padre Atanázio... Kika once saw him leap behind a pillar at the sight of my grandmother, as if Lucifer himself were in pursuit.

And poor Róża too. Nothing like longing for the unattainable. I wonder what she would have done had the young priest lunged at her, consumed with unbridled desire!

———

Every time Róża came to see us in our mews house at number 3, she tormented Kika with a multitude of plans to find her a husband. Her suggestions varied from chatting up the young pianist at the Polish café, to joining every social evening at the library, to loitering by the poshest sports and social club in São Paulo. But the very best plan for Kika according to Róża would be for her to marry her new boss. He was the director of a pharmaceutical company.

Kika had been forced to turn down regular nursing work in a hospital, having developed an acute allergy to rubber gloves. She didn't have to say a word for Wanda to know the depth of her sister-in-law's suffering. The new job, as a PA, was totally against the grain. After the horrors of Siberia and the desert hospital, where Death had been her daily companion, Kika had felt unambiguously that she'd found her calling in the operating theatre, nursing in peace-time, with Life, not Death walking with her, step by step towards a future. That sense of hope and fulfillment was brutally ripped from her in one brief moment, as one day she removed a surgical glove and with it her skin. The allergy to rubber was to dog her for the rest of her life.

As for marrying the boss or indeed anyone, how could she ever get over the loss of PK, the one man who knew her inside out, adored her, and for whom she'd have walked across fire? Their intense young love had swept them up after the war only to hurl them into deep misery when PK made the hardest decision of his life: he left London for Poland, feeling duty-bound to return to look after his mother and younger siblings who'd never be allowed to escape. Several years later, when already in Buenos Aires, Kika received a letter from him, telling her he'd married, but that he'd never forget her, and explaining he hadn't asked her to become his wife because he loved her too much to offer her a dismal future in a Communist Poland under Russia's thumb. Kika who'd have gone with PK to the end of the world, took to her bed for three days clutching his letter and staring at the wall.

———

Life at number 3 was certainly not run of the mill. What is eccentric to some is normal to others. My mother wrote in her memoirs:

'One day my darling husband spent most of the morning attaching dried flowers to coat-hangers, to make mobiles. He put on Chopin's Barcarolle for the dogs explaining to them that Chopin often played the piano in the dark. He maintained the dogs completely understood. Maybe they did. Without opening her eyes, Martha sighed contentedly and wagged her tail.'

As the months rolled by after my family's move to Brazil, Józef did do his best at trying to earn a living in São Paulo. He first had a go at being a businessman by trying to sell his home-made mobiles door to door; next he became a salesman of Parker pens. He quickly fell out with the boss after realising he was spending more traipsing around São Paulo than he made in commission. What followed was the long-cherished idea of bookbinding. A considerable amount of my mother's hard-earned cash was spent on course materials but, before giving this enterprise a chance, Józef enlisted as a trainee carpenter. He narrowly missed amputating his own finger and whilst strolling for days with the digit wrapped tightly in a silk foulard, he entertained all and sundry with anecdotes about the carpentry teacher's rotund wife and her daughter's hysterics at the sight of his wound.

Kika and my mother repeatedly tried to get Józef to focus on his multilingual talents but attempts to use his many languages in order to earn a living failed spectacularly too. During a business conference, Józef produced a catastrophically inaccurate simultaneous translation which resulted in the acquaintance who'd recommended him for the job never speaking to him again.

'Józef's mind must have wandered out through the window to the architectural characteristics of the architrave across the road, or some such thing. He was a brilliant translator, so I have no doubt that the dire consequences were as a direct result of his lapse in attention. Being fired in this way amused my husband no end. Bon mots and laughter pinged off the walls which was delightful, but I knew that the funnier he became the worse his pain, and that it was only a matter of time before he fled away from those who loved him. Maybe we made him feel inadequate at basic survival.'

One evening, in the tiny garden at number 3, my father grabbed my mother by the waist and yanked her into a rousing tango.

'We moved through the precise steps, spines straight and heads tilted, snapping left and right, giving our own overblown interpretation to the synchronised moves, reducing ourselves and Kika to convulsive laughter. When the gramophone screeched to the end of the track there was a sudden silence, bar the sound of Kika's enthusiastic clapping. Józef led me along the few footsteps to the end of the lawn, my hand in his. We sat on the grass, backs against a thick tree stump. We didn't speak. With my head on his shoulder I clasped his hand tighter. There was no moon that evening, which was just as well because neither of us could bear to look at the other's eyes.'

By all accounts, my father Józef frequently lost his patience with his mother Róża when she arrived for lunch, as she often did at weekends, all bundles, baskets, parcels and bags. She unleashed mess and confusion wherever she turned. In private, Wanda would try to remind her husband that although his mother could be dementing, she deserved kindness. After all, when in Siberia life had become a question of survival, she had risen to the challenge.

In Brazil, years after the war, she needed protecting, cosseting, thanking, not lashing out in impatience, but the more my mother and Kika endeavoured to cushion Józef from his ever-present angst, the guiltier he felt about his mother. She was fragile, she'd been terribly brave, she'd shed her foibles and fought for her children like a tiger. Prone as Józef was to extremes of emotion, one day he'd kiss his mother's hands and say he wanted to be buried with her in the same coffin; at other times, letting Róża draw him into shouting matches, they'd both lose their cool. His mother would invariably shriek in a high-pitched tone shouting that Wanda was a saint to put up with him. Once, as they argued, and the tapping of Róża's umbrella grew faster and faster against the tiles in mounting hysteria, my father yelled in Spanish, *'Yo la mato esta vieja!!'* ('I'll kill this old bag!'). On that occasion Kika and Wanda ushered them out through separate doors, threatening to throw buckets of cold water over them both.

Józef never did succeed in banishing the memories of how his childhood had vanished overnight on 1 September 1939. At times Wanda wondered whether to hide the photograph he always had in his wallet. It was of him, aged thirteen sitting on his father's knee in the summer of 1938. One year later their world had changed forever.

My father Józef Mycielski on his father's knee summer 1938, one year before the war

Wanda knew that notwithstanding my parents' shared sense of humour and interests, what had happened in her husband's life since 1939, would forever manifest itself in the form of a seeping wound, poisoning everything between them. In 1952, when I was two, one particular morning brought home to her louder than ever, that my father was increasingly resentful of my existence, and exasperated to feel that 'the poultice for his soul' as he described my mother, was slipping through his fingers.

One day my father barked at her that she was giving me too much attention. As he tried to shut me out of the room, the door slammed. I screamed, my mother wrested the door from him, scooped me up and fled to the garden in tears. She knew he hadn't intended to trap my finger. Józef was never physically violent and he was immediately overcome by regret, shame, guilt and fear. My mother writes:

'Later, when Lala was asleep, the three of us, Józef, myself and Kika, hugged tight in silence, six arms entwined. Something had broken forever that evening and all three of us knew it.'

In that same year, 1952, a year or so before my father left, my two grannies, my parents and Kika were invited to a relation's wedding in a fashionable area of São Paulo. I was left behind with an innocuous former nun who adored babies and who was only too thrilled to spend a few hours at number 3. Wanda was of the opinion the ex-nun was in love with Kika. She always stood a little too close and there was something in the way she blushed when Kika entered the room. My mother suggested to Kika that they really should inform the ex-nun that neither of them was that way inclined. Rather unkindly, my father volunteered that even if Kika reciprocated her urges, the poor woman was SO boring that were she to drown, somebody else's

life would flash before her eyes. Wanda, Kika and Grandma Grażyna roared with laughter whilst Róża looked vacantly on. As extraordinary as it may seem, either she really didn't know homosexuality existed, or she refused to acknowledge it.

Just as they were setting off to the wedding, Józef snapped a photograph of his wife who was wearing a black dress with a fuchsia sash, the silk vertically following her figure and fanning out from the waist down. It was often said that my mother was amongst some of the most elegant ladies at social gatherings. Indeed, she could wear hand-me-downs with great aplomb, adding a strip of fabric to hide a moth hole or a silk flower to conceal a tear that was beyond darning.

My parents and Kika were often described as the life and soul of the party. People would gravitate towards them even if later, amongst themselves, they commented on the excessive thinness of the Mycielskis or the eccentric set-up of their household.

My mother knew that as the months passed, she was becoming increasingly

Wanda Mycielska 1952, São Paulo, Brazil

adept at living on two levels, the joyful and the heart rending. The difference between her and Józef was that the intensity of both emotional states coexisted in her without edging her towards an abyss, whereas it gnawed at his soul.

Wanda could and did function well, rapidly establishing herself as the best-known teacher of English in São Paulo, the one that rich Brazilians tried to bribe if only she'd let them jump the queue in her waiting list. I guess the more my father genuinely rejoiced for her, the more he loathed himself for his inadequacies.

Józef's search for work took him all over São Paulo but soon his fascination with the contrasts of the city overtook the original purpose of his outings. He went out every day, but it was to marvel at this vast metropolis and its gradations from charming simplicity to high sophistication, from squalor to grandeur, from the higgledy-piggledy favelas that had sprung after the housing crisis of the 40s, to the fabulous modernist architecture popping up all over the city. He couldn't wait for Oscar Niemeyer's plans for São Paulo to translate into buildings, entranced as he was by Niemeyer's work, particularly the Church in Pampulha. He often went to Ibirapuera Park, São Paulo's green lung, wandering in that Burle Marx oasis, thrilling at the thought that soon Marx and Niemeyer would together create something spectacular and life enhancing.

Before long he stopped pretending he was looking for employment. He'd come back home every evening, elated. He relished telling his wife and sister how he rode on the red and yellow buses and trams, how he walked the cobbled streets where horse-drawn carts sold bread or fruit and joined in conversations about football on street corners. He enthusiastically recommended 'Café Bola-Bola' to my mother and Kika as the best place to buy sandwiches and *cachaça* for the beggars, and debate various football topics, not least whether Brazil might once more host the World Cup as it had in 1950.

Once he convinced my mother to join him on one of his urban expeditions. She was exhausted through lack of sleep, but she didn't have it in her to say no. It would have felt like snatching an ice cream from a four year old. My parents put me in a pram and strolled along Avenida Paulista gawping at its magnificent villas with luxury cars parked in the drive. My father thrilled at the sophisticated clubs, elegant restaurants, plush cinemas in the city centre. He breathed in the variety of experiences that played on all his senses. This city did not have the breathtaking beauty of Rio, pressed between mountains and sea, but there was a most exciting buzz of a highly cultured growing metropolis. Had Wanda not been so worn out, she'd have shared more intensely in his enthusiasm. That morning, she drew the line at going into the Museu de Arte, a splendid place, to be sure, but they'd done enough for the day.

'Through the museum window, Józef pointed out the ticket girl who let him sneak in for free every week. She didn't see us, but I saw her. He described to me how she'd first attracted his attention by merely leaning over the counter towards a paper clip.'

It would have been impossible for my father not to notice the play of light and shade at her cleavage. My mother was quite sure that brazen and coy, the dark girl could have been his queen and his slave, if only he'd let her. And yet she was touched that my father wanted to introduce them and show off his baby.

'Lala, asleep in the pram, would soon wake and there was a long walk to get back. Besides I had to leave for my afternoon lessons. I left him at the Museum and set off home.'

This very museum was one of my father's very favourite places in the whole of São Paulo. It had opened its doors in 1947 with its first acquisitions, amongst which were canvases by Picasso and Rembrandt. It had become a meeting point for students and intellectuals and thanks to the girl with the not so hidden charms, Józef visited exhibitions by foreign and national artists for free and dreamt of joining workshops and courses on modern art. He was hugely excited by the São Paulo Art Biennial which had been founded in 1951 and was the second oldest art biennial in the world, modelled on the very first one in Venice, in existence since 1895.

My mother and Kika knew that my father's walks through São Paulo were a mixture of this fascination with the country and his own panic about finances. Just like them, he was indeed beguiled and intrigued with the characteristics of the Brazilian people: where could you find such charm, such a desire and hope for progress and the future, even in the face of massive obstacles; such acceptance of fate, such faith in God, such humour? How could they have this peaceful nature, despite the huge difference between rich and poor? How had Brazil managed to develop from a monarchy to a republic without war? Józef enthused incessantly. After all the constitutional monarchy of the Empire of Brazil ended the reign of Emperor Pedro II in 1889 in *a military coup without the use of violence*! Were such peacefulness and courage this people's enduring trait? Yet charmed as he was, my father knew his days in Brazil were numbered. The message from his inner hourglass was unambiguous: he had to leave.

In 1953, as I toddled around his feet or pushed myself between him and my mother, he made a decision with regards to work, a sensible one for the first time since arriving in South America: he revisited the idea of using his languages, bought several dictionaries in a second-hand book shop, but this time he registered with a translation agency and focused on written rather than simultaneous translations. He knuckled down, and in a few months had enough money to buy a one-way ticket to Costa Rica.

The day my father left, Wanda watched a friend's rusty little van disappear around the corner laden with my father, his books and his existential angst. She ran in tears to her priest, seeing herself as a failure for not managing to stop him, but the wise Dominican, who knew my parents well, didn't hesitate: 'Fall to your knees woman and thank the Lord!'

The only male resident at number 3 after that, was a canary called Pedro who, within one week in our household of women, produced a green poo and died.

CHAPTER THIRTEEN

BLOODY DEATHS, REPTILES AND A RITE OF PASSAGE

THE IMAGE OF brain matter on the ceiling is not something you forget in a hurry. Not that I saw it myself, but when I was four and a half there was a conversation about it between my mother and our neighbour's cleaner, Mercedes. I can't tell you with any certainty whether I actually remember snippets of that exchange myself or whether what I recall is my mother telling me every detail about it years later. Maybe both. I certainly remember Mercedes. She worked nextdoor to us for over a decade.

Mercedes thrived on always being the first to deliver sensational information. She'd tilt her neck, simultaneously drawing her chin towards her collarbone and looking sideways at the effect of her words. I can well imagine that on the 24 August 1954 her morbid delight lay not only in announcing that the President had shot himself that morning, but in furnishing some juicy details. My mother could do a very good impersonation of her inching closer, whispering: 'They haven't cleaned the coving yet.'

Mercedes did have a cousin who was one of the cleaners in the presidential Palace of Catete, so it wasn't entirely implausible that said cousin had telephoned her before the news reached the radio, but my mother didn't have the heart to tell her that President Getúlio Vargas had shot himself in the heart so there couldn't have been any brain matter on his ceiling!

No doubt had my father still been in the country he'd have written a eulogy to the dead President. Wanda wondered which slant Józef would have chosen: Vargas the revolutionary? The dictator? The nationalist beacon? The expansionist? The father of the poor? Certainly, Vargas the man of contradictions. Józef might also have penned some little verse about Mercedes the fantasist, Mercedes the one with no sense of proportion: a month previously, to the day, an event had quickened her pulse just as much as the President's bloody death, namely the outrageous injustice when Miss Brazil, Martha Rocha, came *second* in the Miss Universe contest. What was the world coming to?!

With my father's departure, a new *modus vivendi* emerged at number 3 and the dynamics of my family life changed. Where at first there had been five of us, there were now three: my mother Wanda, her mother (grandma Grażyna) and me.

Having blossomed professionally as *the* teacher of English to the rich, Wanda was soon turning people away, incredulous at her two-year waiting list. She took four groups a day of five people each and her fees escalated dramatically, not by her own initiative, but at the suggestion of her students. Twenty people daily, each paying the hourly rate normally charged for one-to-one tuition, was unheard of. The groups met in private houses and the midday lesson included a sumptuous lunch. Her pupils, the *crème de la crème* of São Paulo society, embraced her into their circle, many becoming close friends. My mother was astounded at her reversal of fortune and relieved that she could single-handedly support our household more than adequately.

The pharmaceutical company Kika worked for had moved to Campinas, a city an hour away from São Paulo and, although not particularly enjoying her job, she quickly made friends with colleagues and neighbours in that town. The fact that she no longer had daily emotional demands placed upon her by her brother and mother, gave her regular stretches of respite. She made the coach journey to São Paulo every other weekend, arriving late on Friday when I was already asleep.

For as long as I can remember, the first thing I did on those Saturday mornings was to run into the bathroom where on a freestanding cabinet, next to the hairbrushes, Kika always left a little penny ring for me. I must have been very small because the shelf was at the level of my nose. I wondered every time what colour the stone would be that week. I ended up having so many little rings that I often wore them on every finger and threaded onto a ribbon like a necklace. I adored my aunt Kika as much as I adored my mother.

Grandma Róża continued to come on Saturdays and Sundays, fretting and fussing, bringing offerings infused with love and symbolism. Cheap replicas of riches lost (more penny rings, glass necklaces, gawdy bangles) nestled at the bottom of her bags, in between little parcels of sticky cakes, crumbling biscuits, slices of polenta from the Italian market stall and unripe bananas. Everything was individually wrapped in tissue paper with an elastic band around it. The profound emotional importance of these offerings was there for all to see, in the excitement of her hands and the conspiratorial gleam in her eyes, limpid blue and vulnerable. Food. Glorious food. 'Here, look what I've got for you Lala darling. This one's got coconut all over it. Let's sit in the hammock. Sh... sh... don't let on....'

Grandma Grażyna's approach to nourishment was very different indeed and to this day I cannot understand it. She resented every penny spent on food, so much so that she bought the cheapest produce, the worst possible cheese, the most boring biscuits because, by being unappealing they'd last longer. The fridge was virtually bare and the only things always present were bread, jam and a bowl of jelly, varying in colour every few days. My mouth salivates even now as I think of the wonderful smells of cooking wafting in through my bedroom window from the neighbours next door. I remember hoping madly that they'd invite me for supper which they started doing every so often, after their two little daughters came for lunch one day and went back home hungry. Decades later when as adults, these sisters came to visit me in England, they told me their parents worried incessantly about my nutrition seeing the alacrity with which I set about their food. Kind people. I remember the sound of my spoon scraping against the blue plastic plate and the little flap of peeling membrane at the bottom. I went at it with my spoon to get every last drop of sauce.

I have countless memories of yearning for proper food throughout my childhood. When our maid Dona Laura made me a few little rice fritters she was told by Grandma Grażyna that she shouldn't waste time cooking when there was cleaning to be done. Seeing that our house was very small, and Dona Laura was there every day from 9 to 5, this made no sense. I recall also, a big basket of fruit brought by a friend from his farm: figs, mangoes, avocados, a pineapple, bananas of several varieties, carambolas, jabuticabas. I was allowed just one fig and felt guilty forever when behind Grandama Grażyna's back I stole a second one. I remember my heart beating hard for fear of being caught even though my grandmother never punished me, never smacked me. She never even raised her voice, but I feared her disapproval, which I believed she'd be quite right to express, were she to catch me doing what I knew was wrong. Stealing was wrong, WRONG. I ate that fig so quickly I didn't even enjoy it.

It was perfectly normal in our household that lunch for Grażyna and me could consist of a boiled cauliflower in the middle of the table, with, joy of joys, fried breadcrumbs on the top! I can't say I was hungry as such because I stuffed myself with bread and milk. But I was sickly and anaemic, being dragged from doctor to doctor, having endless blood tests. If only I'd been properly fed, I'm sure all those doctors would have been unnecessary and Grandma Grażyna needn't have worried about my health as she did. As it was, every morning she marched towards me with a raw egg yolk on a spoon. A few drops of lemon juice on it were meant to make it less revolting. She also sometimes grated apples, as one does for babies.

If I woke in the middle of the night, she spoiled me by inviting me to her bed, bringing me cream crackers with butter, tea with lemon and honey, and reading gloriously illustrated Polish books for children until I fell asleep again at some ungodly hour. That bit was heaven as was her smell, cinnamon and sunshine, and the silky feel of her lacy nightdress on my cheek. I felt cherished, but there is no doubt that love and neglect coexisted in my childhood. My mother had lavish lunches every day with her students, my grandmother Grażyna ate well at her frequent bridge evenings at the club, whilst I longed for the weekend, when Mama was home and cooked vast amounts of rice, beans, sausages and eggs for the many beggars who came every Saturday to number 3. I circled round the stove breathing in the aroma of garlic and spices, ready with my plate.

The street market was two blocks down from our house and poor people who came to scavenge around the stalls soon learnt that there was hot food being dished out at number 3. They sat on the pavement, some eating in silence, others putting the world to rights. They were grateful and polite, not least the one who rang the bell to return his plate and asked with impeccable manners whether next time the yolk could be a teeny bit harder. My mother was enchanted with his request and made sure that, from then on, his egg was always *just so*.

One of 'our' beggars will always remain in my mind. One Saturday my mother engaged him in conversation, and it transpired he'd been a professional chef but several illnesses and family disasters later, he'd ended up on the streets. He couldn't apply for jobs as a tramp in rags. 'Come back in three days,' my mother told him. Since there was no man living at number 3, after swooping down on various friends who had sons or husbands in the young man's size, my mother amassed every garment he might need. He did return and, overcome with emotion, holding a canvas bag with the clothes, he went. A week or so later, clean and smartly dressed, he arrived at our door with a big smile. He'd got a job, and he came bearing a thank you gift: a big ripe pineapple. The joy in our household was palpable. Kika was there that weekend, and the two grannies too. Granny Róża slipped a peanut bar into his pocket.

On those weekends when both Kika and my mother were at home, I was in heaven and wanted them for myself. During the week, Grandma Grażyna was my rock. She no longer worked as *dame de compagnie* for Madame Rattlesnake and looked after me. She read to me incessantly, played board games, took me for walks with Philippa (the mongrel who had replaced Martha and Charles after their joint death from some virus).

My mother often came back from work when I was already asleep. If still awake, I cruelly made her pay for her long working hours. I felt a tinge of guilt but I still punished her: having asked her to lie by my side, I'd pretend to fall asleep and then, when she slid gently off the bed and tiptoed across the bedroom, I'd call her, just as she reached the door, thus wrecking her escape! She'd sometimes let out an exasperated sigh at that point, but she always came back to lie next to me until I fell asleep. My poor mother! I imagine all she longed for was a glass of wine and a catch up with Kika.

Kika's life in Campinas was pleasant and she'd made good friendships, mostly with Brazilian work colleagues, several of whom played the guitar and organised evenings in little bars, where everyone joined in the singing. Everyone except Kika that is, as she was tone deaf and wouldn't inflict her voice on anybody. But she was hugely popular, not least for her great beauty and delightful sense of humour.

A certain story about Kika's life in Campinas is memorable: one of her friends was a Pole, Mr Dowbór, whose face I remember but not his first name.... He lived in the same block of flats as Kika, which he shared with Catarina (his beautiful two-meter-long Caninana snake), his iguana Michael and several little water snakes. He once threw Catarina on an unsuspecting guest's

My aunt Kika, 1952

lap. Others suffered similar shocks when in the middle of dinner one or more of the water snakes would slither out of a vase of flowers onto the table. As for Michael the iguana, nothing would give him more pleasure than to sit with his eyes closed, whilst Mr Dowbór stroked his throat after feeding him an egg.

One evening when Kika arrived home from work, there was a dreadful commotion outside, with a hysterical woman, a fire engine with flashing lights and a little crowd gathering by the block of flats. The emergency was not fire. Kika made her way to the 5th floor where Mr Dowbór lived but he wasn't home and the focus of the drama was in one of the flats all the way down the corridor from his, where a sorry sight awaited her: Catarina in the middle of the room, with a noose around her head, being brutalised by a burly fireman. Whether Catarina recognised my aunt I wouldn't know but Kika certainly recognised her and immediately understood what had happened: Mr Dowbór had left his window open and the resourceful snake had slithered along the outside parapet past several apartments until she found an open window. The poor tenant must have thought she was hallucinating when she saw Catarina calmly making her way into the bedroom. Apparently, when the woman called the fire brigade she told them it was an enormous boa constrictor. No wonder they arrived in record time.

Worried that a few more minutes of the noose might spell Catarina's demise, Kika took matters into her own hands, asked the surprised firefighter to step aside, looped Catarina around her neck and took her to her own apartment. She placed the escapee in the bath to await the return of Mr Dowbór. According to Kika, the fireman with the noose was visibly disgruntled to have been robbed of his hero moment. But Kika smoothed things over and gallons of coffee were had by all, with delicious cheese balls freshly baked by the caretaker's wife. I loved that story and asked Kika to tell it again and again.

I didn't miss my father. A year or so after leaving for Costa Rica he flew in and out of São Paulo in one day, en route to a one-off job some gorgeous female had found for him. We had a photograph taken, he made me laugh and he was gone. No major impact.

I know from Kika and my mother that during the 1950s and 1960s my father darted around the world (USA, Panama, Sweden, Costa Rica, Puerto Rico), ricocheting between jobs and beautiful women who adored him and wanted to take him home forever. He always slipped through their fingers. At times gainfully employed, at times in dire need, he once slept for a week in a bandstand somewhere in Central America.

It never entered my mind to ask why he didn't live with us. The only occasion I remember when his absence caused me momentary distress was when at school, a girl asked me about my father's occupation. I didn't know so I just told her that he lived far away. She was surprised, mentioned the word 'divorce' and I felt embarrassed. I imagine in my Catholic school I may well have been the only one in my class whose parents weren't together. Yet I wasn't aware of needing him. I felt loved by the four women in my family and my life was good. Yes, I could have done with some decent food but there was much else in my world that was exciting, interesting and fun.

For a start, there were always people coming and going, often young from abroad who'd been told by friends of friends about the little house in a mews in São Paulo. They knew that although they wouldn't be fed much, they'd be welcome for a night or two. At times this made for unusual combinations like when three art students from Madrid shared floor space with Frère Henri, a monk who lived with the Touareg in the Sahara and wore sandals made from car tyres. I was transfixed with his explanation of how he'd made them.

Another time two very good-looking young Italians spent the night in sleeping bags on one side of the sitting room whilst on the other, were three nuns from the order Les Petites Soeurs de Jesus, a Catholic community inspired by the writings and life of Charles de Foucauld. One of the young Italians turned out to be the Marchese di San Giuliano who a few years later married Fiamma Ferragamo, queen of shoes, daughter of Salvatore.

I often slinked out of my bed to sit unseen on the top step and listen in on conversations that went on downstairs, late into the night. Even though I didn't understand much of what was said, I'm sure some of it sank in. I remember hearing someone talk about Picasso's drawing of a dancer and longing to see it but I couldn't ask my mother the next day because she'd know I'd been eavesdropping instead of sleeping. She'd know because the only Picasso picture I'd ever seen before was a line drawing of a cockerel on a card and I'd been amused by the sound of the name *Picasso*. Any mention of the drawing of a dancer and I'd be found out.

Occasionally Wanda and Kika took me to the vibrant Japanese quarter in São Paulo. Brazil has (to this day) the biggest Japanese population outside Japan because in 1907 a treaty was signed between the two countries, permitting Japanese migration due to a labour shortage in the coffee plantations. Strolling through the Liberdade district at the weekend was magical for me from an early age. I was fascinated by the paper lanterns, cherry blossom trees and colourful Japanese dishes. Because Grandma Grażyna wasn't there to curtail spending on food, my mother and Kika bought me sushi followed by sweet dango and mochi.

Whatever we were doing, the time spent with my mother was so very special for me because when we were together Wanda was totally present, giving me undivided attention, and showing me her love by just looking at me. When she held my gaze she was mine and I was hers. I felt as if honey filled my chest. But she started going away every few weekends to Catholic gatherings. I remember one day accompanying Kika in the car to drop off a washbag for her at her place of retreat. I still feel sad when I recall wanting desperately to get to her but being frightened by the barking of a big dog on the other side of the door. I felt the beast was keeping her from me. Kika handed the washbag through a hatch and took me to Ibirapuera Park to feed the ducks. There was no soothing honey in my heart that day.

Sometimes Mama spent a few days in the slums of Rio where she stayed with Les Petites Soeurs de Jesus. This order never preaches but lives amongst the poorest in the world, only talking about their faith if asked. I like that. What I don't like is what I heard one night when eavesdropping on Kika and Mama's conversation from my top step. I was seven.

My ears pricked up when my mother and Kika mentioned the terrible death of a dog called Laika. I didn't know then that Laika was the first dog launched into space by the Russians, but I was so upset by what I'd heard about her suffering that I started crying. And then, just as I decided to go back to my bed before they heard me, the conversation turned to something that threw me into a total panic. I stopped crying about the dog, and I froze.

My mother was telling Kika that a certain Catholic convent in São Paulo had suggested that if she could make responsible provision for me with Grandma Grażyna and Kika, she could enter their order. There was much I didn't understand but what I did take in was devastating. All I remember from the moments that followed was getting into my bed and falling into a deep sleep. I have recently read that a German study from Zurich University suggests that sleep during the first twenty-four hours after a trauma has a positive impact on highly emotional distress. I can only assume that is true.

I cannot now recall the exact chronology of events connected to this issue, but I discussed it with my mother years later, in my adulthood. Handing over custody of me to my grandmother and Kika could never have happened anyway because without my mother's healthy income Kika's salary wouldn't have been enough. Much more importantly, of course, my mother would never have done it but the mere fact that a nunnery could make such a suggestion is unbelievable.

My mother did want to be a nun, but she knew she'd have to wait until I had my own adult life. She did go to retreats, and she even travelled to the UK to visit Stanbrook Abbey in Worcestershire on numerous occasions. Granted, I didn't have enough time with her during the school year, but it is also true that this was in part counter-balanced by the long and heavenly holidays we spent together by the sea and in the countryside in Minas Gerais.

Minas is a vast state, larger than France, a land of mountains, valleys, caves, waterfalls and the longest rivers in Brazil. It is the land of coffee and milk, cattle and sugar cane, corn, beans, bananas and a profusion of mineral riches. Emeralds from its mines are strong competitors to those from Colombia and colonial art and architecture abound. Cobbled streets and baroque churches are imbued with history and charm. None of that was as appealing to me as Fazenda Esmeralda, the farm that had all the memorable smells, colours, tastes and sounds of my childhood. It belonged to dear Brazilian friends and we spent the whole of the summer holidays there. By 'we' I mean my mother, a boy called André Müller and me. Like me, André was a Polish child of émigrés and our parents' families had known each other before the war. He was a year younger.

Schools broke up just before Christmas and didn't re-open until March, so we had over two months in our tropical paradise. We'd leave São Paulo just after spending a very Polish Christmas Eve at home, with dried mushroom soup, fish with vegetables and tiny little *pierogi* followed by poppy seed cake. This was the one yearly occasion when Grandmother Grażyna rose to the challenge (not by doing the cooking herself but by enlisting a Polish woman from the church).

The table was adorned with candles and flowers, with a handful of straw under the tablecloth as a symbol of the manger. There was always an extra place set in case a weary traveller came by, and tradition demanded that we didn't sit at the table until the first star appeared in the sky. Everyone was given a piece of white wafer to share with everybody else, piece by piece, hugging each other, one by one. No white Christmas for us, instead of snow a hot summer, but there was something magical about opening all your presents after dark. Then, on to Midnight Mass at the Dominicans where the padre, a brilliant preacher, knew just what to say and when to stop. Christmas Day was low key, a lazy breakfast of left-over poppy seed cake, baguette with butter and cupfuls of hot milk with a dash or two of strong coffee. I remember doing the unforgivable: dunking my buttered baguette in the coffee, Grandma Grażyna stating it was uncivilised, and Mama defending me by saying it was *très français*.

Grandma Róża was like a child, excited with all her gifts, wolfing down plums dipped in chocolate, folding every piece of wrapping paper until it became small enough to be rolled into a little tube and secured with an elastic band. After breakfast on Christmas Day she scuttled up the hill to the Igreja do Calvário, where poor Padre Atanázio paid for his sins by giving her his full attention as she showered him with gifts: socks, a rosary, a mock leather coin purse, Polish fudge, a case for his spectacles. He must have lost count of how many of all these he already had as she gave him the same things every year.

For each of us, the summer holiday represented something different: for Grażyna, a total rest from being a hands-on granny. For grandma Róża more visits to Padre Atanázio's church to 'help' him with the holiday bible clubs for children. For Kika, no change, as work in the pharmaceutical company wasn't affected by school term times. For Wanda, total relaxation and time to read. And for me the wonderful food that awaited me on the farm, the freedom of the countryside and the presence of my mother.

Our journey to Uberaba took twelve hours by coach and my mother excelled at entertaining us on the way with games, stories, drawing competitions and *cafuné*. *Cafuné* is one of those words that don't exist in English maybe because the action itself isn't part of anglo saxon behaviour! It means caressing a loved one's hair, affectionately running one's fingers through it, slowly and (this is crucial) *doing so for a long time*. It is done to one's beloved, one's child, one's pet. The fact that there is a word for it tells you a lot about a people.

Once in Uberaba we always spent one night in Dona Elina's house. The farm we were heading for was her family's, run by her son and daughter-in-law Marcos and Edilia. There are several memorable things I remember about Dona Elina: she always wore black and at the first sound of thunder she paced up and down the veranda praying out loud, frantically fingering her rosary beads. She wouldn't stop until the storm subsided. I can't blame her: her brother had been killed by lightning whilst talking to her on the wind-up telephone and one of her farmhands had met the same fate whilst riding a horse across an open field.

Someone I remember very well was Dona Elina's *criada*, a lovely girl of eighteen or so when we first met her. Her name was Maria and she'd been brought from the interior to Uberaba at the age of ten to work in the house. This was common in Brazil in the 1950s and 1960s: it was really a case of child labour. These girls, the *criadas* weren't paid, or if they were, the sums were paltry. They had a roof over their heads and more food than their poor families could afford, but they worked alongside the older maids in the household. Dona Elina always had a *criada* on the go and was strict with them, demanding total respect. The redeeming feature was that she made sure each of her *criadas* was offered a course which would give them a skill: cook, seamstress, embroiderer etc, so if as adults they wanted to leave her employ they would be able to support themselves. This was by no means the case in other households.

The eighteen-year-old Maria was shy and beautiful. I remember observing her courtship in the porch of Dona Elina's Uberaba house. Her suitor was thin, dark-haired, lugubrious and always came with a large black umbrella. I assume he had a good job because Dona Elina wouldn't have approved of him otherwise. I think there was a big age difference between them, and Maria seemed frightened. A year or so later, when we came back to Uberaba, Maria wasn't there. I shall never forget the reason: the well-mannered serious man had murdered her. All I know is that it had been a *crime passionel*.

Arriving at Fazenda, Esmeralda was pure joy. First, we ran to greet Marcos and Edilia, and then, dumping our belongings in our room, we chased each other to our favourite carambola trees: there were two, one André's one mine. We played in the brook, rode from a very early age on horses with huge saddles, wearing no hats, galloping cross country unsupervised along rows of gigantic bamboos. We had spectacular falls, dusted ourselves off and mounted straight back. Totally unaware of the dangers of our riding style we nevertheless knew not to sit by the bamboos because snakes and spiders, many venomous, lived within them. We wore knee length boots all the time for that reason and buying new ones every year in Uberaba before getting to the farm, was a particular pleasure.

I recall the pride André and I felt when in spite of our age, we were allowed to accompany the cowboys on occasional all-day treks leading a huge herd of cattle to another farm. It was hot, gruelling and exciting. We ate like them, out of *marmitas* (stacked shallow pans filled with different foods) and drank water from brooks.

On some evenings, following days of work that didn't require long distance riding, the cowboys gathered around an open fire, roasting corn on the cob and *manioc*, and making music into the night with guitars and *cavaquinhos*. A *cavaquinho* is a type of ukulele but with steel strings and the music we liked best was the *Desafio*, an improvised musical conversation between two vocalists. On the nights when we joined them, they invariably made the lyrics about us, making André and me feel very honoured, and also thrilled to be mistaken for siblings. They sang about Mrs Vanda and her children: '*Dona Vanda e seus meninos*'. We'd go to bed with the smell of smoke in our hair, full tummies and tunes and lyrics to remember.

My mother spent most of the day in a hammock reading the many books she'd brought in a large canvas army bag. Anything and everything: Polish, French, English and Italian classics, biographies, Philosophy, History, Latin American prose and poetry, children's literature, satire, science. Whenever she could she read them in the original language. There were books for us as well, but we were far too busy during the day, so we read in our beds by candlelight and oil lanterns. Not good for the eyes, but it was magic. If it was extremely hot, or if there was a full moon, we could hear the buzzing and clicking of cicadas outside, mingling with shrieks of nocturnal birds that often spooked us. We'd then abandon reading and huddled under the bedclothes giggling and enjoying the frisson of the mysteries of the dark.

One enduring memory of a daytime sound was the rustle of ripe mangos falling through the leaves of the majestic trees and landing with a thud on the ground. We'd hear it from our hammocks during siestas after lunch. The chattering of flocks of parakeets and macaws often woke us from our slumber, sometimes prompting us to lazily leave our hammocks and collect the fallen fruit in the cool shade of the canopy of the mango trees. Or we stayed in our hammocks, watching in wonder as hummingbirds of different sizes came to feed from the red and yellow flowers that hung above our heads like bunches of grapes. On one occasion we remained motionless for what seemed like a very long time, as indeed did my mother who watched in awe as a tiny hummingbird hovered two or so inches from her red mouth, clearly mistaking it for a flower. She was deeply moved.

We often consumed far too many cashews. Not the kidney shaped cashew nut (or cashew seed that hangs from the fruit) but the fruit itself, used in compotes, preserves and countless puddings, or to make juice that one drinks on its own or as a mixer with the sugar cane spirit *cachaça*.

Cashew balls were one of the many treats I got on my birthday which, being in January, was always spent on the farm. The person who most spoiled me was Ló, whose mother had been a slave. Before the abolition of slavery in Brazil in 1888, the Law of the Free Womb was introduced in 1871 which meant that babies born to slaves were born free. Dearest loveliest Ló was one such baby, a very old lady when I was a child. She had bandy legs, no teeth and she spoiled me rotten on my birthdays by cooking all my favourite things: pulled chicken, rice and beans, round slices of aubergines deep fried in egg and breadcrumbs, golden chunks of roasted manioc, cucumbers with lemon. The very favourite savoury dishes were anything made out of palmito, or heart of palm. One can get it in a tin, which is delicious in salads or in gratins and soufflés with a white sauce and cheese. But the really wonderful taste is that of unprocessed palmito, the actual inside of the tree trunk of a palm, roasted in the oven.

As for sweet food, there is nothing like the little sweetmeats made for every party. Christenings, birthdays, engagements, weddings, indeed any celebration wouldn't take place without the *docinhos* with names like *bem casado* (well married), *beijinho de côco* (little coconut kiss), *olho de sogra* (mother-in-law's eyeball). Fudge, eggs, coconut, peanuts, passion fruit, chocolate, pineapple are some of the ingredients used, with vast quantities of sugar. Ló made endless varieties of coconut puddings and sweets for me, year in year out, plus the inevitable coconut birthday cake. Nothing I loved more than coconut. I shall never forget that loving old woman, the link between the colonial era of slavery and my new world.

Leaving the farm was always a wrench, but we knew we'd be back. And we had other holidays and long weekends to look forward to: those on the beach.

One beach holiday in particular sticks in my mind, for it was a major rite of passage in my life. Mama and I were staying in a tiny little fisherman's cottage right by the sea and I must have been around seven years old. Not only did I still suck my thumb, but I had a small piece of well-worn blanket (called Godela) that I twisted around my fingers. I woke one morning, having made a decision: I informed my mother over breakfast that this was the day when I would become grown up. I would stop sucking my thumb and I would burn my Godela.

My mother suggested that maybe I'd prefer to first stop sucking my thumb and, given time, reconsider my funeral pyre plans. She pointed out the finality of such an action, but I had made up my mind. Mama offered to stand by my side as I carried out the deed, but I told her this was something I had to do alone.

I can almost feel now the hot sand on the soles of my feet as I walked from our little verandah towards the sea in what felt like slow motion. I had Godela in one hand and a box of matches in the other. I stopped just short of the water, my heart like a bird thrashing about in a cage. It took several attempts to light the match and I had to dig out a little hollow in the sand to protect the flame from the sea breeze. I was aware of my hands moving slowly and methodically. I was very frightened of the feeling of bereavement creeping up on me but there was no going back. As the unmistakable smell of burning wool reached my nostrils and Godela was no more than a little pile of charred fibres, both the sense of deep loss and the feeling of triumph blended. The bird in my chest broke free.

Pratigí beach, Brazil

CHAPTER FOURTEEN

LARKS, INVENTIONS AND A MILITARY COUP

FOR SOMEONE WHO wanted to be a nun, my mother was wonderfully uninhibited when answering questions about sex. When a friend from school told me that if you want to make a baby you have to go into a bathroom with a man and sit on his lap for an hour, Wanda put me right with no embarrassment, tailoring the explanation for my age. As I got older and wanted more detail, I'd say to her: 'Mama, come sit on my bed. Let's talk about men!' Without fuss, she'd make herself a cup of coffee. 'OK. What do you want to know?' I'd then ask the most detailed questions which would have made a grown man blush, and without batting an eyelid she answered them all. She always stressed that with love it was beautiful. I couldn't quite see how that could possibly be, but as bizarre as it all sounded, I believed her.

When one day we suddenly came upon a man exposing himself by the greengrocer's, she held on to my hand, walked on without altering her gait and said loudly: *'Oh look, it's just like a penis. Only smaller.'* This must have been an old joke she'd heard somewhere before, and an enduring one because I heard it again decades later. I can't quite recall what she told me afterwards but what I do remember was the man's face. He looked as if he were about to cry and I felt sorry for him.

The Profumo affair was another example of my mother's calm approach to wayward matters of the flesh. She didn't actually give me articles about it but when I found a magazine with riveting pages of text and photographs, instead of forbidding me to read it, like some of my friends' mothers, she talked about it. I don't remember how she negotiated the topic, but she did so truthfully and in a manner suitable for an eleven year old. I was more interested in the fact that the story involved a Russian spy; and when Mercedes (who'd so excelled in her accounts of President Vargas's suicide) cornered me to furnish lurid details, my blasé response was that I knew everything from my mother anyway.

Most of my chats with Mama though, were very different: they often concerned ethical and spiritual questions (Are stealing and/or lying *always* wrong? Why does God let people suffer? Why are there poor people in the world? Why do hungry people come to our house every Saturday?)

Mama answered as best she could, noting that there isn't always an answer for every question, but that what matters is to continue searching. As for hunger and poverty, she hoped naively that in the bigger picture, by some godly interference, Brazil would blossom to the benefit of all. Politics and Economics were not her forte, but she envisaged that in this New World where fate had placed her after the war, her child could have a decent future and social justice would eventually prevail.

There were hopeful signs in the mid-1950s: Brazil was experiencing unparalleled economic growth and the rates during President Kubitschek's tenure were spectacular, three times those of the rest of Latin America. Political stability attracted much foreign and domestic investment both achieving new highs. It was an exciting time, its best symbol perhaps being Kubitschek's most audacious idea of moving the capital from Rio de Janeiro to the interior. With the aim of opening up the vast rural interior to modernisation, the Congress approved the plan in 1956 and a year later work began. Brasília was built in three years at an astonishing pace, twenty-four hours a day, seven days a week, to the magnificent designs of architect, Oscar Niemeyer. Wanda, like everybody else, hoped that the untapped hinterland of Brazil would be linked to the rest of the nation and indeed it was. Approximately eleven thousand miles of new roads were built, the automotive industry mushroomed to add to the already hugely impressive industrial production of steel, the electrical and communication industries etc. There was, however, a heavy price tag to bear. To meet some of the costs Brazil started printing more and more money. Inflation soared, the cost of living tripled in five years and attempts by the IMF to encourage more orthodox financial methods failed.

Blissfully unaware of the complexities of running a country, I was growing up in a place which in spite of its problems was blossoming in national pride: every Brazilian world cup victory was an occasion for a national holiday, and we all danced in the streets. Pelé was a hero. To a lesser extent so was Maria Esther Bueno who won Wimbledon in 1960. More often than not Miss World and Miss Universe competitions had Miss Brazil finalists and when Miss Brazil won the title of Miss Universe in 1963 and 1968, the whole country erupted in celebrations that went on for days.

Culturally, Brazilian music, both classical and popular, reached well beyond South America and became internationally celebrated and acclaimed. The classical composer Villa-Lobos conducted major international orchestras in America and Europe as they played his works. Hugely popular were his Bachianas Brasileiras, in which he combined Brazilian folk music with Bach.

As for popular music, the birth of Bossa Nova quickly permeated the whole country and palpably became part of Brazilian identity. It linked us all. The music of Edú Lobo, Antônio Carlos Jobim, João Gilberto, Sérgio Mendes, Chico Buarque sounded from radios, little music bars and restaurants, and countless youngsters, myself included, had guitar lessons at home.

There was also a high-quality output in the Brazilian Film industry, and brilliant directors like Carlos Diegues, Nelson Pereira dos Santos, Glauber Rocha, focused on rural poverty and underdevelopment, the urban favelas and the Alagados in the North. Brazilian literature too became internationally recognised and works by both pre- and post-war novelists were translated into many languages.

My own reading in the 1950s, consisted of Polish classics for children, and the books of Monteiro Lobato, the best children's writer in Brazil. I particularly loved his books because the main protagonists, a boy, a girl and a rag doll called Emilia, had met Peter Pan and Tinkerbell in Kensington Gardens and had been given a magic powder that could transport them in time. I was right there with them, being whisked off to fascinating places and centuries. In 438 BC we had supper with Pericles and Aspasia, watched the sculptor Phidias overseeing the final touches on the Parthenon, talked at length with the architects Ictinus and Callicrates about their Doric columns. Disguised as shrubs, we sneaked up Mount Olympus to find Zeus really worried about his demi-god son Hercules and the hatred Juno, Zeus's wife, harboured towards him. Not only that but we had the privilege of watching Hercules attack the Hydra with as much fear as he'd have shown had the Hydra been a lamb.

I shared all this excitement with my very best friend namely my rag elephant Zuzuquinho. We were inseparable when I was little. Maybe because I was an only child, I told him everything, and he took on a very distinctive personality. I truly believed that we communicated at a deep level. I remember telling him one day that truth wasn't always very nice but that I always wanted to know it because if we're patient and do our best, all truths, the nice ones and the not so nice ones will end up making up one huge wonderful truth and then we will know everything, understand everything and…. and… Other children thought I talked nonsense when I said things like that but Zuzuquinho understood everything. As indeed did my mother. So much so that she wrote a book for me, or rather she helped my rag elephant Zuzuquinho write it. And lo and behold, she won the highest literary prize in Brazil for it (Prêmio Jabutí). The famous literary critic Leonardo Arroyo wrote that, '*Wanda Mycielska's book is being singled out by the critics as one of the most expressive to appear in the realm of children's literature for considerable time.*' Whereas Professor Lourenço Filho one of Brazil's most important educators of the time stated, '*Her narrative shares many qualities with good English literature for children and in other ways reminds us of St Exupery's Little Prince, but with greater ease.*' Even Guilherme de Almeida one of the most prominent critics and poets of the time wrote a long letter to Zuzuquinho which was published in the *Estado de São Paulo*, the fourth largest newspaper in Brazil. Mama, Zuzuquinho and I were in countless newspapers, even on TV. Wanda observed the ensuing accolades and media attention with detachment and could barely conceal her incredulous amusement when sharing the stage at the Municipal Theatre in São Paulo with the luminaries in the other categories also collecting their prizes.

I was quite blasé about the book's success and didn't need to reread it because there was nothing new in it for me. After all it was about our life. But reading was indeed my passion, worth interrupting only for more chats about the past with Grandma Róża, who was far more forthcoming than Grandma Grażyna. Whenever I sat in the hammock with Róża and urged her to tell me more about her childhood in Lentvaris, she forgot her foibles and could talk for hours. I heard the same stories again and again and although they inevitably ended up being about loss, they also paradoxically gave me some curious sense of security: these stories *were there*, in her mind and now in mine and nobody could take them away.

Róża talked about her brother Stetysz more than about the youngest, Eugeniusz, who was nearer to her age; maybe because she was hugely proud of Stetysz's inventions and patents. Between 1954 and 1959 he had at least eight patents granted internationally and although this was completely above my head and of no interest to a child under ten, I listened politely as she read me extracts from his letters. I came to appreciate them much later.

Stetysz could have made a fortune had he had some basic business sense. He didn't: instead of negotiating royalties he sold his designs for one-off payments.

I was far more interested (but only momentarily) to hear from Grandma Róża when I was ten, that Stetysz had just been given an important role in the Catholic religious Sovereign Military Order of the Knights of Malta. I latched onto the word *Knight* and imagined my great-uncle walking about in chainmail and a vizor. I was hugely disappointed when told this was not so and glazed over when Grandma Róża elaborated.

As an only child and an increasingly avid reader, I soon moved on from time travel with Peter Pan's friends, to weeping with Marie Antoinette in the Conciergerie, or Emma Hamilton after Nelson's death. Not content with the existing letters from Napoleon to Josephine I wrote imaginary ones to add to the collection. And I compared notes on the romanticised historical novels my mother bought me, with our maid Toninha who replaced Dona Laura when the latter retired (on full pay from my mother).

Toninha had been a prostitute before she came to us. Thrown out by a 'good Catholic' mother for getting pregnant at fourteen she'd had little choice. I can't remember where my mother found her, only that she was in her forties when she turned up, with a big smile, and long black hair. Two memorable things about her that stick in my mind, are the ostentatious opulence of her buttocks and the insatiable curiosity of her brain. She borrowed all my books and spent more time discussing them with me than cleaning. Nobody in our household minded and we all adored her.

Toninha was the one to coax me to stick to Saturday Polish School. Although I liked most of the other Polish youngsters who, like me, were children of émigrés, I wasn't hugely amused at joining in Polish folk dancing. We all spoke Polish amongst ourselves anyway, rather than Portuguese, and I didn't feel I needed the prancing about in national costume to confirm my Polishness. But according to Toninha, any place that could bring me more knowledge was not to be sniffed at. Unbeknownst to Grandama Grażyna, she made me coconut balls for the afternoon break, which I guiltily stuffed under my embroidered ethnic Polish waistcoat before setting off and promising Toninha to learn something new that day.

Toninha also came to my rescue in some unexpected ways. One day I decided my bedroom was a little dull and painted large brightly-coloured flowers all the way up, along the climbing plant growing up the wall, nearly to the ceiling. Grandma Grażyna was horrified. 'It looks like a brothel,' she barked. Toninha very politely intervened: 'It doesn't Dona Grażyna. I never saw art like that in any of the brothels I worked in.' She took the wind right out of my grandmother's sails and all three of us laughed. Mama said that evening that my painting was very nice and then tackled my request for a definition of a brothel.

I suppose, compared to my friends at school, I was a fount of information when it came to matters that they were embarrassed to ask their parents about. But I'm glad to say that wasn't the only reason we all got on so well in my convent school. My best friend Sylvia and I worked hard from an early age and had good grades, but we were also naughty and therefore popular. We slid down banisters and dared each other to burst through the swing doors into the cloister. The excitement lay in not knowing whether or not there'd be a nun on the other side as we did so. The nuns, sweet and ineffectual, were often exasperated by us, but couldn't get really cross because we were polite and hard working. And we didn't start smoking behind the chapel until much later!

1961 was the year I fell in love. I was eleven and he was fourteen. It was true, deep and real. We met in secret on an empty plot of land near my house where we sat and held hands, talking about life, love, death, God and the universe. Or not talking at all in an easy unembarrassed silence which enveloped us in the enormity of what had happened to us. Our mothers knew about it but pretended not to and when Mama parked her car in front of his house where she held one of her English classes, she'd leave the door unlocked so he could sneak in and get my letter from a box placed on the back shelf of the boot, and leave his for me. With one of them he left his photo, barely bigger than a postage stamp. A dark-haired serious boy; my boy.

His father was against it and this speaks volumes of Brazilian society as it was then. It wasn't our age that worried him, since often alliances were made amongst the offspring of super rich landowning families when the *namorados* were in their very early teens. Usually the boy would be a year or two older, sometimes not, sometimes much older. The problem for the *pater familias* in question was that he worried this romance would eventually lead to marriage and I was far from his ideal as a wife for his eldest son. The only child of a divorced mother, with no vast estate, this had to be nipped in the bud. Many tears were shed. Not only then but a few years later when I was about sixteen, hope again flickered only to be snuffed out once more.

~

Playing truant in my teens with my best friend Sylvia was a harmless and amusing exercise. The aim was perfectly simple: to spend the day swimming in the country club, or window shopping in the then fashionable Rua Augusta, and eating vast amounts of *mumude* (vanilla icecream, with hot chocolate sauce and peanuts pulverised with sugar). Nothing more sinister than that. Yet we were seen by our contemporaries as wonderfully brave and we were the only two girls in our school who dared engage in such larks.

The problem was escaping. We had school ID cards which were stamped every morning on arrival and at five when leaving. There was absolutely no way of leaving through a door so the two of us devised a wonderful plan. At least once a week, in the mid-morning break we'd take our sandwiches to the bottom of the garden, where scaling the 6 ft wall was quite a feat as it involved clambering over Our Lady's grotto, on to an overhanging branch, swinging on to the top of the wall and lowering ourselves on to the pavement on the other side. Coming back was far harder with a leg-up on to the wall from one and much pulling up from the other. On a memorable occasion, when Sylvia was already on Avenida 9 de Julho, and I was still astride the wall, a sweet senile little nun appeared from behind the holy grotto and said: 'My child, didn't you know you need permission to leave school premises?' 'Yes of course sister, but I'm not leaving, I'm coming in.' My answer was clearly the perfect one. I hopped back in and helped the old thing hobble down the path back to the school buildings. Sylvia had to wait a fair amount of time before I could sneak back and help her return over the wall.

Over and above such antics, 'The Testicles' were the most entertaining aspect of our school days and, in our adolescent years, they featured very strongly in our daily life. Not only that but they were numbered. This wasn't a case of some unsavoury and precocious sexuality but simply an example of teenage creativity in devising alternatives to academic work. At first, we tried the usual forms of distraction: puzzles, crosswords, wicked cartoons of teachers and so on. Then, one day, we hit upon the best of all: questionnaires. *And what*, you may ask at this point, *what pray* do schoolgirls' questionnaires have in common with an intimate masculine body part? The answer is simple: not a lot. Except perhaps that they are equally private, to be shared only with a chosen friend. But when it came to our questionnaires, there was a little more to it than that. For us they were tests. And as the early ones produced were rather short, we first called them mini-tests, then testlets and finally..... yes.

I shudder to think just how many hours were spent devising, answering and marking testicles. But the risks we took were nothing when compared with the fun we had. One section was always in a multiple-choice format: schoolgirl thinking at its silliest most of the time.

Q *If you HAD to make a choice, which of the following would you choose?*
  a) chewing a live cockroach
  b) eating your dog's poo
  c) spending a night with Mr Silva (Latin master. The most repulsive man I think I have ever seen)
Or

Q *You must choose one. There is no escape:*
  a) sitting in a dark cellar for five hours surrounded by snakes
  b) licking Jeremy's acne
  c) being raped by Mr Silva (Poor man. Little did he know about just how often he featured in our testicles)
Or

Q *Who would you prefer to get intimate with:*
  a) a man with a beautiful nose but a hideous **** covered in warts?
  b) a man with a beautiful **** but a *hideous nose covered in warts?*

Not all our questions explored the most repulsive dimensions of sex.

Q *When you make love for the first time would you like it to be:*
  a) on a bear skin in front of an open fire?
  b) on a sunny deserted beach?
  c) in a luxurious bed at an expensive hotel?

Or (abandoning the multiple-choice style)

Q *Describe how you imagine your first honeymoon night in no less than three hundred words.*

This aspect of our testicles reflected yearning fantasies and little more. Sylvia and I were good gals at a convent school, and these were the 1960s in Brazil where macho ideals still reigned supreme. We went out with boys, but after moonlit necking sessions in cars they would depart to join a call girl or two in their bachelor pads, whereas we, flushed and starry eyed, climbed into our virginal beds alone and dreamed.

There were still other parts of the testicles that would make even the mildest feminist despair. These usually required 'yes' or 'no' answers.

Q *Do you think a woman should go to university? Do you think living with a man out of wedlock would sully your name? If your boyfriend forbade you to wear a mini-skirt would you obey him?*

Our testicles also contained utterly meaningless items, examples of nonsense for its own sake. Like this one: *Write down the first sentence that comes into your mind.*

The response here was one of Sylvia's: 'Please help me to put my Clark Gable in the fox.' For some reason I have never forgotten it.

Others could, at a pinch, be classed as questions of an ethical nature:

Q *You are on a desert island with your husband and your baby and food supplies have run out. Which of the two options below would you choose?*
    a) chop your husband into little bits and feed him to your baby.
    b) chop your baby into little bits and feed him to your husband.

My position in this gruesome dilemma was expedient if not very maternal. When challenged, I explained: 'I could make another baby with my husband, whereas the reverse would be impossible.'

I'm glad to say that Sylvia and I were prone to the occasionally serious thought:

Q *Are you in favour of abortion? Are you scared of God? Do you support Lyndon Johnson? Do you sympathise with the Vietcong? Could you adopt a handicapped child?*

The answers to these, showed us as a bit more than just two giggling dumb blondes in their teens, even if these questions were grossly outnumbered by the likes of Jeremy's acne, Mr Silva's anatomy, dog poo and honeymoons. Nevertheless, I'm embarrassed to say that what was going on politically in Brazil didn't figure in our testicles, nor in my conversations with Sylvia. The testicles may be a little vignette of Brazilian macho society at the time, but not much more than that, which surprises me. After all, in the mid to late 1960s, when the population was estimated at 90 million, 60 per cent of those living in the South, including the industrial triangle of Rio de Janeiro-São Paulo- Belo Horizonte, lived on 20 per cent of the land and earned 80 per cent of the national income. Yet the appalling poverty in the rest of Brazil was indescribable. Actually, these were estimates that masked a much worse reality: in São Paulo itself less than half of the population was registered so it was impossible to accurately calculate the rate of unemployment.

The economist Ladislas Dowbór (son of Kika's friend, the Mr Dowbór of Catarina the snake and the iguana Michael) when interviewed by the distinguished journalist Sanche de Gramont, pointed out that there were essentially two Brazils: an industrial one inside an underdeveloped one. In the modern sector there were gleaming factories where reasonable salaries were paid to fewer workers, yet there was still a huge migration from the countryside to the cities, searching for an Eldorado, creating an ever-growing slum population.

For me as a teenager from a household where conversations centred mainly on the arts and where politics were seldom mentioned, I felt good when we helped poor people, as indeed we did, but I didn't seek out any possible connections between the vast latifundia and the appalling poverty. I spent some of the best holidays one could dream of on enormous and luxurious farms of some of our friends, not worrying about anything.

One such farm belonged to the same family who owned the one already described by me in an earlier chapter, but it had a completely different character. The simple one, belonging to Dona Elina's son Marcos, provided a magical tropical paradise where nature and a simple country life with no electricity enticed and captivated. The one belonging to Dona Elina's daughter and son-in-law on the other hand was pure luxury. It was in the State of São Paulo near the town of Araçatuba. Dona Elina's daughter, Esmeralda, was my mother's dearest friend (who had offered to be my guardian had my mother died whilst I was still a child.) She was a most beautiful woman, often mistaken for her six children's sister. Brave is the parent who christens their baby Esmeralda as there is no guarantee the child will be beautiful. An Esmeralda with the looks of Quasimodo would be most unfortunate. But our Esmeralda more than lived up to her name. I adored her. I even wanted my thumb to curve like hers, longed to have hands like hers, to walk like her.

The arrival at Esmeralda's farm from São Paulo was in one of their private Cessna planes which landed by the swimming pool. The house sprawled through vast rooms furnished in a stylish and comfortable mix of modern furniture with light-coloured colonial pieces not least a wooden altar used as the sideboard in the dining room. The rooms were linked by terraces with hammocks and abundant flowering creepers, offering a harmonious choice of spaces in which to lounge or entertain, or indeed to clinch enormous business deals. I remember once or twice seeing powerful-looking men in discussions with Esmeralda's husband in his study, filled with a most impressive array of trophies and prizes for his world-famous cattle.

Meals were gargantuan, and delicious, served at the table by a young lad who, at weekends and on special occasions wore white livery with large monogrammed gold buttons. Many would wince at such opulence on a farm in the middle of nowhere, yet we all know that appearances can deceive and far from it being a blatant example of ostentation on Esmeralda's part, it was actually a sign of her kindness. The boy, in question, José, was the child of one of her farmhands, an awkward youngster of about fifteen who was being beaten and abused by his family. Esmeralda plucked him from his terrible situation and installed him in the servants' quarters of the main house. She invented jobs for him so that he could earn something and thus develop some feeling of self-worth. He was put in charge of polishing anything polishable: shoes, door-knobs, hinges, window locks, even keys. Once he stopped cowering every time someone approached, Esmeralda asked him to tell her his dream, the highest thing he'd like to achieve in his life. 'A uniform with gold buttons', was his stuttered answer. She gave him his dream, he reached his pinnacle and blossomed.

José and the rest of Esmeralda's employees were lucky. They had good houses, good medical care, good education in the farm school. This was by no means the case throughout the vast latifundia up and down Brazil. Be that as may, it made me happy to see José so settled, and the care

Esmeralda showed those in her employ. I lapped it all up – the scents in the air, the riding and swimming, the exquisite food and the pride with which the cooks showed me how it was made, the happy banter in the kitchens. And even though my home was in the concrete jungle that was São Paulo, my Brazil was the rural paradise of hummingbirds and toucans, macaws and parakeets, an abundance of varieties of fauna and flora, extraordinary fruit, cowboys, horses, alligator hunters, palm trees, spectacular scenery. Although sounding like a kitsch travel brochure it was a land of sea and sun, of football and Bossa Nova, of carnival and girls from Ipanema, of sweet friendly people with humour and faith in God. This aspect of Brazil was indeed real, moving, enthralling and life enhancing.

Juxtaposed with this reality there was another, very different one. On 31 March 1964 the then President João Goulart (who was proposing to introduce agrarian reform and to remove Brazil from the latifundial economy) was deposed by a military coup. Inflation at the time was running at almost 100 per cent. The elites feared Brazil was going to become another Cuba and the large landowners and conservative politicians supported the Generals.

In the years that followed the coup, constitutional rights were suspended, there were widespread and arbitrary arrests, imprisonment with no trials, rape, castration and murder not to mention systematic torture and a book-burning mentality. Long lists of prohibited reading considered 'dangerous' included even the likes of *The Red and the Black* by Stendhal. Our large canvas army bag (which we always took to the farm with our reading material for the holidays) took on a different role. In the dead of night, Mama, Kika and I drove to the bridge over the Tietê River that flows through São Paulo and threw the canvas bag and its contents over the side. I shall always remember that splash. I was fourteen and my heart constricted as I watched what looked like a human body, a murder victim, being disposed of.

When two of my mother's students disappeared without trace and notwithstanding the fact that I was a teenager and far from a militant anti-junta rebel, she decided it was time to send me abroad to improve my English.

CHAPTER FIFTEEN
DARKNESS AND LIGHT

MY MOTHER USED an appealing carrot to convince me that it would be great fun to spend a few months with a large Polish family in Canada and go to a lovely school nextdoor with their children. She'd travel with me to settle me in, The Beatles would be giving a live concert in Montreal in September 1964, and I'd see proper snow for the first time come Christmas.

It turned out to be a disaster: from the moment we arrived, an old flame from London blitz days got wind of my mother's presence in the city and pursued her relentlessly, spoiling what little time I had with her before she returned to Brazil.

When she left, I soon found out that there were great tensions in that family, that the children made no effort at all to make me welcome and the nuns in the school were beastly. I didn't even get to see The Beatles in the flesh but only on a big outdoor screen, having slashed my knee on the ice whilst running to get there. My misery was only made a little less dire by having someone else to concentrate on: a rotund housekeeper in her fifties, who the children's parents had taken in from Poland to look after their five offspring. Some of them were so unkind to her that she regularly wept in my arms as I hugged her and stroked her thinning hair. She called me her angel from heaven and by focusing on her misery my own became lighter, albeit only for brief periods.

I cried myself to sleep every night and sent desperate letters to my mother begging her to take me away; just like she had done when she was left in the unpleasant school in Rabka during her parents' divorce. I even wrote to a friend of my mother's pleading for her to urge her to come for me. And then... a glorious relief! I was informed my father was coming to see me! All would be well, I'd tell him how unhappy I was, and he'd be my saviour! He had been sending me amusing letters on and off during the years and now I was going to finally see him face to face.

I knew within an instant of his arrival that he wouldn't be able to help me in any way. I hadn't clapped eyes on him for ten years and from the moment he walked in, to the moment he left later the same day, he stared at my face and repeatedly asked the same questions: 'Do you love me? Do you love me? Do you ever miss me?' He'd press me to his chest so hard I could barely breathe. I felt hugely sorry for him, but I wished the hands on the clock could move faster and the taxi would come to take him to the airport.

I was plucked from my misery by my mother's kind and loyal half-sister Eva who lived just outside New York. She flew in and took me home with her, but my relief didn't last long as I was thrown into a much worse situation.

My aunt and her husband lived in a one-bedroomed flat in a block where my uncle was a caretaker. He was a highly intelligent man who, if it hadn't been for the war, could have easily had a career in Politics in Poland, but in the USA he was only able to hold a lowly job due to his anti-talent for languages. His English was virtually non-existent and there was no hope whatsoever of it ever improving. My aunt Eva on the other hand had a very satisfying position in a publishing company in New York and was gone all day. Because there was no room for me in their tiny apartment, I slept in a vacant flat at the end of the corridor, where I had a bed, a chair, a lamp and a clothes rail. Little did my aunt know that whilst she went to work, I was being molested by her husband who came into my room every morning to ensure I was up in time for school. I hardly slept, kept the light on, and remained fully dressed in my uniform to minimise what I knew was coming. There was no rape but a nasty experience, repeated almost daily, which poisoned everything. I couldn't tell aunt Eva and I couldn't phone my mother without being overheard. There were no mobiles then of course which would have given me some privacy. Between writing a letter to my mother and her arranging to have me sent back to Brazil, almost a month went by. It was an eternity.

I feel I can mention this event because both my aunt and her husband are dead, and they had no children. I'm not hurting any innocent parties. My aunt never knew, as my mother kept quiet. Eva would have been utterly devastated as she adored her husband, or she simply wouldn't have believed it. Had my mother gone to the police, would there have been a case? I very much doubt it. His word against mine and no proof. It was brushed under the carpet. I just hope I was the only one, and that he didn't do the same or worse to any other child.

Of course, there are degrees of sexual abuse, none of it acceptable, some much worse than others. Nowadays we're more aware of it but maybe then it was much more prevalent than people thought. Even with my very sheltered upbringing this wasn't the only instance. I and all the other girls in our Saturday Polish school well remember how the father of one of the Polish boys would stick his hand up our skirts whenever he had the chance. We were under ten years old when he started. Most of us told our mothers but nothing was done. Again, it went straight under the same carpet.

The father of one of my Brazilian schoolfriends who suggested sharing the school run with my mother, kissed me on the mouth the first (and last) time Wanda left me by his gate. I told her. Same problem: should she have told his pregnant wife and destroyed her? The police wouldn't have been able to do a thing. No proof, my word against his.

I can and will mention one instance where something could and should have been done: there was a priest doing the rounds of the RC Schools in São Paulo addressing young teenage girls in great detail, about sexual activities we should not engage in as good Catholics girls growing up. He used lurid descriptions of activities none of us had even imagined. We did run to our class mistress afterwards and the old nun was appalled. I'd bet my bottom dollar that she took it no further than her gasps of 'Meu Deus, meu Deus! Dios Mío! Dios Mío!' in both Portuguese and Spanish. As for our mothers, none of them including mine tackled the issue. I'd like to think that today they would have joined forces and gone to the Bishop/a lawyer/ the press, but they didn't. I don't know whether one can partly excuse their inaction on the grounds of the times. The carpet and the broom were indeed ubiquitous.

It goes without saying that the above actions are completely inexcusable, yet the fact remains that in spite of them, my life was not destroyed, nor have I been unable to relate healthily and happily to men. I agree with the use of the term *sexual abuse* when referring to what was done to me by my uncle, but I deplore lumping together under the same label (or indeed the label of *sexual harassment*) actions like, for example, putting an arm around someone's waist. Of course, if asked not to, were the person to persist, then harassment would be an appropriate word; but I think the pendulum has swung too far and is killing the joy of harmless flirting.

After my return from the USA, 1965 brought more holidays on the farm and long weekends on the beach in Rio or Guarujá, many with my dearest Polish friend Monika Koszutska. We wore the same clothes and pretended to be sisters, devoured icecreams made from tropical fruit and bought lots of fabulous new sandals. It was also the year my mother and Kika took me to Poland for the first time. For a youngster who'd never been to Europe, let alone Poland, it was the most extraordinary experience. Grandma Róża had mixed feelings about us going and had no desire to join us. The last time she'd been in Poland was when the Germans invaded in 1939 and she, her husband Władzio, plus my father and Kika, had fled East from the German frying pan into the Russian fire. For my Mama and Kika 1965 was the first time in their mother country after the war.

The greyness of Communist Poland was extremely depressing. A drably dressed population in worn out shoes, queued in front of awful government shops with chronic shortages of basic foodstuffs. Plaques all over the city marked sites where countless people had been shot during the German occupation. I was appalled by the grim blocks of flats, many with no lifts, with people living cheek by jowl and several families sharing one kitchen and one bathroom. When my mother threw out a pair of laddered stockings, the schoolfriend of hers we'd gone to visit, fished them out of the wastepaper basket embarrassed but thrilled that she'd be able to darn them for her daughter as a birthday present. We left most of our own clothes behind for them after that. My mother was in tears as we said goodbye. To add to the sadness of seeing what it was like to live in Communist Poland, she'd been told by her old school friend that more than half of their classmates had died in the Warsaw Uprising of 1944.

Our visit to the dilapidated estate near Poznań where my grandma Róża had moved to from Lentvaris after her wedding to Władzio Mycielski (and where my father and Kika had spent their childhood) was both devastating and very moving. The house was no longer there but many trees were and one of them showed the marks made by generations of children's shoes on the forked tree trunk, as they climbed to the top branches. That was the very tree my father had once jumped from in one of his attempts to fly.

An eerie slow-motion feeling enveloped us as we walked. Kika suddenly noticed a little old woman waddling in front of us, in typical peasant clothes: a skirt nearly down to the ground and a big scarf on her head. 'I know this gait,' Kika said and called her surname: 'Sikorska!' The old woman turned around. Before I could fully realise what was happening, Kika and she were weeping in each other's arms. Sikorska then tried to curtsey to all three of us. Kika cupped her elbows and stopped her mid-bob. Soon we were in her tiny cottage with her extended family: Sikorska's children and grandchildren had been brought up knowing all about my family, their dog had been given the same name as my father's last dog, and above their tiny fireplace a portrait of my grandfather dwarfed the room. It had been rescued from the house before it burned down. *'You must take it with you,'* they urged us. We categorically refused. They more than deserved to keep it. *'Come back to Poland!'* they pleaded. *'We'll help you! We'll start again!'* The thought that *they* wanted to help *us* was hugely touching. One of them brought an armful of meadow flowers, wanting us to take them to Brazil for Grandma Róża, and by the end of the afternoon we could barely see, so swollen were our eyes from crying and so close our hearts to bursting.

The visit to the basilica of Holy Hill in Gostyń was no less overwhelming. That was where, all those years before, desperate for help to overcome her mental health issues, Róża had knelt in front of the miraculous picture of Our Lady, between her husband and mother-in-law, both holding her hands, both joining in her prayers. When Mama, Kika and I arrived, we were met by the Abbott with great ceremony as descendants of the founders. We were taken to the vaults where I watched in disbelief as a monk lifted a coffin lid and I found myself staring at a great-great ++ grandmother in a purple dress and *fichu*, shin bone showing, the rest of her leg and her hands like my mother's fine Italian leather handbag. So many ancestors lying there, so much heroism and sorrow. Another great-great ++ grandmother's coffin is there too, to this day, surrounded by those of her husband and three sons. In a letter from her to the future king Frederyk Wilhelm IV (who as a Prussian was her country's enemy but was also her personal friend) she wrote: *'The mother country has been kind to me. I gave her five sons, she gave me back two.'* Three of her sons were awarded the Virtuti Military, the highest Polish military decoration for outstanding combat merit. On a par with the Victoria Cross it is one of the oldest military orders in the world still in use.

I felt as if my heart could simultaneously break and fly. We stood in the sepia light, surrounded by coffins. I could hear Kika's gentle sobbing and suddenly a curious calm enveloped me. I belonged under blue Brazilian skies, my birds were macaws and toucans, mango was my fruit. Yet there, in Poland, in the musty air of a catacomb, I was home.

The coach that took us from Poznań to Warsaw gave Mama and me three or so hours of respite, a lull before the next emotional charge. For Kika it brought an additional maelstrom. Heaven and hell. PK, her PK, the man she hadn't seen since they'd parted in London in 1945, boarded the same coach. He'd heard she was in Poland and had sent her a message. He could only leave his wife for those few hours. He didn't know that the letter he'd sent Kika in the 1950s to Argentina was always in her missal; that agonised letter explaining he hadn't proposed after the war not because he didn't love her but because he'd felt duty bound to return to Poland to take care of his mother and young siblings. He had nothing to offer Kika other than a grim future in a communist Poland. He'd felt he loved her too much to put her through it.

'Don't look at them darling,' my mother said to me on the coach. PK was sitting at an angle on the edge of his seat, holding Kika's hands in his and they were both weeping. I don't think they said much. I just remember his eyes, his well-worn coat and, when we arrived at Warsaw coach station, Kika's face when he turned around one last time, before disappearing in the throng. (Years later when Kika died, I put all his letters in her coffin.)

In Warsaw, we left Kika in the tiny room we had rented. Mama took me to finally meet the man I then thought of as my grandfather, namely Zygmunt Karpiński, Grandma Grażyna's first husband, and officially my mother's father. When I look at my photos with him, I'm filled with sadness as what I see is a brave and kind man whose heart had been broken forever, and who for the sake of others had pretended otherwise. He must have known that my mother wasn't his child and that therefore I wasn't his granddaughter, yet he was gracious and generous to us both, Mama and me, until his death.

Meeting Grandma Róża's older sister Zofia and her husband in Warsaw, after our visit to Zygmunt, was almost unbearably poignant, as if one were buffeted simultaneously from every direction. Kika smiled heroically whilst her eyes spoke volumes. I watched the sweet old couple sitting at the shabby formica table with a large faded print of Lentvaris behind them. My mother pretended to deal with a wayward lash in her eye. Photographs of Zofia's younger days flashed into my mind: Zofia as a shining dancing light; as a nurse during World War I in the Red Cross army hospital in Lentvaris; as a bride marrying her beloved Klemens. They smiled at us and poured tea. Leaping at us from the walls, were photos of their only son Moryś, my father's favourite first cousin, killed in Auschwitz at the age of nineteen.

The next day there was more to come: the final onslaught on our emotions was a visit to the Gestapo Headquarters in Warsaw, which was opened in 1952 and is called The Mausoleum of Struggle and Martyrdom. I was winded when seeing the four group cells and ten individual ones where Polish patriots and resistance fighters were brutally tortured and very often died of their injuries, even teenagers and pregnant women. These cells were left untouched after the war so that as a museum, people could better imagine the full horror. How many prisoners went through the Gestapo headquarters in Warsaw I don't know but human ashes found in the basement after the war weighed 5,578.5 kg (12.298 lbs). And vast numbers were non-Jews. In her book *Holocaust Forgotten – Five Million non-Jewish victims* (2012), Terese Pencak Schwartz states that in the Holocaust, approximately eleven million lives were lost in all, five million or so of which were non-Jewish (three million Christians and Catholics). The scratched messages on the wall were unbearable to see. Names of loved ones, desperate goodbyes, a few words from prayers. The most famous one is the following:

> *It is easy to speak about Poland*
> *It is harder to work for her*
> *Even harder to die for her*
> *And the hardest to suffer for her*

Before leaving the museum with bleak darkness in my heart, I saw a large book on a lectern with scores of signatures. It had been brought on foot from Germany in a pilgrimage by a group of young Germans in expiation of the sins of their parents' generation.

Before returning to Brazil we stopped for a few days in Sweden to rest for a couple of weeks with friends who took us to their lakeside log cabin in Töksfors. It was the form of therapy we needed after the deeply distressing emotional time in Poland: total relaxation, fabulous smorgasbord lunches, sauna and swimming.

'Swimming' is actually not at all an accurate description of how we communed with the lake. My mother refused categorically to go anywhere near the sauna and gazed lazily at the lake from the terrace, wrapped in a vast mohair shawl, with a book opened on her lap. Kika and I embraced the sauna, but the 'swimming' turned out to be no more than a mad dash into the freezing lake and out again. On one occasion, Kika and I chose to do so naked, with shrieks of delight, knowing full well that if our friend's father (a stern Presbyterian pastor) were to see us he would have been appalled. Kika giggled afterwards, explaining she'd kept her pearls on out of respect for him! My mother took a photograph of us, having first hurriedly brought us two coats for the sake of decency. We were so cold in the water that she had seconds before we emerged out of the lake, pastor or no pastor. I was fifteen and Kika thirty-nine, but we squealed like schoolgirls, shutting our minds off to the recent emotional upheavals. Kika was Phoenix, yet again rising from blood red ashes.

In August 1965, the Auschwitz trials ended with six life sentences. I saw the headlines on the newspaper stand near our house in São Paulo, whilst my little pocket radio played *The Girl from Ipanema*, which had recently won the Grammy award as the record of the year. Not for the first time, nor the last, did I wonder how to hold both in my mind simultaneously. The evil darkness of Auschwitz and the sunny joy of Ipanema, both in my head at the same time, conjured a sharp image of incongruity, like watching some gruesome murder being committed under a glorious blue sky.

After our return from Europe, Grandma Róża didn't particularly want to talk to me about the past for a while. Maybe because, over the years, she'd shared with me everything there was to share about Lentvaris; maybe because I was becoming less receptive as I grew older and had less time with her; maybe because the places where Wanda, Kika and I had just returned from, in the West of Poland, were unbearably painful for her to focus on. It was there that she'd had the best and the worst of her married life with her beloved Władzio and where her mental issues had overshadowed their happiness. She still came to see us often, not least every weekend, with her bundles and rustling papers, her holy pictures and half eaten chocolates, frequently asking my opinion on how to best show her affection to Padre Atanazio at the church on top of the hill. Her adoration of the long-suffering priest went on for years, until he was moved to another parish. His successor was very nice, but Grandma Róża's round blue eyes seemed dulled after his departure.

Kika moved back to São Paulo because of her bad health and the first of many major operations. Having her in the same house was wonderful. Not only could we look after her during her recoveries but for me it felt like having two mothers.

We stopped going to the Dominicans for Mass on Sundays because several of the monks were becoming more and more outspoken against the military dictatorship and eventually some were arrested. My Mama, Kika and I spent many Saturday afternoons on Rua Augusta (the street where I played truant with my friend Sylvia). Going to the cinema was a high point: Audrey Hepburn, Cary Grant, Natalie Wood, Claudia Cardinale, followed by coffee and *fios de ovos* (very long strands of sweet deliciousness made from egg yolks strained through a special funnel on to boiling syrup).

In 1966, I was far less interested in world affairs (like for example Indira Gandhi becoming Prime Minister of India, or Harold Wilson winning the general election in the UK) than in the fact that Claude Lelouch's *A Man and A Woman* had won the Palme d'Or at the Cannes Film Festival. And at the same time as lusting after Paul Schofield in *A Man for all Seasons*, as Sir Thomas Moore (what a hero, standing up to Henry VIII and dying for his beliefs!) I was suddenly aware of the attentions of young men.

In Brazil at the time, girls were given huge parties for their fifteenth birthdays, wearing long dresses and Cinderella shoes, in wonderful marquees, no expense spared. A celebration, a coming of age, these were introductions into society and indeed into the marriage market. Several of my friends met their future husbands this way. I remember dancing with boys at such balls, realising just how intoxicating a man's smell could be, not to mention the wonder of moving cheek to cheek to the sound of songs like *The Shadow of your Smile*. One boyfriend followed another, many proprietorial in a Latin macho way, one even not wanting me to wear a mini skirt on outings to the cinema with my mother, because men would ogle my legs. When an article came out in a magazine about daughters of postwar emigrés coming out into society, he was not amused at my photograph in an evening dress.

I don't remember many political discussions with any of my boyfriends, nor comments about the increasing brutality of the Military Junta. Life went on: academic work, parties, taking my dog Philippa for walks, sunbathing in Rio, smoking behind Our Lady's grotto or the chapel at school; and steaming up car windows late into the night on top of the hill of Morumbí in São Paulo, where couples parked side by side. Sometimes the police knocked on the windows and moved us on.

At home, Grandma Grażyna carried on begrudging food but otherwise being wonderful and looking after us in various other ways, not least securing our family finances. My Mama handed over her earnings to her and she protected the money in what she considered the best way possible: by burying it. She had no faith whatsoever in the banks and to beat the appalling inflation she exchanged vast sums into dollars and buried them in tightly packed jam jars. An enduring image in my mind is Grandma Grażyna walking to the bottom of our diminutive garden with a trowel and a little bucket of clothes pegs, digging up the jam jars and hanging the dollar bills on the washing line for airing. This had to be done regularly, in rotation, as the washing line could never fit all the dollars in one go.

Being practical was certainly one of Grandma Grażyna's qualities. Being unflappable was another. When she had a mastectomy, she had an extremely long curved scar (starting at the front and ending on her back) which would have upset most women. She showed it to me and, looking at herself in the mirror, said theatrically: '*Je suis une femme mutilée!*' (I'm a mutilated woman) and burst out laughing. Declaring that, like a dog, she'd heal in no time, she never gave it another thought. She just got on with it.

From the autumn of 1968 there was a huge increase in guerilla activity in the largest cities. More than a hundred banks were robbed, army barracks were dynamited, as were warehouses belonging to American companies. Revolutionary speeches were broadcast from radio stations taken over by the guerillas who also succeeded in releasing jailed terrorists from a prison in Rio.

I remember Kika coming back from Campinas one day, where she'd gone to visit friends, including Mr Dowbór and his reptiles. She reported that his snake Catarina was in cracking form, that his son Ladislas Dowbór had returned from Lausanne as an Economics graduate and that his father was very proud of his son's intellectual prowess. Little did any of us know then what was about to transpire.

By this time, I'd met Alan Matthews, the man I was to marry. I was eighteen when we were introduced and nineteen when we tied the knot. Compared to the rich landowning Latin macho boyfriends I'd had up to that stage, he immediately scored a thousand points for being an Englishman and multilingual. My mother had everything arranged for me to spend a year in London, live with a relation in Kensington and go to Bedford College to broaden my horizons but, in love with my Englishman, I categorically refused.

One evening in early 1969 the young Ladislas Dowbór came for dinner. He was scholarly and spoke quietly. I was just short of my nineteenth birthday and unpolitical as I was, it was nevertheless blatantly obvious to me that Ladislas Dowbór's intellect was formidable. I listened intently whilst he discussed the situation in Brazil with Alan, my husband-to-be.

Shortly afterwards, in March, I walked into a shop and saw a large poster with a photograph of Ladislas. **WANTED**, the poster said. *LADISLAS DOWBÓR, KNOWN AS NELSON, ONE OF THE HEAVYWEIGHTS OF THE TERRORIST ORGANISATION, A DANGEROUS COMMUNIST ASSASSIN RESPONSIBLE FOR THE DEATHS OF MANY HEADS OF FAMILIES. HELP US PROTECT YOUR CHILDREN. WARN A POLICEMAN AS SOON AS YOU NOTICE HIS PRESENCE.*

On 21 April 1969, Ladislas Dowbór was arrested and taken to the interrogation centre run by the counter terrorist army squads. The words over the door into the torture room read: 'Here there is neither God nor human rights'. He was an important catch and was appallingly tortured for seven weeks until the German Ambassador in Rio, von Holleben, was kidnapped by the guerillas and released in exchange for Ladislas and twenty-seven members of his group. I remember a photograph in the papers of them disembarking in Algiers on the 15 June 1969.

The Pulitzer Prize winner, French journalist Sanche de Gramont interviewed Ladislas Dowbór in 1970 in Tangiers. In a piece entitled 'The Transformation of Moral Idealism into Violent Revolution', de Gramont is less concerned with Brazil than with *'the mysterious process by which a pleasant, scholarly young man from a middle-class background is transformed into a revolutionary'*. He describes Ladislas as having *'the quiet authority of the natural leader'* and concludes that he *'was dangerous not because he had a gun and was willing to use it, but because he is one of those rare persons who carry the notion of moral consistency to its logical outcome'*.

I wonder whether de Gramont kept in touch with his interviewee over the years. Since 1982 Ladislas Dowbór has been Professor of Economics at the Catholic University in São Paulo, the very city where he was a high-level terrorist leader. He has been a Consultant in development planning in many countries and to countless institutions including the UN, has written over forty books, and has a vibrant interactive website. Many of his interviews and talks can be seen on Youtube.

By 1970, when Sanche de Gramont was writing up his interview, I was married and living with Alan in a little flat not far from the house I had shared with Mama, Kika and Grandma Grażyna. She dropped by one evening unannounced, which was very uncharacteristic of her. Alan wasn't there. I poured her a drink and, unprompted, she started talking. There was no practical, matter of fact discourse but a quiet appraisal of her life. She shared with me her guilt and deep regret at having left Zygmunt Karpiński for Antoni Dygat, destroying two families, causing such terrible distress to so many people. She then asked for a few sheets of blank paper which she signed at the bottom, saying they could come in handy, and she handed me a receipt for the dry cleaner where some clothes needed collecting. She told me the money for the milkman was in the left drawer in the kitchen, got up, made a sign of the cross with her thumb on my forehead and left. I was dumbfounded and rang my mother. Something wasn't right with Grandma. She was the last person on the planet to have premonitions. She actually ridiculed them.

The next day, being driven to Rio de Janeiro for the weekend by a dear friend, Grandma Grażyna was killed in a car crash.

—⁓—

In Brazil people are buried within a day. The arrangements were organised and paid for by the husband of the friend who'd been driving and who'd survived the crash with a minor cut on her forehead.

Grandma Grażyna's funeral was extraordinary for several reasons. First of all, she'd have been astounded at the numbers of people present. She was so hugely popular that mourners of all ages and various nationalities descended on the sprawling hilly cemetery, stunned and in tears.

Then there was the family grave she was joining: it wasn't our own, but belonged to Prince Roman Sanguszko's chauffeur, Władysław Bryg, who had deeply touched Grażyna years earlier when he'd told her there would be plenty of space for her in his family tomb. For years he and Grażyna used to giggle that this was by far the nicest invitation she'd ever received.

The committal itself was a supreme example of black humour. Grandma Grażyna would have howled with laughter. As shocked and distraught as we were by her death, one couldn't help watching the proceedings as one does a black comedy. The grave was at the very bottom of the steep graveyard, too far to carry the coffin, which was placed on the proverbial and undignified 'tea trolley'. As it gathered momentum, the attendants hung on to it for dear life and just managed to guide it to the grave without hitting the many corners en route. At this point serious complications arose as the coffin wouldn't fit into the tomb. One could hear the bumps and thumps of my grandmother's body in the coffin as the graveyard attendants tried different angles but to no avail. Understandably my mother was becoming more and more distressed and was led away by two dear friends some distance from the scene, to await a resolution. Finally, realising that no amount of manoeuvring would make the coffin fit in the available space, there was only one possible option. With a few more thumps the coffin was extricated and placed on the ground, and whilst two attendants stabilised the head end, the third one vanished for what seemed like an eternity, to reappear with a saw in one hand and a cigarette in the other. He pressed down one knee on the coffin, placed the cigarette behind his ear and started sawing. My grandmother was finally buried with her bare feet poking out. I'm sure if this were to happen in England today, there would be a lawsuit demanding huge compensation for the whole family (maybe even for all those present?) As it was, we went home to grieve, to reminisce and to raise a few glasses to the indomitable Grażyna. The hole she was leaving in our lives was vast.

There were now just Kika and my mother living at number 3 in the mews. After grandma Grażyna's death, the colourful and delightful maid, Toninha, was finally allowed to cook properly. Too late for me, but a good step forward, nevertheless. My mother and Kika often asked her to sit down and join them for breakfast and gave her more and more books to read. Toninha called my mother 'Boss' and marvelled at their relationship, unheard of in other households.

In September 1970, I found out I was pregnant. A new light shone bright on my horizon. Grandma Róża was ecstatic and added a new focus to her hoarding: baby clothes. Her eyes brightened, and we met often, making plans to one day, in the distant future, tell my children about Lentvaris.

CHAPTER SIXTEEN

DECAY, REDEMPTION AND HOPE

I MUST HAVE radiated happiness as I flew towards Costa Rica in June 1971 with my one-month-old baby, Joanna. I was in heaven, in love with my first child, oblivious of the rest of the world, looking forward to introducing her to my father. I hadn't seen him for seven years, since those few unhappy hours in Montreal in 1964. The least I could do was to bring him his first grandchild.

I was met at the airport by an elderly Polish couple in a rusty Jeep who explained that my father was waiting in their house and that we'd be staying there for a few days. I sensed they wanted to tell me something but maybe they took pity on me. I was clearly exhausted after a flight of not much sleep, indeed a whole sleepless *month* after a swift but brutal labour. I only became aware of our impending arrival at our destination when Joanna began crying and the Jeep started bumping along a dirt track that hadn't seen rain for a while (in spite of June being the official start of the rainy season). It was very hot.

The house was little more than a decaying shack. A bedraggled dog scratched itself lazily on the veranda, watching a gecko about to pounce on a large insect. It paid no attention to me. Chickens pecked and scratched at the ground; large motionless flowers didn't look real in the haze. This was no tropical paradise.

My father was nowhere to be seen. The kind Polish man unloaded my baby paraphernalia from the Jeep, and I carried Joanna into the house. As they led me along a dark passage towards what was to be my room I saw my father on the floor next to an empty bottle of vodka, barely conscious, with the look of an old man, rather than the forty-six year old he was. I can barely remember walking past him and placing Joanna on the bed to change her nappy. She began screaming for my breast and all I could think of was to feed her and protect her from the heavy pall of decay and misery around us.

I could see in the kind faces of the Polish couple that they viewed me as the last hope for Józef. In that moment I knew that I wasn't there for him to experience the love and the joy of bonding with a first grandchild. As the woman mopped his face with a wet flannel and my tears dropped on to

Joanna's head, I felt a rising anger towards him. I wanted to feed my baby as I always did, in an atmosphere of calm and cosiness, humming lullabies, letting my love flood into her with my milk. Instead she was absorbing my anguish and the sound of my sobs.

I hated him for a few moments, then came the guilt for feeling that way, followed by an ocean of pity. When he sobered up enough to approach us, he didn't even look at his granddaughter. He focused on my face and, just like seven years before in Montreal, he asked repeatedly, *'Do you love me?'* I rinsed Joanna's nappies, left them to soak in a battered metal bucket and fell asleep looking at her face next to me on the iron bed. Some odd sounds woke me in the middle of the night. The generator was off. I lit the candle and went towards the source.

The bathroom had no glass in the window, only vertical metal bars, and the moonlight cast their shadow on the cement floor. Józef was on his knees, bent over the bathtub, sobbing his heart out, washing Joanna's nappies. I went back to bed and howled into my pillow.

'He won't last long at this rate,' the old man said to me the next morning and I knew what I had to do: take Joanna and myself out of there, phone Kika and my mother in Brazil to warn them and change my flight back home.

Within a month my father was flying to São Paulo on a ticket paid for by my mother, and Kika was about to embark on long years of physical and emotional suffering with demands relentlessly placed upon her which would have broken many. She'd always wondered about how and why God drew such tortuous patterns in her life, yet she never resented Him, never asked 'Why me?' For her a much more appropriate question would always be 'Why *not* me?' Alongside this resilience, her sense of humour survived. Her attitude was that God himself had a sense of humour and wasn't he frightfully kind to share it with her!

When Joanna was six or so months old and I was pregnant with my second baby, my mother did what she'd been waiting to do for years: she left Brazil and became a contemplative Benedictine nun in Stanbrook Abbey in Worcestershire. Many in Brazil thought she'd left to join some mysterious lover in England.

Less than a year later, when Joanna was one and my son one month old, Alan, I and the children left Brazil for the UK where Alan had a place to do a post graduate course at Manchester University. The house in the mews in

São Paulo was sold and the proceeds shared between Kika and me. Granny Róża's dreary little cottage was also disposed of, and Kika bought two small adjoining flats on the ground floor of a four-level building. Grandma Róża moved into one and Kika with my father Józef into the other.

I felt we were all deserting Kika: Grażyna dead, my mother following her star, me following my man, and Kika, with her appalling health, left with the burden of having her loopy mother and alcoholic brother to look after.

Kika understood that for Wanda becoming a nun at Stanbrook was simultaneously a huge wrench and an imperative. Yet I'm ashamed to say that this was a time when I went through a period of resenting both my parents. I resented my father for being the reason Kika was going to continue having a rotten life, and I felt abandoned too, not least because my marriage to Alan was rapidly deteriorating. I was only twenty-two and I wanted my two mothers, Wanda and Kika, to put their arms around me. Kika couldn't take me under her wing, and my mother had chosen Stanbrook Abbey over me. It wasn't quite like that of course and Wanda assumed I didn't need her anymore as I was a married adult and had my own life to lead. But that was the way I felt. It was the loneliest unhappiest time of my life.

My mother wasn't the only nun in Stanbrook who had been married. There were two others: the beautiful Irish singer Mary O'Hara, and another whose name I can't remember, who kept her husband's trouser press in her cell to iron her veil. The difference between them and my mother was that they were widows whereas my father was alive (and kept sending my Mama his poems to review as she was the only person whose opinion he sought).

Wanda Mycielska, Stanbrook Abbey 1973

I suppose there were other ways in which my Ma wasn't a typical nun. When I brought my tiny children to see her on a grey and rainy day in 1973, I winced at the wide counter that prevented us from hugging, and I could feel a rising childish hostility towards the nuns who had stolen her from us. At this point Joanna requested loudly: '*See navel. See navel.*' Without batting an eyelid my mother lifted her habit and showed it.

In 1974, before I had actually accepted that my marriage was over, my mother again faced a wrench and an imperative: she longed to remain in the nunnery but I was in pieces, barely able to look after my children. On the day she left Stanbrook Abbey and came to my rescue, she bought a Christian Dior wig and a cashmere twin set en route. She arrived in my house in Manchester looking a million dollars. She was jolly well not going to look like a nun when she no longer was one.

Nobody could have guessed Wanda's intense distress at having to abandon the contemplative life she had chosen and in which she'd felt completely content. My Mama took over the running of the house and the care of the children, dedicating to them every minute of the day. What she couldn't do for me when I was a child, she could now do for my children. She more than rose to the occasion. There is no question that she sacrificed herself to the demands of real life rather than to the nun's cell and I know that in this she was heroic.

Grandma Róża wrote regularly, letters of much love. Here is one she sent to my mother, in 1975 soon after Wanda left Stanbrook:

'My beloved daughter-in-law: I have five minutes to hug you from the bottom of my heart because Theo is leaving in a moment and I enclose $30 which are meant to be only for clothes for you. It's not much but you'll buy yourself something. It will give me huge pleasure. Don't spend it on anything else, I ask you that it will be something for you only. My hug is as strong as my love for you. May God keep you. Róża'

In November 1976 she wrote to my five-year-old daughter Joanna:

'For loveliest Joanna, my very very beloved great-granddaughter.
Thank you so much for the wonderful photograph and the little drawings. They are lovely and a very precious gift for me. You both

look fabulous on those beautiful ponies. You've brought me much joy.
I would so love to be with you my darlings. My hugs for you are as strong as my love. Give a big hug to Mama, Daddy and your Babi.
(Babi was my children's name for my mother)
Your loving great-grandmother Róża'

I once asked Kika whether she thought Róża would one day consider coming to us in England for a while, to see us and to give Kika some respite. The answer was categorically, no. Grandma Róża was petrified of the idea of flying and would only pluck up courage to do so if it were ever possible to go with me to Lentvaris... Those thousands of hours spent in the hammock with her over the years when I was a child in Brazil, flooded back in a wave of nostalgia; a nostalgia also for Lentvaris itself, that felt very much mine – not only Grandma Róża's, even though I had never been there. Ah... if only I could have scrounged a pinch or two of that magic powder from Peter Pan that made time travel possible.... As exasperating as Róża could be with her hoarding and fussing, I missed her. I pinned two photographs of her on the inside of my wardrobe. One holding me in 1950, the other holding my daughter in 1971.

When, finally, Alan's life took him to a new start in Portugal, my children in effect had two mothers: Wanda and me. This meant that I too could strive for a new beginning. The Lucie Clayton Model Agency offered me work and Manchester University accepted me for a BA Hons Degree in Psychology. I did model for a year but then had to make a choice and chose the latter.

I have to laugh when I think of my modelling days. Lucie Clayton was a top model agency in London but before you think 'Jean Shrimpton and David Bailey', mine was the Manchester branch and for the first three months I was doing ads for tea sets, bedding and other such marvels in mail order catalogues. I think my very first assignment was sitting cross-legged in a satin evening dress, elbow on one knee, chin resting on my hand, looking dreamily at a New Home 613 Automatic sewing machine, ('superb elegance, a dream come true'). You could barely see me in the brochure due to the arty fading.

Modelling days, 1974

Then, to my amusement it was decided that legs were my thing. I couldn't quite understand it because apart from being long and slim, one is thinner than the other and one knee points inwards. I thought they were bonkers. Buy hey presto, I got 'them pins' in *Vogue*, NOT I hasten to add, in a glamorous fashion shoot but in an advertisement for Vernon Humpage snakeskin sandals. It was a full page add and I made the photographer laugh so maybe this was what led to slightly better work: big ads for Kendal Milne (The Harrods of the North!), their music department, their cashmeres and the like. I also did some fashion shows, all 'Paris turns' and arms akimbo, strutting around and feeling a fool.

On a serious note though I clearly remember becoming obsessed with weight and although I was perfectly slim, I feared putting on a single ounce. Nobody at Lucie Clayton ever advised any of us to diet but I often ate nothing but a few Digestive biscuits with cottage cheese and then fell into bed with the room swaying around me. When the agency suggested that I move to London to forge a proper modelling career, I said a polite thank you and joyfully leapt into the arms of Academe. At this point, one of the boyfriends I had after my divorce, pinched my best modelling photos which I only realised after he'd departed for the Antipodes.

I loved my three years at University. I was twenty-five when I started and therefore classed as a 'mature' student. There is no doubt that those of us who had children and other commitments studied far harder than many of the nineteen year olds. After graduating I became a research assistant in the same department and Wanda continued to be the mother figure whilst I worked and tried to fathom why so many men were appearing out of nowhere. I had the classic impostor syndrome both with regards to looks and intellect.

As looks go, a little voice in my head kept telling me: *They think I'm attractive, but I know I'm not.* Even when modelling. This fortunately didn't last too long but with regards to brains I still felt, for years, that I was a fraud. *They think I'm clever, but they're wrong. My upper second must have been a mistake. It's a matter of time before I'm found out.* It was only when I got accepted by Mensa that this particular hang-up faded a little. You don't need a degree in Psychology to surmise that an absent father and a failed marriage had contributed to that.

<center>~~~</center>

There is no question in my mind that Kika and Alcoholics Anonymous saved my father's life. He arrived in Brazil from Costa Rica, a drunken wreck, no longer able to function at the most basic of levels, let alone hold down a job. All he could just about manage was to write the poignantly beautiful poetry he'd produced for years. His full recovery from alcoholism took a considerable time during which Kika didn't only deal with him but also with his companions from taverns and bars: on more than one occasion she'd wake in the middle of the night to find several alcoholics boozing all over her little flat. One of the regulars was a huge black man with few teeth who looked extremely threatening to put it mildly, and who had the marvellous name of Hércules da Silva. He too came through eventually. After a few months of Józef's eventual sobriety, his beloved dog Oscar was run over and he was on the verge of going on a grief-fuelled binge, but Hércules sat on his bed all night with Kika and between them they helped my father weather the storm.

Józef's triumph over his addiction was precarious of course, as being on the wagon always is, but the fact that he was sober and that I was an adult, transformed our relationship completely, even though it was long distance. He was working freelance as a translator and helping a bookbinder nearby a couple of days a week. He wrote to me regularly, funny clever letters, and to my children too. I was glad for him because he clearly felt that he was making up for lost time, but I'm ashamed to say that I was nevertheless glad I wasn't the one taking care of him. Poor Kika. Never a moment to herself, keeping an eye on her two neurotic dependants, working full time between bouts of bad health and operations. Her faith, her humour and extremely kind and protective Brazilian friends kept her going.

Grandma Róża was broken when news reached her of her brother

Stetysz's death from pneumonia. It was 1976. She'd had a loving letter from him from London only a few weeks before in which he'd expressed the hope of soon being back home. During one of our rare, and in those days expensive, international phone calls, Kika told me Róża had been sitting in the hammock with a photograph of herself and her siblings in Lentvaris, running her finger over Stetysz's face again and again. I wished I could have been sitting there with her, in 'our' hammock under the bougainvillea.

⁓

In 1981, a very special man unwittingly saved me from a potentially rather tricky fate: working for Robert Maxwell in Oxford at Pergamon Press. His name was John Wilbraham, he was nineteen years older than me and he'd recently been left by his wife. He had three sons, close in age to my children. What first struck me was the twinkle in his very kind eyes. On the very first day of our acquaintance, when in the middle of our conversation I mentioned my plans to move to Oxford, the twinkle left his gaze and he said quietly. *'Please don't.'* And I didn't.

Our marriage was blessed by a bishop on a hugely happy rainy February day in 1983 in Woodhey Chapel in Cheshire, no doubt causing one of John's ancestors much outrage. Lady Wilbraham, chatelaine of Weston Park, wife of Sir Tomas Wilbraham, was reputed to have been the first ever woman architect. She had built Woodhey Chapel in 1698 and must have done summersaults in her grave when we married because, according to John, she loathed Roman Catholics with a passion. And there was I, a left-footer, not only in her holy place but having an Anglican bishop officiating. Poor Lady Wilbraham!

Ours was an unusual celebration as Woodhey Chapel is in open countryside. There is a wonderful photograph from above of the Bishop of Stockport and Canon Archie Douglas, fully robed for the occasion, standing in the middle of a field. Our guests, wearing the traditional morning coats for the men and smart hats for the ladies, were requested to wear gumboots. The local press wanted to do a feature along the lines of 'And the bride wore wellies' but we declined. We dodged cowpats and giggled under large umbrellas. The choir from Chetham's School of Music, where John was a Governor and Feoffee, sang the *Ave Verum* magnificently. It was a memorable and extremely joyful day, the start of thirty-five years of a very happy marriage.

Kika and Józef sent moving letters for our wedding, and John was to keep the one from my father in his briefcase forever. Grandma Róża sent a parcel. It was waiting for us on our return from our honeymoon in Vienna. Heart-shaped sweets wrapped in velvet and lace, a holy picture of St Joseph of Cupertino, a black and white photograph of Lentvaris church and my father's poem *The Golden Apple of Samarkand*. Grandma Róża had copied it by hand on a piece of parchment.

I was told by Kika that there had been an almighty row between my father and Grandma Róża, the latter maintaining she should be the one to copy the poem on parchment because it had been her idea, and the former yelling that he'd written the poem in the first place so it should be him. It took Kika some nifty mediation in which she finally managed to convince them that if copied by Róża this gift would become from them *both*, the author and the calligrapher; and that what mattered most after all was the symbolism in my father's poem which had its roots in the steppes of Kazakhstan.

Neither Róża, nor Józef and Kika would ever forget the day when they were released from the Siberian labour camp at the end of the war and the initial relief was swiftly replaced by the fear of having no idea which direction to walk in, where to find the nearest source of food, how to survive. Then someone said that there were good apples in Samarkand and at that moment the golden fruit became their symbol of hope and direction.

It is sad that this poem isn't in my father's printed booklet, and that the parchment version was eventually eaten by mice in an English attic. Yet what will last in me forever is the symbol itself: even after all the horrors, my father, the starving boy in the Siberian steppes, still had the capacity to hope.

CHAPTER SEVENTEEN

NAME-DROPPING, BEREAVEMENT AND JOY

ETON, THE RIFLE Brigade, the London Stock Exchange. John Wilbraham, this most conventional British gent got himself an offbeat foreign wife. *Exotic* some said: born in Argentina, brought up in Brazil, of Polish blood. I didn't feel at all exotic; I was just me and I rejoiced in John's huge charm, lack of arrogance, warmth, his social ease and diplomacy, his kindness, humour, capacity for fun and that ability (alien to anyone except the British upper class) to dress like a tramp when in casual mode. His favourite piece of clothing was the sweater his father had died in, with an ever-increasing ratio of holes to yarn.

John's predictable career path started veering off most delightfully, just before we were married. His working life threw us into an international world of musicals, theatre and films, starting with his involvement with Goldcrest Films at the time of *Ghandi* and *Chariots of Fire*. Andrew Lloyd Webber's musicals followed, with John helping raise the finance for productions in the UK, Germany and the US, not least *Cats, Starlight Express* and *Phantom of the Opera*. He co-produced several West End plays and raised the finance for others.

We travelled a lot: the Cannes Film Festival, The American Film Market, visits to first nights and anniversary parties of Lloyd Webber productions in various countries. We had private dinners with colourful creative people, some delightful, some not. We met countless actors, many household names, the cream of theatre and film. One of the Hollywood greats and his wife (a dear old friend) came and stayed with us in Yorkshire; we stayed with them in their houses, were generously included in many of their public and private celebrations, not least their small and very low-key wedding in their home. This is the point at which I could drop endless names, but I won't. There is no room in my memoir for self-aggrandisement by association. Suffice it to say that we found some of the greatest and most distinguished to be the most self-effacing. As indeed was my husband: his love of the performing arts had started early and for someone who'd been an enthusiastic amateur actor, his post-stockbroking career brought him much fulfilment; and yet, when *Who's Who* sent him forms to fill in, he couldn't be bothered and threw them in the bin.

In these glamorous and interesting settings, John's disregard for the most basic of sartorial standards provided much mirth, for me at least, as other mortals were usually unaware of the circumstances. The best example was when, in Germany, John was sitting next to Hildegard Kneff in a TV studio being interviewed about some play or other and a persistent rustling noise kept interfering with the sound system. I noticed that this happened every time John moved in his seat. The same occurred when after the interview we sat in the bar having an apéritif. I was only able to investigate when we were in the lift and I could carry out a hurried inspection of my husband's crotch. The seam in his trousers had come apart, probably weeks before, and instead of telling me, he'd taken it upon himself to 'mend' it with parcel tape!

My mother as the third adult in our household was invaluable and my life with John and our children was made infinitely easier by having her in the granny flat. The boys, John's and mine, were in boarding school but my daughter and our ever-growing band of rescue mongrels needed an efficient and loving presence during our absences.

When we were at home, we weren't on top of each other because the granny flat was at the far end of what was a large Georgian house. My mother's territory was past the green baize door, along the dark corridor with the old servants' bells, the butler's pantry and other servants' areas of yore. She didn't for a moment feel pushed out but relished having her own space away from us all. As for the rest of us, although there were three televisions in our house, it was in her granny flat that everyone congregated to watch.

I do believe that although my mother had wanted to be a nun forever, she did find happiness in her life with us. This was I'm sure due to her inherent acceptance of what she saw as God's will and her mother's mantra: '*Be a weed. Wherever life throws you, GROW.*' She became passionately interested in the Universe and Quantum Physics, and the relationship between Science and Religion. What 'lies beyond' fascinated her and she'd get hugely excited with every new TV programme on these topics. Her shelves were full of books by writers like John Polkinhorne and Richard Feynman and her enthusiasm was infectious. Above her bed was a quote by Feynman: '*I'd rather have questions that can't be answered than answers that can't be questioned'.* This very much applied to her faith which was never blind or categorical.

When we were away, Wanda rose to every occasion in our household where rescued mongrels reigned supreme and she actually moved into our huge double bed to be nearer to my daughter's room and, just as important, to give moral support to the dogs who all had their baskets in our bedroom. There was never any tension between Wanda and John, nor indeed between her and me. She was completely undemanding, never gave opinions unless asked, and the three of us were equally blessed with not being moody.

⁓

It was a joyful December when Grandma Róża's older sister Zofia was allowed by the communist regime in Poland to come to the UK at our invitation for two weeks over Christmas. I'd met her only once previously, when I was a teenager and her husband Klemens was still alive. When, all those years later, she came to our house in Cheshire, she was ninety-two and travelled by herself. The tiny little figure arrived with stacks of copies of family papers and photographs for me to keep, including microfilms from the National Archives in Warsaw: a treasure trove and the chance for me to compare Grandma Róża's accounts with hers. The Lentvaris I knew from Róża's accounts in my childhood, was the same as great-aunt Zofia's; and she was able to give me additional details of their life, my poor grandmother's mental problems and the period between the two world wars.

Almost as wonderful as having her presence among us, was great-aunt Zofia's gift to me, namely a book, one of thousands from the library in Lentvaris. I wasn't particularly interested in the subject matter (Gogol's historical novella *Taras Bulba*) but the fact that it had belonged to my great-grandparents Maryńcia and Władysław Tyszkiewicz was magic. I felt I had been given a little piece of Lentvaris of my own to keep. Little did I know at that moment what an extraordinary and precious surprise that book would reveal several years later.

I know we gave great-aunt Zofia a memorable Christmas. We pampered her as much as we could but what she gave me was infinitely more, and I don't refer to the leather-bound volume. That tiny fragile ninety-two-year-old person showed me her enviable inner strength, a humbling tranquil acceptance of both the horrors life had thrown at her, and of the continuing hardship her remaining years inevitably held in store.

Great-aunt Zofia Potocka neé Tyszkiewicz, Christmas 1985, Cheshire

When I took her to the airport I wondered if I'd ever see her again. As she was wheeled through the boarding gate, I knew that whilst I was going back to a wonderfully comfortable and beautiful house, to people who loved me, she was returning to her reality in a Communist country, up three floors without a lift, to a poky empty flat with only photographs of the two people who'd mattered most: her husband Klemens and their only son Moryś, murdered at the age of nineteen at Auschwitz. I cried all the way home.

Less than two years later John had meetings with Film Polski in Warsaw with the view of using Polish locations for some British films. We were both more excited about seeing great-aunt Zofia again than the appointment in the film office. What I remember most about the latter was being given a loo roll by one of the employees since there were none in the grim lavatories and each person had to bring their own.

We only had a couple of days in Warsaw and we spent every possible moment with great-aunt Zofia. We'd brought her suitable gifts, things that for us in the West were commonplace but for her were luxury: warm tights, tins of Nescafe, soap, hand cream and shampoo. In Communist Poland you could only buy such wonders in Pewex, the chain of government shops which accepted American dollars and other hard currencies, but not the country's indigenous *złoty*, thus making basic items inaccessible to the majority of Poles.

Great-aunt Zofia was nearly ninety-four at the time of our visit, and we witnessed first-hand her daily struggles and her courage. Even John found it an effort to carry her shopping up three flights of stairs. She had to do it daily, come rain or shine, because one big weekly shop would have been impossible for her to heave all the way upstairs. The shopping itself was a challenge to start with as it involved standing for very long periods in interminable queues often finding that the choice of groceries was dismal. In the winter, with the pavements thick with snow and sheet ice, walking was a very hazardous affair. I'm surprised she didn't fall more often. Younger friends did help her when they could, but they too had their own hardship and responsibilities. Her brother Eugeniusz's family, most of them living in Sweden, showed her great kindness, but none of us were in the same country for hands-on assistance.

On that last visit, we took great-aunt Zosia for dinner to our hotel, stocked up her cupboards with staples and delicacies from Pewex and left her wads of dollars which she pushed into the hollow inside the terracotta sculpture of her mother, my great-grandmother Maryńcia. When we hugged goodbye, I think we both knew we wouldn't be seeing each other again.

The image that most sticks in my mind from that final and brief encounter is of her sitting in her diminutive kitchen, alone at the tiny table for two, with that large faded black and white poster of Lentvaris as the backdrop. In that photograph, the person I see is not my great-aunt Zofia, or a newly married Countess Zofia Potocka, but Zofia Tyszkiewicz, the young girl who ran along the paths of Lentvaris park with her younger sister Róża before either of the wars tore their world apart.

<p style="text-align:center">~~~</p>

Back in the UK, I often thought of how very different my life was from my grandmother Róża's. The most fragile of the three, she would never get rid of her vulnerability. Kika, in spite of her appalling health, was emotionally strong and my father, no longer in the grip of alcoholism was living as happy a life as he could: he had a sweet adoring female in his life, a kind beautician ten years his junior, with whom he didn't live but who he spent long weekends with in a little house on the island paradise of Ilhabela. With stunning beaches, waterfalls and unspoilt Atlantic rainforest, two hours away from São Paulo, Ilhabela was the place where he found contentment.

The delightful house had been bought by his girlfriend with a small contribution from him and Kika, and the mid-1980s were the happiest for him in decades. Kika and Róża often came to the island too, they ate freshly caught seafood and drank non-alcoholic juices made from a variety of tropical fruit; Józef wrote poetry, lay in the sand with his love and left it to Kika to manage their mother's worries about spiders and gekkos and whether, were there to be a storm, the palm tree would or wouldn't crush the house. Józef even became less combative with Róża when she droned on about him not having married the beautician. Fortunately, even Grandma Róża reserved that particular conversation for when they were alone. Just as well because Kika overheard him, more than once, telling their mother that he couldn't possibly marry the sweet woman because she had a loo seat with metallic goldfish set in transparent turquoise. (I can reveal that now because she is dead and had no children!)

The *modus vivendi* of my beloved Brazilian trio became as good as it could be and Kika found again in my father the brother-in-arms of their childhood, the ally who'd been *hors de combat* for so long, during his alcoholic years.

And then, in 1988 after a peaceful day watching the surf, my father had a massive heart attack and died in Kika's arms. He was sixty-three. He is buried on Ilhabela, in its unpretentious little cemetery with whitewashed graves, tropical trees and the smell of the sea. His gravestone reads JÓZEF MYCIELSKI, POET.

⌇⌇⌇

My father's death was the start of a long and increasingly difficult phase in Kika's life, *à deux* with Grandma Róża, whose sole focus she became. In addition to our visits to them in Brazil we were kept abreast of events in their life, largely through friends, as Kika would never complain.

Over the years, as our five young grew up, our house was a lively and social place for people of all ages. There were plenty of bedrooms so countless friends came to stay, formal and informal parties took place; there was tennis, croquet, swimming, clay pigeon shooting, much dressing up and John larking about in funny hats; scores of Opera singers practiced in the walled garden and in the shower, during the weeks that they spent with us every summer, for the Clonter Opera Summer Schools. The Fourth of June at Eton for John's boys, and Exhibition Weekend at Ampleforth for my son (another Jozef) were exhausting but delightful family occasions.

We had holidays and/or short breaks all over Europe, Africa, Brazil, the USA, Australia, and, for John and his sons, countless visits to the battlefields of Normandy. Half term, when the boys were home from boarding school, saw John in high octane bonding with them. Another idiosyncrasy of a certain section of British society, this was alien to my upbringing in Brazil, where you only sent your children away to board if they were delinquents. You bonded at home, day in day out, in normal daily interactions, rather than cramming it all into short slots of time. Turbo bonding didn't come naturally to me, but I can't deny it was enormous fun.

A couple of luxury cruises were unexpected treats for John and me when we travelled for free in exchange for John's talks: one about his ancestor, entitled 'William Penn, a man ahead of his time'; the other about the risks of investing in the theatre, 'Angels can lose their wings'.

My own solo trips to Brazil were always a mix of bereavement exasperation and joy. Joy at being with Kika and Grandma Róża, seeing the former, braver but weaker with every one of my visits, and the latter increasingly vague and emotionally demanding. Exasperation at not knowing how to help. How long did the Almighty plan to test Kika so?

The maid Toninha kept coming to their flats, able to clean less and less as Kika's and Róża's joint hoarding became an assault course, an ever-narrowing slalom route for successive vacuum cleaners, all of which died of dysphagia. Amazingly, when Kika was invited out by friends, she somehow managed to dig up just the right clothes, jewellery and bloody-minded positivity to shine.

The feeling of bereavement that kicked in every time I arrived in Brazil was twofold. One was predictable, but even though it was the same every year, it still hit me: my childhood was no more. The wonderful garden in my old school (where Sylvia and I had larked about by Our Lady's grotto) had been sold to developers. The tree Grandma Grażyna had planted in front of number 3 in the mews had been cut down. Banana sellers' carts no longer existed. Friends from my mother's generation hadn't been preserved in time but looked disturbingly older.

The other feeling of bereavement was very real and appropriate: in spite of the end of the Military Dictatorship, killings continued for years. Toninha's fifteen-year-old son was shot by the police. Four friends had been widowed in their early thirties. One husband was shot in his office for refusing to hand over the combination to the safe. Another had been defending his wife from an attacker on the doorstep. A third was killed surprising a robber in his house in the middle of the night.

Sylvia, of The Testicles, had the worst experience of them all: she was waiting for her husband to come home from work and take her and the children out to dinner. He was late. A phone call from the hospital didn't alarm her unduly when she was told he'd had an accident and suggesting she came over. Knowing that driving in the rush hour was painfully slow, she imagined he maybe had a broken leg or a few stitches on the head. On arrival, when she mentioned his name, she was casually told to go to a certain cubicle. She had their children with her. There, two feet protruded from under a white sheet. Her husband, who'd stopped at the traffic lights, had made a fatal mistake: instead of handing his watch to the thief who pointed his gun at him through the window, he stepped out of the car.

Soon after his death a woman turned up with a child and Sylvia's world fell further apart. She'd thought she had a fabulous marriage whilst for years he'd been living a double life with another family in Rio. Sylvia's doctor recommended a Trauma Clinic. She checked in but didn't stay more than a day as her instinct for self-preservation kicked in. It was clear to her that the stories of some of the other patients were not going to help her in any way. The young pregnant woman in the adjoining room had gone to shop for baby clothes with her mother and on returning earlier than expected, they'd found her husband in bed with her father.

＊

As the years rolled by, our five children searched for their individual paths, planned their gap years and university courses, chose or fell into their careers, got married, produced children of their own. Once they were all ploughing their own very different furrows in different parts of the world, John, I, my mother and seven rescue dogs moved to North Yorkshire to a smaller Georgian house, a haven on the edge of the Lower Derwent Valley Nature reserve. We had views to the horizon of never ploughed, never fertilised water meadows, some ridge and furrow, and a mediaeval cobbled pond. We made fifteen acres totally dog proof. People with horses don't bat an eyelid at spending money on extensive fencing to keep them in. We didn't see why doing the same for dogs would be considered extravagant. The sight of mongrels from horrible beginnings running free through the meadows with no possibility of getting lost was pure bliss. We frequently sat on a bench on the edge of the ha-ha, watching the sunset with a glass of wine, with the dogs at our feet or parting the meadow grasses as they chased each other. We waited for the Barn Owls to appear overhead, their mesmerising faces looking straight down at us. They didn't disappoint. This was an area with one of the highest concentrations of Barn Owls in Europe. In the wet season, when the water meadows became a massive lake as far as the eye could see, large numbers of swans flew to and from their favoured feeding ground.

Meanwhile in Brazil, Grandma Róża died a few months short of her 100th birthday, in 1998, with Kika holding her hand. She thought she was going to Lentvaris. I'd like to think she was.

Grandma Róża's death came just under a decade after Józef's; long exhausting years during which Kika looked after her singlehanded. When suddenly she no longer had anyone sucking her dry it wasn't freedom she felt, just a deep and heavy exhaustion, an ocean weighing her down into oblivion. She slept for a week. Kind friends brought her food, and in the first days, took it in turns to sleep in her flat; no mean feat to create a space amongst the heaps of clothing, books and amorphous piles of belongings, not to mention the overweight cat.

In Kika's last five years in Brazil she endured another operation, missed more and more days of work (sorting the young Prince Sanguszko's genealogical files) and became increasingly eccentric. Her humour prevailed. '*Why,*' she once said, '*Why can't I lie on a chaise longue in satin bedclothes, surrounded by lillies, quietly coughing into a lace handkerchief? Why do I have to be at the mercy of my bowels? Give me consumption any time!*'

The only time when laughter was not forthcoming was if anyone doubted her belief in the sensitivity of cats. She told me a story ('*Gospel truth*', she said) of a cat belonging to a pilot who had died in a plane crash. Not only did the cat scream at the precise moment the crash had occurred, but it then committed suicide. How, pray, had the feline killed itself? By jumping upwards with all its might, deliberately cracking its head on the ceiling. She was cross with me for several days after my reaction.

When it became untenable for Kika to look after herself and unfair for me to rely on the kindness of Brazilian friends, John announced without hesitation that there was an obvious and wonderful solution: to bring her to England to live in the cottage in our garden. He wrote her a most moving letter that convinced her to accept. She, like my mother, felt better knowing that they could financially support themselves, but this in no way minimised John's kindness. Not everyone would leap at the thought of living in such close proximity to two mothers-in-law.

I set off to Brazil, knowing I wouldn't be seeing John and my mother for weeks. At the end of it would be the joy of being able to look after Kika. The process of packing up her flat and organising the move however, ended up taking me two months and was comparable to one of the twelve labours of Hercules. I felt uncomfortable at the necessary deception involved but there really was no other way. Truth is not always the best option.

CHAPTER EIGHTEEN

LOVING LIES AND A
TREASURE REVEALED

THERE WERE CLOSE to two hundred bottles of dried up nail varnish in a large box in the utility room. Kika was adamant she would need them in England, just as all her paperwork was indispensable. Piled high all over the flat, stuffed behind furniture or in plastic bags under the bed and the sofas, nibbled by cockroaches and mice, most of it went back decades. There was even a receipt from Dr Scholl's, dated 1975, for my father's ingrowing toenail. Kika wanted that too. I very quickly realised the enormity of my task.

Thank the Lord for the very dear friends who adored her and had kept an eye on her for years. They put me up in their spacious house and every morning, after a sumptuous breakfast, I was driven to Kika's flat and collected in the evening in time for dinner.

I was acutely aware of the major emotional upheaval the move was going to be for Kika and I was determined not to bulldoze through her feelings. She needed to feel that the decision as to what she was to bring was hers, even if it could not be so.

Since she wanted to pack up the entire contents of the flat '*to sort it out in the UK*' I managed to convince her that we should look through every single item one by one, so that we could discard what she didn't want, mend what needed mending, clean what needed cleaning and arrive in the UK with everything tickety boo. I devised a system of boxes: things to throw away, things to give, things to take. She did the segregation. At the end of every day the boxes came with me to our friend's house where Kika thought I would be getting them ready for the removal company. The reality was that I disposed of approximately 80 per cent of her belongings. There must have been at least thirty bowls and boxes of various sizes full of a mixture of sticky elastic bands, sweet wrappers, rusty pins, chipped marbles, dried up tubes of glue and so on. In this respect, over the years, Kika had morphed into Róża. It was hoarding on an unimaginable scale.

Of course, personal letters and photographs would come, as would a lot of her books, her pictures, a few small items of furniture, many knick-knacks and her favourite saucepan. I packed twenty issues of *Paris Match* but not the hundred or so that she wanted to take. As for her clothes, out of over thirty pairs of identical black trousers, I selected five; out of forty or more dresses I picked ten, and so on. The sheer quantity of clothing was beyond imagination. Even if she'd been a tidy person, she would have needed twenty or more double wardrobes to house it all.

I took all the clothes that were to come with us to the Japanese laundry to be cleaned and mended and Toninha spent days washing everything else that was wearable, filling more and more gigantic plastic bags. It goes without saying that she did this in our friends' house so that Kika wouldn't know and she had the pick of it, before distributing the rest in the poor area where she lived. For Toninha, Kika's departure was the final curtain for a very long era, but she was grateful that I didn't leave her high and dry: I found her a job in a very good and unconventional household.

The date for our departure approached and I became increasingly worried about Kika's beloved old cat because she was adamant that she would drug him and smuggle him on board in her hand luggage. For Kika, rehoming the feline was out of the question. There were several eminently suitable prospective owners, not least Kika's enchanting vet, Marcelo, who the cat was named after. To distinguish between them, the cat was referred to as Marcelinho. There could not have been a better home for Marcelinho than Marcelo's.

Once Kika categorically refused even that, I could see no solution. The aeroplane tickets were booked. Kika became more and more agitated. Although normally I wouldn't resort to negotiations and bartering with the Kingdom of Heaven, I took to praying to St Francis for his intervention. He obliged and one sunny morn Marcelinho was run over. He was killed instantly which was a blessing for all concerned, not least Marcelinho himself who was not only old but very sick and should have been put down long before.

Marcelinho had a beautiful funeral in the Country Club, in a box filled with flowers, some cat biscuits, and his toy mouse. Our friend was a member of the Club and she slipped one of the groundsmen a nice bribe to double-up as grave digger. There was a moment when I had to bite the inside of my cheek when, to everyone's disbelief, the man offered to sing a funereal hymn for the deceased. At the same time, my heart went out to Kika who stood by the grave, thin and sombre, leaning on her walking stick.

Life had dealt Kika so many lessons in detachment that one more was simply yet another occasion to use towards her spiritual growth. Marcelinho's death was serious and painful for her and despite the loopiness that had crept up on her over the years, she had a sane and private spiritual core which drew her deeper into her faith. She didn't talk about it but every so often a few words would give one a precious glimpse.

The final month in São Paulo became easier and Kika was much calmer. My system of dealing with her belongings kicked back into gear and ended with a wonderful flourish: when I delved deep into the last shelf in the last cabinet on the last day, I tried to pull out a metal vessel which showed some resistance. It turned out that the rubber tube at the bottom had become sticky over the years and had firmly attached itself to the wall. As I pulled, it brought with it a big chunk of plaster. Kika was delighted: *'That's where it is! The enema bucket!'* She was insistent that we should take it to Yorkshire because enemas were all the rage and I could give it to one of my neighbours!

Our dear friends put on a wonderful send off for Kika: a huge lunch party in their garden, with countless tables and flunkies and all her favourite food. It was moving and beautiful. The only thing marring it for me was that we had to continue lying for a little longer: Kika was expecting to receive countless crates by sea. As it was, only three were delivered. The final lie was that some got lost by the shipping company.

Sometimes the end does justify the means. I'm sad that we as a family had to resort to devious methods in Kika's last big step into her new reality, but it was done out of love, so that finally she could be looked after and have no more worries apart from her ever present ill health.

Almost as soon as we arrived in North Yorkshire, Kika set about charming her new coterie of doctors. She was in pain virtually all the time and feared another bowel operation, but she was no longer anguished. I don't think the GP will ever forget their first meeting. As he inserted his finger up her bottom she asked: *'Wouldn't you rather have been a florist?'*

Kika loved being taken to Castle Howard, to feed the ducks in Newburgh Priory, to the Ferryboat Inn in Thorganby for a sandwich. She derived much pleasure from watching tiny boats sail by under the huge weeping willows. Outings to the local supermarket were most exciting. She took ages choosing stacks of unsuitable food and I waited for as long as she needed. Mice never set up home in her cottage because we cleaned it frequently and thoroughly, replacing her gastronomic treasures just as she'd left them. Being able to look after her was a privilege.

Whilst Kika longed to be taken for outings, my Mama read incessantly, painted charming primitive paintings that people wanted to buy, and scribbled her memoirs under the cherry tree. She also re-wrote in Polish the book she'd originally written in Portuguese about my rag elephant, for which she'd won the highest literary prize in Brazil. She re-did all the illustrations.

The Polish version came out with much publicity in Poland, partly because of my mother's connection with her biological father Antoni's family. It made good copy: Wanda's half-brother was the famous writer, Stanisław Dygat, whose wife was a notorious Polish film star (Kalina Jędrusik), and whose daughter Magda Dygat was and is a well-known writer herself. My mother's half-sister Danuta was married to Witold Lutosławski, acknowledged in his obituary (by Charles Bodman Rae in *The Independent*) as '*one of the most significant composers of the 20th century. His works have earned a place in orchestral repertory unequalled by those of any other contemporary composer*'. Only four months later the same writer for *The Independent* was to pen the obituary for Danuta herself. '*Her role was not only that of providing background support...*' '*Danuta Lutosławska has too often been overlooked.*' For more than forty-five years my mother's half-sister was her husband's draughtswoman and copyist of the full scores of most of his major works.

Whatever the reason for the noise created in the Polish press about my mother's book, it brought her a lot more satisfaction than when the Brazilian original had won the literary prize. She allowed herself to enjoy it this time round and I was immensely happy for her. Our joint pleasure at her success was just one more little tile in the full mosaic: my adult relationship with my mother was extremely close and uncomplicated, where the overriding emotion was an easy and free-flowing love.

One evening, when Wanda was looking through our bookshelves, she came upon the little tome from Lentvaris that great-aunt Zofia had given me on her visit: *Taras Bulba*. She was flicking through the interesting prints depicting Gogol's Cossack protagonist, when I noticed something poking out of the spine of the book. As I tugged, out came a yellowed calico tube, hand sewn with tiny perfect stitches. Before even daring to guess who had inserted it in such a hiding place, I was snipping at the stitches with the greatest of care. My mother and I stared at the contents in disbelief as they spilled out onto the desk: one large diamond, and many small diamonds and emeralds.

Two things were undeniable: the gems had come from Lentvaris and great-aunt Zofia hadn't known they were there when giving me the book as a memento. This could only mean that these precious stones had belonged to my great-grandmother Maryńcia Tyszkiewicz, and that they had been part of something bigger. I could barely breathe.

During both wars countless people dismantled jewellery in order to have smaller treasures with which to barter. Items were buried, bricked up, concealed about the person, or in less easily detectable portable objects. The spine of a book had clearly been a good choice.

My head throbbed at the thought that it was perfectly possible these precious stones had been part of the very earrings that Grandma Róża had once been allowed to touch with one finger, just before her parents stepped into the carriage for yet another glittering night out. Of all her mother's spectacular jewellery those earrings had been Róża's favourite throughout her childhood. They shone brightly in her memory for ever as a magical symbol of her grand and untouchable mother, who she had on a pedestal and whose affection she craved.

The stones we found in the book were the same as those in the earrings: emeralds and diamonds, and I was told by a jeweller the next morning that they could be dated by their cut to the early 1900s. It all fits.

My only sadness is that Grandma Róża didn't live long enough to share such a poignant event with me. I wonder also where the other three large diamonds from the earrings ended up. I imagine they were used by my great-grandmother Maryńcia to barter with either Germans or Russians. They might even have saved lives.

I had the large diamond set in a ring, and the small stones in a wide eternity band. Not only is Grandma Róża with me when I wear them, but my great-grandmother Maryńcia Tyszkiewicz from Lentvaris is with us too.

CHAPTER NINETEEN

ADIEU

'MR MARTIN WILBRAHAM, *please come to the information desk',* the airport tannoy called my husband. John didn't respond. Why did his parents register him as Martin John if they intended to call him John? This was a frequent source of irritation, and if referred to as Martin it sometimes took a few seconds for him to react. He was once flown there and back on the same day just to prove that John Wilbraham and Martin John Wilbraham were one and the same. A solicitor's letter wasn't acceptable to the client who paid for John's seat on Concord.

This time John was called because of his sub-standard attire. His passport had been found on the floor at the Duty Free having fallen through the torn lining of his back pocket. From that day onwards I took it upon myself to be personally in charge of the maintenance of all his clothing. He drew the line at the sweater his father had died in and I was categorically forbidden from taking it to the Invisible Mending. He was also rather wounded when I put his ancient British Warm Military Coat on the scarecrow. The lining was held together by dozens of safety pins, and I'd had to stop the car en route to the airport and force him to run in and out of a gentlemen's outfitters to buy a replacement. He didn't at all see that in most countries people wouldn't understand how a tramp could be lecturing them on film finance.

John loved buying me fabulous clothes, but every suggestion about upgrading his own wardrobe met with incomprehension. This disregard was more than matched by his total lack of interest in cars. An extraordinary wedding in Cap Ferrat is a great example. To set the scene, at the religious ceremony, a personal message from the Pope to the bride and bridegroom had been read out from the pulpit; the guests included the likes of Adnan Kashoggi and members of the Niarchos dynasty; the bride and her family were decked out in Valentino (who kept an eye on every fold of silk throughout the evening). Gloria Gaynor provided the music and sang the night away yards from our table; heavily armed security personnel in camouflage kit lurked in large numbers in the vegetation, others with discreet walkie talkies mingled with the catering staff. The size of the precious stones adorning the women was on a par with Catherine the Great's (some might have easily belonged to the Russian Empress once upon a time). It goes without saying, that John and I were the plankton at the bottom of that particular pond. There was nothing to embarrass us about our clothes that evening but our mode of arrival was another matter.

John had rented the cheapest car he could find for the evening: a minute little bright red Ford, which when delivered to our hotel tickled me pink by its incongruity with the occasion. As we turned up at the gates, charming armed security men checked our passports and our invitations and motioned us through. A few yards into the bride's spectacular home, a hand appeared through the car window with two large glasses of champagne on a tray. I think it is accurate to say that we were the only people without a chauffeur. Being handed two glasses of champagne when sitting in comfort in the back of a car, was a charming way to be greeted. To drive, like I was, whilst trying to hold on to the bubbly, changing gear at the same time and laughing was no easy task. I assume that my spectacular faux jewellery from Butler and Wilson fooled only those who hadn't seen us arrive! At the end of the evening we all stood by the balustrade, watching the newlyweds depart in an enormous yacht. As the festivities drew to a close, our little red Ford was brought to us with the same efficient flourish as were all the Bentleys, Rolls Royces and Porsches.

It is true to say that there was an enjoyable aspect to all our travels and breaks over the years. By no means were all of them glamorous. One delightful long weekend took us and one of our dogs to a little hotel near Southbourne where they only accepted bookings from people with at least one pooch. If you didn't have a dog, you'd be refused entry even if it were a bank holiday. The food was abysmal, the beds made one wish one had married a chiropractor, the noise of the plumbing in the wall behind our heads made sleep an unattainable dream; but the owners were charming and the other guests delightful. The one we most bonded with was a lorry driver who'd come with his dog Stallone, having left his wife at home with their rescued battery-farm chickens. We had lovely chats with this fellow guest and went for joint walks with his dog and ours in the New Forest and along the coast.

Regular visits to Provence were also a tonic even if staying with one particular friend was an ordeal due to the abominable cuisine. His alcoholic butler had been a chef on the *Belgrano* and the two of them produced food that became legendary for its awfulness (apart from the figs and tomatoes from the garden). The worst of our friend's table practices that I witnessed myself (coming down for a glass of water after dinner when he was clearing up) was the pouring of the dregs from twelve or so wine glasses back into the bottles for the next day. Year after year we all came back because we were very fond of him and because his milieu in Provence was fascinating. Visiting his friend, artist Nancy Negley for example, more than made up for the off-putting aspects of those trips. Her art was an inspiration as was the fact that she'd bought the house opposite hers which had belonged to one of Picasso's great muses, Dora Maar.

One autumn when our dear Provence friend was in England, he was on his way to stay with us and several other households in the North when he fell asleep on the Circle line, en route to King's Cross Station. He had a small case and carrier bags laden with French cheeses as gifts. At some point, unbeknownst to other passengers, his slumber must have gently transported him to another dimension because his death was only noticed at the end of the day. It was a kind departure from this planet for him but for all his friends from all over the world, it was the end of an era.

In between our travels I wrote a few articles, did translations for Manchester Polytechnic, and interpreting for Manchester Crown Court. What engaged me most, however, was to start translating into English

the substantial archive material about my Grandmother Róża's family. Although my son and daughter speak Polish, I knew that if future generations were to be interested in their Polish roots, they'd need an English version. This self-imposed task lasted twenty years on and off and eventually received a large boost from the extensive research and resulting books written by historian Dr L. Narkowicz about the Tyszkiewicz family.

John and Lala 2005

In the intervening years, both Kika and my mother became frailer of course, but they were a delight together. A photograph on my mother's 8oth birthday speaks volumes. I can remember exactly what Kika was saying: she was explaining that because of her extremely kind and loyal nature she would never ever abandon her very best of all her friends: Nicotine.

Wanda Mycielska's 8oth birthday, North Yorkshire 2005

It was precisely because of Kika's unconditional devotion to cigarettes that her last operation (a growth on the end of her beautiful nose) couldn't be done with a general anesthetic. She had COPD and her lungs wouldn't have been able to take it.

The surgeon was unsmiling and just as he approached Kika's face with a syringe she said to me in Polish: *'I've got to inject some life into this man; I'm going to sort him out. Just watch me!'*, whereupon she addressed him in English with a twinkle in her eye: 'Mr So and So. *You're about to destroy my one ambition in life'*. The bemused consultant politely asked her to elaborate, *'To be a magnificent corpse!'* came the reply. The doctor did smile and became instantly human.

That evening John suggested Kika had dinner with us rather than in her cottage. She at first declined out of decorum because she'd been told that the wound should have no dressing. She quickly found a solution though, which involved an eggbox, a length of elastic and holes for breathing. The photograph (opposite) remained on the surgeon's noticeboard for some time.

A couple of years after Kika's nose operation, she was diagnosed with dementia and at one point the social services organised some days of respite care so that I could have a rest. On my first visit to Kika she told me *sotto voce* that every night a naked man jumped up and down in her

Kika Mycielska 2005

doorway. She was completely serious. I told her not to worry, there, there, I'd tell the nurses. *'NO!'* was her loud protest. *'It's his human right!'* And she burst out laughing. In spite of her dementia the humour was still there.

A few days later Kika informed me that the naked man had got into her bed the night before. I relayed this additional hallucination to the matron who on this occasion didn't giggle at all and went into professional protocol mode, to tell me it had actually been true! Her words were along the lines of: *'In view of the behavioural shift in the patient's actions, my duty was to implement rule x etc'.* All she meant was that the old boy had been moved to another ward.

Kika's dementia progressed as did her COPD and then, in 2011 she broke her hip. This was the year of the saddest goodbye for me and my children, when Kika, my mother and a much-loved dog all died within six months. It was not *Au Revoir* this time, but the final *Adieu.* I was sixty-one, yet I felt orphaned. My father was dead and now both my mothers.

Neither death was premature: Kika was eighty-four and Wanda eighty-five but the latter was mentally firing on all cylinders so the loss of sharing our lives with her was particularly hard. She'd had several mini strokes over the years, but she recovered from them every time, until the last one. There is no doubt that fate was kind to her in the manner of her death. Had a stroke left her unable to read, write or speak it would have been a living hell.

Sorting my mother's room after her death was bizarre. It felt as if she were about to walk in with a spring in her step to pick up another paintbrush or her book of *Fiendish Sudoku*. Amongst the tomes weighing down her shelves was one about 'emotional intelligence' by Geetu Orme. Wanda had been one of the subjects in the author's research and she'd had the highest score in the country.

I was not surprised by the outpouring of affection grief and gratitude from friends of all ages. My mother had an uncanny ability to 'read' people which affected many of them forever. She never advised anybody, never pontificated, yet somehow, she made their lives better. Below are some examples of what people wrote after her death.

'I was forty years old and a robot when we met. Her friendship and love made me human.'

'She saved me from myself.'

'At a very low point in my life she pulled me back up and set up a permanent parapet, so I never fell into that hole again.'

'She was the first person ever to make me believe that I was lovable.'

'She taught me to give real meaning to what I do.'

'Her beauty and serenity, mixed with her intellect, faith and humour, were an intoxicating force and a rare combination. She exuded such warmth, reassurance and love that you felt completely peaceful in her presence.'

'She was one of the most compassionate people I've ever met. She had an enormous amount of grace, humanity and dignity and a fantastic sense of humour.'

'Her hunger for Truth and search for the Beyond were never pious. She was on an exciting adventure that drove her deeper and higher into the unknown and closer and closer to truly understanding the rest of us.'

'She taught me by being, not by preaching or judging.'

'She sought the best in all she met.'

'She had no idea whatsoever of how remarkable she was.'

Tempus does indeed *fugit*, birth and death are the only certainties in our lives, clichés are clichés because they are true, yet all these particular clichés were not helpful with our bereavement. What did help, yet again, was humour.

During Kika's funeral my four-year-old granddaughter, Lidia, pointed at the hearse in great excitement. *'THAT's the car I want!! The windows are so big that I'd be able to see EVERYTHING, and I'd fit in all my teddies, my dolls and my bags! Pleeeeease Daddy, sell our car and buy one of these!'* Kika would have thought this a perfectly sensible request.

This same grandchild once telephoned me with news that her mother had bought her the best black plimsolls EVER. *'I love them so much, SO MUCH, that I'm going to wear them to your funeral,'* she announced. *'Better crack on before she grows out of them,'* was my husband's swift advice to me.

Nobody was cross with Lidia. Death mustn't be a taboo and the candour of a four year old is disarming. What's more it didn't at all mean she was indifferent. Some days later she asked her mother: *'Why is it that when I talk to Babi she doesn't answer?'* (my granddaughters called my mother Babi). Joanna's response was perfect. She told Lidia that maybe if she closed her eyes and was very quiet, she would hear Babi's answer in her heart. Lidia ran to a place halfway up the stairs where on the wide windowsill she and her sister Anousha had placed my mother's photograph, her watch, her scent. She sat there with her face in her hands, eyes closed, for a long while. She ran back delighted: *'It worked Mummy!! I heard her! I heard her! Babi said to me – Lidia, I would love to cuddle you and to have you on my knee, but I can't because I'm dead.'* She then walked quietly upstairs and put her whole face in a zip-up bag full of my mother's scarves to breathe in her scent.

It is a given that any normal person knows light and darkness coexist, as do pathos and humour, pleasure and pain, life and death. With *weltschmerz* as my companion from an early age, I have a debt of gratitude to my family, not least Kika and my mother, for the fact that this potentially crippling empathy with world pain has not been allowed to crush me. They were the strong ones. I've had it easy. I do believe that it is because of them that in my own life, humour firmly holds hands with *weltschmerz* so that I can trot merrily on.

***

Lentvaris came back into sharp focus after Wanda and Kika died and I resumed the translating of my family history into English with renewed vigour. When eventually I got to the descriptions of the parks and gardens of Grandma Róża's childhood, the name of the designer Édouard André (1840–1911) resurfaced and I metaphorically slipped and tumbled into the magical world he had created.

One evening I googled his name. The surname Tyszkiewicz popped up within the text, and a click or two later Florence André, Édouard André's great-granddaughter, materialised on the screen, talking about Édouard's own garden in La Croix-en-Touraine. I promptly emailed her, and she didn't delay in sharing my delight: *her* great-grandfather had designed *my* great-grandfather's gardens just under 120 years before and suddenly we'd found each other. She told me about the correspondence between Édouard André and my Tyszkiewicz relations and rejoiced in the fact that they had made time to understand each other's visions. *'We must meet,'* she said when we spoke on the telephone.

A few months later, in June 2017, an envelope arrived for me with a Lithuanian stamp. It was an invitation from the Édouard André Club in Lithuania, the Lithuanian Association of Landscape Architects, Vilnius Gediminas Technical University and Klaipéda University. At Florence André's suggestion, I had been included in the list of guests for a conference about Édouard André's son entitled: *'The Times of René André (1867–1942) a field of creativity of landscape architects from greenery to town planning'*.

I was thrilled. The two great-granddaughters, Florence André and me, both exactly the same age, wouldn't merely meet but would walk together through Lentvaris, in the footsteps of our great-grandfathers, Édouard André and Władysław Tyszkiewicz, in my grandmother Róża's childhood paradise.

At the end of September, I boarded the aeroplane exhilarated. With me was a dear friend, Victoria Agnew, who in 1994 had been part of the team that founded the World Monuments Fund in Britain. Not even the sock breath of the man in the seat beside us could dampen my joy. I was only hours away from stepping back a hundred and nineteen years, to 1898, the year of my grandmother's birth and of Édouard André's design for Lentvaris. Grandma Róża settled comfortably in my heart as the plane took to the skies and I was filled with what I can only describe as elated peace.

CHAPTER TWENTY

PARADISE REGAINED?

I FELT AN instant rapport with Florence André when we met at the very pleasant Shakespeare Boutique Hotel in Vilnius. I was prepared for the emotions that our visit to Lentvaris would bring but not for the welcome I received when arriving at the conference. The venue was a few miles from Lentvaris, in Trakų Vokè, one of the three other Tyszkiewicz estates in Lithuania for which Édouard André designed the gardens and parks. Trakų Vokè, had belonged to Jan Tyszkiewicz, my great-grandfather Władysław's first cousin.

The participants in the conference were specialists and academics in the fields of landscape architecture, urban planning, geography, art history and botany with the main focus on the functions of public gardens, the role of green spaces in urban design and the revival of historic parks. The conference was conducted in three languages: Lithuanian, English and French.

During the proceedings, Dr V. Deveikiené (Chief Specialist for City Landscapes in Vilnius, Vice-President of the Lithuanian Association of Landscape Architects, and President of the Club Édouard André) introduced me to the conference as Władysław Tyszkiewicz's great-granddaughter. I don't know what I had expected. Maybe a few curious glances in my direction. I was certainly completely taken aback by the attention given to me as soon as the first coffee break was announced. On their way to the refreshments

some hovered, taking a closer look at me, whilst others asked me to sign their conference brochures and to be photographed with them; one even told me that to meet me was like touching history. I was moved and grateful.

Great-granddaughters, Lala Wilbraham and Florence André, Lentvaris 2017

I met not only the experts at the conference but also volunteers who are passionate about Édouard André's legacy, and who work tirelessly to help restore what they can in the Tyszkiewicz gardens and parks.

The day after the conference (Sunday, 1 October 2017), at the invitation of the vicar, Florence and I attended Mass at the Church of the Annunciation of the Holy Mother of God, built by my great-grandfather in Lentvaris. He is buried in its crypt. The date on the front of the church (1906–2006) marks its 100th anniversary with 1906 being the year in which the first (wooden) version was consecrated, not the later brick building built in the style of the fifteenth century Maria della Grazia in Milan.

The church was packed. Father Petronis invited me into the pulpit and explained who I was. I felt emotional but calm when I addressed the congregation. Their eyes were on me and many came up to me after mass. A little girl curtsied and presented me with flowers. Father Petronis asked whether he could take a photograph of me with his mother.

These were 'moments in aspic' as Kika used to say, and when Florence and I found ourselves outside the church, there were many more people as there had been a religious procession before we had arrived for Mass. Father Petronis introduced us both, this time to the much larger gathering consisting of Lithuanians and Poles. I felt Florence was a far more important guest than me, not only due to her relevance to Édouard André's legacy in all four Tyszkiewicz estates, but also because without her I wouldn't have been standing there in the first place. It was a day to remember and I can't thank her enough for having made it possible.

On the morning of our visit to Lentvaris, I felt simultaneously sombre and excited. I was aware that in part this would be painful; but before turning to Grandma Róża's childhood home, the other three Tyszkiewicz estates (Palanga, Trakų Vokè and Užutrakis) deserve a brief mention here, not least because one can then compare their restoration with what the situation has been in Lentvaris:

Palanga is today the most popular Lithuanian seaside resort. The park and gardens were designed for my great-grandfather's brother, Feliks. The site was magnificent, between the Tyskiewicz forests that stretched as far as Prussia and the beaches on the Baltic shore. Today Édouard André's creation is the Palanga Botanical Gardens (financed by the town) and the restoration is poised for its final stages. The palace became the Palanga Amber Museum in 1963. Restored by 2015 largely with EU funds, it has been visited by more than eight million people.

Palanga 2019 by Audrius Venclova (Shutterstock)

Trakų Vokè, where the conference was held, has received grants for the restoration of the gardens from the EU (85%) and the Municipality of Vilnius (14%), and work is progressing.

Trakų Vokè by kind permission of Marius Jovaisa

As for **Užutrakis,** my great-grandfather's brother (Józef Tyszkiewicz) had owned this estate, built on a promontory between the lakes Galvė and Skaistis. It was entrusted to Trakai National Park management in 1995. It is now a museum restored with grants from the EU Structural Funds, the Republic of Lithuania, the Lithuanian Ministry of Culture and the Polish Ministry of Culture and National Heritage. The work was coordinated by the Wilanów Palace Museum in Warsaw. Užutrakis today hosts guided tours, art exhibitions, concerts and weddings.

Užutrakis restored, photograph Rolandas Misius (Alamy)

Sadly, **Lentvaris** in the twenty-first century is the most neglected and least protected of the four Tyszkiewicz estates in Lithuania largely because of its multiple ownership. Parts of the estate belong to the Municipality, some to locals who have been allowed to buy the buildings they had squatted in since the war, yet other structures had become a kilim factory in Communist times. The resulting bureaucratic confusion has meant that funds that have come from the European Union for the other three Tyszkiewicz palaces and parks are not forthcoming for Lentvaris. Most of the estate buildings are in ruins, many beyond repair. There is little hope of arresting their decay, let alone restoring them to their former glory.

In 'The Role of Historical gardens in city Development- from private garden to public park. Édouard André heritage case study 2014', Dr Deveikienė writes that Lithuania has ratified, or approved a number of International Conventions, Treaties and European Directives. *'This makes the urban planning in Lithuania an integral part of the process and network of management of sustainable development in Europe';* yet she adds that there are still many inadequacies in the *'legislative instruments stipulating the processes of implementation of urban renewal projects.'* Certainly, Lentavis, which has been on the Cultural Heritage list since 2008, is an example of how worthy cases can and often do fall through the net.

Nevertheless, with Lentvaris palace itself, the situation is encouraging: a young businessman, Ugnius Kiguolis, has bought it with the view of restoring it as a hotel. Although he was only allowed to buy the palace and nothing else, good news came during my three-day stay for the conference: he received a partial grant, to be matched by him, for the very extensive renovation.

From the point of view of Édouard André's legacy, the gardens and park are areas of great interest for garden designers, botanists and dendrologists. Aerial photographs show how, if left to her own devices, mother nature invades what she can, taking with her former vistas and with them the balance intended in a planned landscape.

Lentvaris after decades of neglect (Shutterstock)

My 2017 visit to Lentvaris, however, was not a professional analysis but a personal pilgrimage. The fact that Florence was by my side and my grandmother Róża in my heart, shaped this visit for me and I was determined to allow my imagination to travel in time.

As we walked along the meandering paths, up and down the undulating terrain, the setting for some of the events described to me in my childhood by Grandma Róża were instantly recognisable. The grotto, in particular, conjured up an instant image of Róża as a child: so *this* was where she had slipped, got wet, and where her beloved nanny Paniunia had wrapped her in a warm rug and made her feel safe. And *this* was where happy picnics took place with her cousins from Użutrakis and Trakų Vokè. I could almost hear her voice telling me about it in our hammock when I myself was a child.

Lentvaris grotto 1905

Lentvaris grotto 2017
Sitting L to R: Florence André, Lala Wilbraham, Vaiva Deveikienė,
Standing: Victoria Agnew and sitting behind Florence, Rasa Puzinienė

The water tower had less happy connotations as that was where, when playing hide and seek, Róża had a panic attack when she became trapped inside. She never found out whether one of the other children had deliberately held the door shut or whether there had been something wrong with the latch and the children had actually rescued her. I walked around the tower slowly, imagining just how scary it would have been for a nervous little girl to be in that dark space.

Water tower photo by Rasa Puzinienė

One of Grandma Róża's favourite views of the house was from 'Café Riviera' where she often gorged on cakes and hot milk with honey, whilst waiting to go boating on the lake. As I stood looking across the water at the tip of the spire, I compared what I was seeing with an image of what this view had been in my grandmother's childhood.

Not far from 'Café Riviera', in a secluded pine wood, nanny Paniunia would often stop with my grandmother for a quick prayer in the tiny open-air chapel. There had never been any walls or a roof in this chapel, just wooden benches on faux root legs and an image of Our Lady of Częstochowa in a faux roots frame. An oil lamp burned night and day, and everyone was welcome. Like everything with Paniunia, whose God was a kind and merciful one, moments in the chapel were soothing for Róża. She told me so. There was little for me to see in 2017 but I could well visualise them there and as I stood in that tranquil place I thought of them both.

Grandma Róża loved it when Paniunia pretended to chase her around the narrow paths that encircled the two *rond-points* in the *parterre*. She remembered those games, even though she must have been quite small. In the middle of each of the two *rond-points* there was a column. I found it more difficult than anywhere else in the park to visualise Róża in that area since the plants that were meant to be kept low, as the word *parterre* implies, now form sky-high barriers, blocking out all vistas. The only feature I could recognise in the 1990s photograph was the column.

Parterre in Lentvaris 1900s

Parterre in Lentvaris 2017

As we meandered along the paths, through views of both decay and beauty, I absorbed the Tyszkiewicz spirit still present in those trees, those grounds and in what is left of the buildings. Maybe because I am a Slav, I allowed myself to feel that my grandmother Róża was with me and I urged us both to turn away from the distressing aspects of my visit and search for the uplifting ones which give one hope. It wasn't difficult to find them: there are large numbers of people dedicating themselves to furthering the understanding of André's principles of garden and park design, to melding his and their own visions of urban and rural development, to restoring and preserving these parks without freezing them in time. These people haven't given up on Lentvaris. Yes, they've got their work cut out, but teams of botanists, historians, architects, garden, landscape and urban designers along with many passionate volunteers, do what they can in the hope that all four Tyszkiewicz parks will work in perpetuity as exceptional public ones, sustainable and integrated in current urban development.

Mock-up of Lentvaris by Architect James Norman Ferguson 2008–2009
(it doesn't show the glasshouses)

My great-grandfather Władysław Tyszkiewicz died in 1936, before being banished from his beloved Lentvaris which is what the Second World War brought to the rest of his family. The decline in wealth and power for magnates like the Tyszkiewicz, had started with the First World War, the Bolshevik war, the world stock market crisis and the agrarian reforms of 1929. The last nail in the coffin was the Second World War. Family palaces, estates, collections of cultural treasures assembled over many generations were confiscated or destroyed by Stalinism. I'm glad my great-grandfather didn't live through that. Yet, if we gloss over certain pages of history, I believe that the notion that what is left of his creation can in some ways be useful now, in modern day Lithuania, as part of the country's heritage and used profitably for the common good, would sit well with him. As the Vilnius newspaper *Kraj* (1902 nr 50) wrote: '*Count Władysław Tyszkiewicz is relentlessly driven by the family's all-consuming commitment to public service.*'

When I left Lithuania and headed back home I was in a daze but a few days later I was able to ponder on the extent to which such a whistle stop visit had enriched me. It has deepened my sense of history, linked me irrevocably to my grandmother's world, sharpened my perspective by increasing my empathy with people across centuries, not least those in Lithuania today. It brought into focus the strength of the human spirit, the striving towards a chosen direction against all odds. It also gave me new and genuine friendships that I know will last into the future.

When we parted, Florence André and I were already planning her visit to me in the UK. She came in 2019. We rejoiced in each other's company, visited gardens and houses, cried together watching the Notre Dame fire on TV. Since then we have kept in frequent touch and are now looking forward to my visit to her house when Covid 19 loosens its grip. She will then be able to show me Édouard André's own garden in La-Croix-en Touraine.

A few days ago (September 2020) I was sent a photograph of Lentvaris taken in May, showing the scaffolding now on my grandmother's childhood home. The news about the restoration of Lentvaris Palace is good: the owner, Mr Ugnius Kiguolis, has truly engaged with the work. The total cost of the restoration is estimated at 7 million euros and the goal is for the building to offer a hotel, a museum, restaurant, café, a laboratory for the production of natural scents and other organic products, and a so called 'art incubator', where art and business are brought together, where it is possible to meet artists in their studios, attend talks, concerts, exhibitions and movie screenings, enjoy interactive entertainment, and generally learn about the creative process.

Additional information has reached me that a few of the other buildings, including the water tower, are now also for sale: another reason for hope that maybe someone with vision will take up the challenge.

My message to all emigrés and refugees is: adapt, integrate and learn to belong again, but don't lose your identity; to my granddaughters Anousha and Lidia: look for the bigger picture; and to everyone everywhere: don't underestimate the value of humour. It can help us step back, providing a psychological distance that makes the unbearable a little less daunting.

For my grandmother and her children in 1941, dreams of the golden apples of Samarkand symbolised their hopes for a future far removed from the cruelty and privations of a Soviet labour camp. For me, writing in 2020, the plans to restore and redevelop Lentvaris hold the same significance. Hope is nourishment and it starts in the dark.

Lentvaris, photo by Rasa Puziniené

APPENDIX 1

CHART OF POLISH VS LITHUANIAN NAMES

POLISH	LITHUANIAN
Tyszkiewicz Pronounced Tish kay vitch	Tiškievičiai
Landwarów Pronounced Landvaroof	Lentvaris
Wilno Pronounced Veelno	Vilnius
Waka Pronounced Vaka	Trakų Voké
Zatrocze Pronounced Za tro tshe	Užutrakis
Połąga Prounced Powonga	Palanga
Kowno Pronounced Kovno	Kaunas
Troki	Trakai

APPENDIX 2

ZYGMUNT KARPIŃSKI AND THE POLISH BULLION RESERVES

It is incomprehensible that my mother's official father, my grandmother Grażyna's first husband Zygmunt Karpiński, seems to have been whitewashed from history. Modern accounts and articles on the fate of the Polish Bullion Reserves don't mention his name at all amongst the names of people who, although an important part of the actual physical transportation of the gold, were much lower down the pecking order.

In 1958, The Commission for the Coordination of Studies of World War II events at the History Institute of the Polish Academy of Sciences, produced a booklet entitled '*Losy Złota Polskiego podczas Drugiej Wojny Światowej*' ('The Fate of the Polish Gold during World War II'), published by the National Scientific Publishing House, where it states that **Zygmunt Karpiński** '*as a director of the Bank of Poland in charge of foreign affairs, took part, both in Poland and abroad in all decisions concerning the fate of the Polish bullion reserves*'. *The study is based on both Karpiński's accounts and on materials in the archives of the National Bank of Poland*'.

In this booklet it is stated that: '*In March 1940 a book was published in London by Methuen & Co Ltd, entitled 'The Polish Gold' containing countless false accounts of the proceedings. The authors Robert Westerby and R. M. Low – neither of which was known to the Bank of Poland, stated in the introduction that they based their information on official reports as lodged with the Polish Government, which did not correspond to the truth. It is not known whether Colonel Matuszewski or Colonel Koc furnished them any information. The true nature of the events was in itself so extraordinary and exciting that there was no need to add sensational fantasies as invented by the authors of that book. The progress of the Polish Bullion Reserves was a topic of great interest to the foreign press who reported many interviews and descriptions which weren't always accurate.*'

Below are two interesting documents which clearly demonstrate the extent of the powers of attorney given to Zygmunt Karpiński by the Bank of Poland, both from the 9 September 1939. The first is the Power of Attorney given to Dr Karpiński as the sole attorney in charge of the Polish Bullion Reserves. The translations are below them.

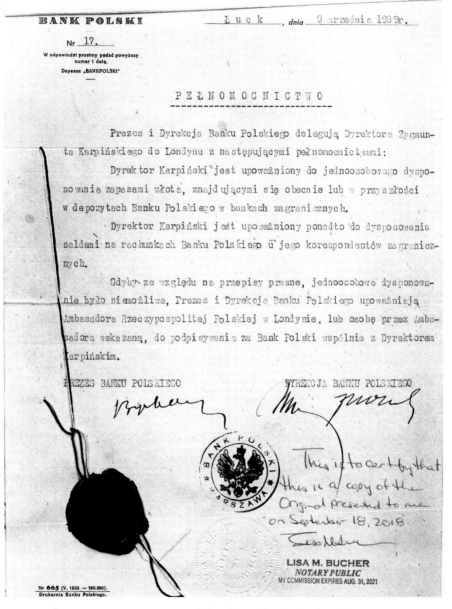

Power of attorney given to Z Karpiński by the Bank of Poland as the sole attorney in charge of the Polish Bullion Reserves

BANK OF POLAND

No. 17

Please provide the above number and date in your reply.

Cable messages to: 'BANKPOLSKI'

Łuck, 9 September 1939   POWER OF ATTORNEY

The President and Directors of the Bank of Poland hereby delegate Director Zygmunt Karpiński to London with the following powers of attorney:

Director Karpiński shall have the authority to solely administer the current and future gold reserves of the Bank of Poland deposited in foreign banks.

Furthermore, Director Karpiński shall have the authority to administer the balances in the accounts of the Bank of Poland at its foreign correspondents.

Should the sole administration be impossible due to legal regulations, the President and Directors of the Bank of Poland hereby authorize the Ambassador of the Republic of Poland in London or any person appointed by the Ambassador to sign on behalf of the Bank of Poland together with Director Karpiński.

PRESIDENT OF THE BANK OF POLAND	DIRECTORS OF THE BANK OF POLAND
[Illegible signature]	*[Two illegible signatures]*

[Impression of a round ink stamp bearing the Polish state emblem: BANK OF POLAND, WARSAW]

[Handwritten note: This is to certify that this is a copy of the original presented to me on September 18, 2018.]

[Illegible signature]

[Impression of a rectangular ink stamp: LISA M. BUCHER, NOTARY PUBLIC, MY COMMISSION EXPIRES AUG. 31, 2021]

[Impression of a round seal: LISA M. BUCHER, NOTARY PUBLIC, STATE OF CONNECTICUT]

No. 665 (V. 1939. – 100,000) Bank of Poland Printing House

BANK POLSKI

Nr 18

W odpowiedzi prosimy podać powyższy
numer i datę.
Depesze „BANKPOLSKI"

Ł u c k , *dnia* 9 września 1939 r.

Do Pana

Zygmunta Karpińskiego

Dyrektora Banku Polskiego

w m i e j s c u .

W związku z udzielonym Panu pełnomocnictwem z dnia 9 b.m.,
dajemy Panu następujące instrukcje:

Sumami podnoszonymi z tytułu tego pełnomocnictwa może Pan
dysponować:

1/na rzecz agentów Rządu Polskiego dla spraw zakupu,których
to agentów charakter zostanie stwierdzony przez Ambasadora
Rzeczypospolitej Polskiej w Londynie lub w Paryżu,

2/na wszelkie koszty związane z dokonywaniem transportów
złota Banku Polskiego zagranicą i inne koszty bankowe,

3/na osobiste wydatki.

PREZES BANKU POLSKIEGO   DYREKCJA BANKU POLSKIEGO
/-/ B y r k a   /-/Barański /-/J.Nowak

/Pieczęć okrągła Banku
Polskiego/

Za zgodność z oryginałem
Łuck,dnia 9 wrześ   r.
B A N K   P O L S

*This is to certify that this
is a copy of the Original presented
to me on September 18, 2010.*

LISA M. BUCHER
NOTARY PUBLIC
MY COMMISSION EXPIRES AUG. 31, 2021

Nr 665 (V. 1939. — 160.000).
Drukarnia Banku Polskiego.

Power of attorney

232

BANK OF POLAND

No. 18

Please provide the above number and date in your reply.

Cable messages to: 'BANKPOLSKI'

Łuck, 9 September 1939

To Mr. Zygmunt Karpiński

Director of the Bank of Poland

at the same address

In connection with the power of attorney granted to you on the 9th of this month, we hereby provide you with the following instructions:

You are authorized to use the sums put at your disposal under the power of attorney:

1/ for agents of the Polish Government for the purpose of purchases, provided that the agents have been identified as such by the Ambassadors of the Republic of Poland in London or Paris,

2/ to cover any costs related to the transport of the gold reserves of the Bank of Poland abroad, and any other bank charges,

3/ for personal expenses.

PRESIDENT OF THE BANK OF POLAND	DIRECTORS OF THE BANK OF POLAND
[*Illegible signature*]	[*Two illegible signatures*]
/-/ Byrka	/-/ Barański /-/ J. Nowak

/Round ink stamp of the Bank of Poland/

I certify this to be a true copy of the original
Łuck, 9 September 1939
BANK OF POLAND
[*Two illegible signatures*]

[*Handwritten note*: This is to certify that this is a copy of the original presented to me on September 18, 2018.]

[*Illegible signature*]

[*Impression of a rectangular ink stamp*:

LISA M. BUCHER,
NOTARY PUBLIC,
MY COMMISSION EXPIRES AUG. 31, 2021]

[*Impression of a round seal*:
LISA M. BUCHER,
NOTARY PUBLIC,
STATE OF CONNECTICUT]

No. 665 (V. 1939. – 100,000)
Bank of Poland Printing House

ACKNOWLEDGEMENTS

My thanks go first to my dear friend Becci Howard for encouraging me to write about my family history for a readership wider than my relations, and for introducing me to Hugo Vickers. Thanks to Hugo for putting me in touch with Tom Perrin and to Tom for suggesting literary consultant Lynn Curtis. Lynn helped me to structure my book, and to find the right 'hook' on which to hang the narrative. Thanks to her, what at first seemed daunting, quickly became crystal clear. She (and Covid lockdown) pressed my button.

Thanks to writer Caroline Chapman for her encouragement too, not least for bringing my story to the attention of Lord Strathcarron, Chairman of the Unicorn Publishing Group. And thanks to Lord Strathcarron himself, of course, for taking me on and saying that mine was a story that needed to be told.

Dr L. Narkowicz who has written several books about various branches of my grandmother's family, accessed private archives, memoirs and conversations with several members of the Tyszkiewicz clan. She followed through with her extensive and meticulous research of numerous national, regional and press records. I am grateful for being able to rely on her research of those sources.

The Golden Apple of Samarkand wouldn't have appeared in its present form without the inspiring friendship between me and Florence André, the two great-granddaughters of the men who shared and fulfilled a dream in 1898. It was thanks to Florence that I was able to visit Lithuania for the first time and to walk by her side through the magical world of my grandmother's childhood.

I must thank also the many people in Lithuania who did what they could to make my visit not only enchanting but informative, furnishing me with invaluable material for my book: Dr Vaiva Devekiené and her team, and Rasa Puziniené, who was such a wonderful example of the generosity of passionate volunteers striving to preserve their Lithuanian heritage.

Thanks to Richard and Gillian Mawrey of the *Historic Gardens Review*, for agreeing that part of the article I wrote for their journal (*Nostalgia, Empathy and Hope*, November 2018) appears in this book in chapter 3 (A Very Special Garden).

Thanks too to the wonderful designers: Piotr Suchodolski for the book cover and Vivian Head for the interior design.

INDEX